MOVING INTO
ADULTHOOD

Themes and Variations in Self-Directed Development for Effective Living

Gerard Egan
Loyola University, Chicago

Michael A. Cowan
Processus
St. Cloud, Minnesota

Brooks/Cole Publishing Company
Monterey, California

Other Books by Gerard Egan

Encounter Group Processes for Interpersonal Growth/**Face to Face** The Small-Group Experience and Interpersonal Growth/**The Skilled Helper** A Model for Systematic Helping and Interpersonal Relating/**Exercises in Helping Skills** A Training Manual to Accompany The Skilled Helper/**Interpersonal Living** A Skills/Contract Approach to Human-Relations Training in Groups/**You and Me** The Skills of Communicating and Relating to Others

Other Books by Gerard Egan and Michael A. Cowan

People in Systems A Model for Development in the Human-Service Professions and Education/**People in Systems** Personal and Professional Applications

Brooks/Cole Publishing Company
A Division of Wadsworth, Inc.

Printed in the United States of America

10 9 8 7 6 5 4 3 2 1

Library of Congress Cataloging in Publication Data

Egan, Gerard.
  Moving into adulthood.

  Bibliography: p.
  Includes index.
  1. Adulthood.   I. Cowan, Michael, joint author.
II. Title.
BF724.5.E36   155.6   80-15876
ISBN 0-8185-0406-4

Acquisition Editor: *Claire Verduin*
Manuscript Editor: *Robert Rowland*
Production Editor: *John Bergez*
Interior Design: *Ruth Scott*
Illustrations: *Carl Brown*
Typesetting: *Graphic Typesetting Service, Los Angeles, California*

Preface

Moving into Adulthood: Themes and Variations in Self-Directed Development for Effective Living presents an integrated picture of the developmental tasks confronting individuals during the transition to adulthood—roughly, between the ages of 18 and 23. Our intent has been to make contemporary theory and research on this important segment of life available to our readers in a way that allows them to assess systematically their own developmental status and needs. Since the developmental tasks considered here continue to be faced in one form or another throughout life, the book is also intended to encourage people over 23 to review the ways in which they worked through these tasks during their moving-into-adulthood years and the ways in which they are dealing with these tasks now that they are at a different life stage.

In a previous book, *People in Systems* (Brooks/Cole, 1979), we described how human development over the life span is bound up with the social systems in which it occurs. These human systems include small, immediate ones, such as families, friendship groups, and classrooms; larger organizations and institutions, such as the economic system, various forms of government, and the media; and, finally, what has been called the largest or most influential of the systems, the pluralistic culture in which our lives are immersed. In *Moving into Adulthood* we systematically apply the people-in-systems model to one segment of the life cycle—the years of transition into adulthood. We show the structure of ten key developmental tasks, the resources needed for their mastery, and the ways in which the social systems of life affect the development of people during the moving-into-adulthood years.

Our approach in this book is a practical one that stresses personal applications of theory and research. In each chapter on a developmental task, the reader moves from self-assessment, to the development of "working" insights into the task, to concrete action planning. Structured group-interaction steps are woven into each chapter to facilitate the kind of guided discussion with peers that can enrich each student's learning.

Moving into Adulthood can be used as the main text in courses designed to help young adults develop a personal, action-oriented awareness of key concepts in psychology and the other social sciences. It is particularly appropriate for courses in personality development with a self-help or self-development focus. Those who teach such courses as psychology of adjustment, personal development, or adult development will find many of the issues typically dealt with in these courses recast here in a developmental and social system perspective. The book will also be useful to instructors who wish to supplement a basic theoretical text with one that offers a personal, pragmatic approach to adult development.

As our subtitle suggests, human development is characterized by common themes and individual variations. All of us face the same tasks, but we do not all develop in the same way or at the same pace. This book does not promote conformity. It does, however, suggest that life-style choices have both personal and social consequences. Becoming aware of these consequences helps individuals to make choices they can live with.

A special word of appreciation is due to several people whose reviews of the original manuscript of this book were most helpful to us: Richard Breen, Yakima Valley College; David Cella, Loyola University (Chicago); Robert Conyne, Illinois State University; Richard Lundy, Pennsylvania State University; Robert Osterhouse, Prince George's Community College; and James Zullo, Loyola University (Chicago). We would also like to acknowledge the work of our production editor, Robert Rowland, of Brooks/Cole. His efforts in connection with this text and our previous joint effort added much to the final products.

Gerard Egan
Michael A. Cowan

Contents

Exercises

Chapter 13

CHAPTER

What Self-Directed
Human Development Means

In this chapter, we describe what is meant by the term *human development.* We introduce four themes that recur and serve as organizers throughout this book: challenge, support, working knowledge, and life skills. Then we explain the four elements of the process through which you can become more self-directed in the pursuit of your own development: (1) reflection on your experience and behavior, (2) systematic analysis of developmental tasks, (3) structured group interaction, and (4) personal-action planning designed to translate reflection and analysis into action. Next, we offer a means of analyzing the social settings in which the developmental events of your life take place—settings that can influence those events profoundly. Finally, we discuss the values this book promotes.

What Human Development Means

This book focuses on human development—especially psychosocial development—that takes place between ages 17 and 23. It deals directly with your growth as a person in your relationship to yourself, including the ways in which you've come to think and feel about yourself, as well as the way in which you act toward yourself—kindly, harshly, critically, self-indulgently, realistically, compassionately, cautiously, and so on. This book also deals directly with your growth as a person in your interactions with others in all the social settings of life: at home, at school, at work, in the neighborhood, at parties, at church.

Although this might be the first time you've taken a formal look at this subject as one of the important issues of your life, informally you already know quite a bit about human development. Since this book focuses on self-directed human development, it will help to understand from the beginning what is meant by the term *human development* as it is being used here. In this context, an understanding of human development includes an understanding of the following notions: predictable stages, biological maturation, stage-related developmental tasks, the gradualness and continuity of development, the cumulative nature of development, themes and variations, human development in human systems, developmental crises, and development and culture. We will now discuss each of these notions briefly.

Predictable stages. Human development takes place in relatively predictable steps or *stages* (Levinson, Darrow, Klein, Levinson, & McKee, 1978; Newman & Newman, 1979). For instance, the stage you've left behind is called early adolescence. You are presently in a transitional stage; the stage toward which you are headed is called early adulthood (from age 23 to 30).

Biological maturation. Your development includes the ways in which you grow and mature physically. We won't dwell on *physical changes* in this book; they are more important in earlier stages of development and later in life. However, the way in which you relate to your body is very important.

Stage-related developmental tasks. At each stage of development, there are certain kinds of growing to be done, knowledge and skills to be acquired, and psychosocial accomplishments to be achieved. These are called *developmental tasks.* Learning to trust others, to speak a language, and to participate in group learning are examples of developmental tasks that you've already confronted. Learning how to live more independently and get a clearer sense of your own values are tasks you are presently facing. Finding a full-time job or choosing a career and establishing a family or some other form of extended personal commitment are tasks you will be facing in the near future. Coping with retirement is a task that lies in the distant future. In this book, ten interrelated developmental tasks are presented for your exploration.

The gradualness and continuity of development. You're aware of the fact that you've changed in many ways over the course of your life. You can look back and readily see *differences* in yourself as a first grader, a junior high school student, a high school senior, and now as a college student. At the same time, you also can see *similarities* in your various "selves" as you've grown and developed. The concept of constant, gradual *change* over time, coupled with a sense of *continuity* or *sameness,* is central to the image of development presented in these pages.

The cumulative nature of development. Human development is incremental and cumulative. This is true not only biologically—first you had to be carried, then you could crawl, and finally you walked—but also intellectually and psychosocially. The fact that you developed the ability to think more abstractly in early adolescence gives you the ability to plan your future with greater clarity and conviction. With the maturation of your emotions, you're able to relate to others with an intensity not possible before.

Themes and variations. Although there are predictable stages of development, not everyone develops at the same pace or in the same way. One person might reach a stage of sexual maturation at age 10 or 11 that another person won't reach until age 14 or 15. Human development is age-related, but not age-specific. Although people in our culture tend to experience developmental events at certain times of life, significant individual differences can and do occur. These differences have important practical implications. A model of human development should not be rigidly applied to everyone indiscriminately. Such a model, including the model presented here, is a general framework for analysis, understanding, and planning.

Human development in human systems. Human development doesn't take place in a vacuum; it has a *context.* The way in which you develop depends on the quality of challenge and support you receive in your family, school, workplace, neighborhood, and peer group. Organizations and institutions in the areas of government, business, education, the professions, and religion exercise a profound influence on your development.

Developmental crises. First of all, the term *crisis* comes from a Greek word meaning a "dividing." When you're faced with a developmental task or challenge, you can go backward, you can stagnate, or you can move ahead. For example, when you're faced with the developmental challenge of establishing intimate relationships with members of the opposite sex, you can intensify your relationships with members of your own sex, stay on the edge of mutual heterosexual relationships, become more and more isolated, or move ahead and experiment with new kinds of relationships, opening yourself to both hurt and joy. It's a "dividing time"; developmental crises are crossroads.

Second, usually there is some anxiety associated with developmental tasks, because they seem so big when you approach them for the first time. Since these tasks place demands on you, they often generate periods of stress; therefore, the term *developmental crisis* can refer to the kinds of normal turmoil associated with facing these tasks. It's sometimes difficult to distinguish normal developmental turmoil from the abnormal stress and anxiety associated with emotional disorders.

Development and culture. The meaning of the word *development* varies with cultural context. The particular developmental map presented in this book refers to contemporary North American society and to the subculture of people who attend two-year or four-year colleges. In many ways, development is what a particular culture or subculture says it is. Such cultural relativity needs to be recognized.

Developing a Personal Working Knowledge of Human Development

Psychologists are greatly interested in the period of life in which you now find yourself. In developing their theories and conducting their experiments, they've amassed a great deal of information dealing with many different aspects of your life. We believe that much of what they've learned can be of real use to you as you pursue the developmental issues associated with making the transition from adolescence to adulthood. Currently, much of this information is available only in highly academic, technical language, and it tends to be scattered in a variety of books and journals. In this book, we attempt to present some of the principal findings of these social scientists in a systematic and integrated way. By "principal findings," we mean the kind of information about human development that will help you to prepare yourself for the various tasks of life, from developing intimate friendships to preparing yourself for job or career intelligently and effectively. Moreover, we provide experiential learning exercises to help you apply the information presented here to your own life in practical ways.

This book invites you to ask yourself questions such as: "What specific developmental issues am I currently dealing with?" "What practical knowledge and life skills are called for by these challenges?" "What can I do to gain the working knowledge and skills I need?"

The Role of Challenge in Human Development

Human development can be defined as movement toward greater complexity, competence, and integration as a result of challenge and support experienced in the important settings of life.

Complexity refers to the development of all the aspects of yourself—your thoughts, feelings, values, hopes, dreams, choices, and behaviors—in the context of, and in interaction with, the various levels of social systems or settings of your life. Complexity is seen in the array of developmental challenges that are reviewed in this book.

Competence, as we shall see more fully in the following chapter, refers to the ability to *accomplish* important life tasks or attain life goals consistently. A competent individual is able to use such abilities as learning how to learn and interpersonal, decision-making, and problem-solving skills to achieve developmental goals.

Integration results when developmental tasks are put together in order to produce a valued and meaningful life-style. From another perspective, integration refers to the development of a self that gives consistency and unity to all these different tasks. (Chapter 13 will help you to integrate all the tasks discussed in this book.)

Development, in other words, occurs as we experience demands within our families, friendships, schools, workplaces, and communities for progressively more complicated behaviors, attitudes, values, and ways of managing our feelings, provided that such settings also supply us with the resources we need to cope with such demands.

An illustration of developmental challenge can be seen in the ways in which life after high school differs from life during the high school years. In college, you're on your own in ways that you were not in high school. (Your peers who haven't gone on to college also are more on their own, but in different ways.) Since you're still in school, you notice how college differs from high school. Students in college don't "mess around" in the classroom the way students often do in high school. The assumption is that you're in college because you *want* to be there, not because you *have* to be there. You're expected to manage your own behavior both inside and outside the classroom in order to achieve academic goals that you (at least in part) set for yourself. Those who have not gone on to college are expected to become adept at managing their own lives, too, but whereas you are making decisions with respect to courses to be taken, they are making decisions with respect to full-time work.

Your family probably exercises less influence or control over your life now than when you were in high school. This is especially true if you're living away from your family for the first time. You're presented with the challenge of making decisions that will fashion your own style of life. You choose your courses, your friends, your daily schedule of work and relaxation, the intensity of study time, and the ways in which you use your leisure time. You're faced with the ongoing dilemma of balancing the personal goals that brought you to college with the pressure of peers and other significant people in your life. If you have to work to support yourself, you're faced with the task of integrating school, work, and social life. You might find that you have little time for social life or that the demands of work leave you with little energy to give to school; you have to manage the resulting frustrations.

The area of *values* becomes more and more challenging at this time of life. As you encounter individuals whose perspectives on personal morality, religion, alcohol, other drugs, and sex differ from your own, you're forced to reflect on your own values and make very concrete decisions. If it had occurred to you only in rather vague or abstract ways that a significant number of people in the world have opinions and values that differ from those you acquired from your family, local church, and community, then encountering this diversity in your peers might be a disturbing or even disorienting—that is, challenging—experience.

The question *"What's ahead?"* is part of the ongoing challenge of the college years. For many, the issue of career choice remains "hidden" during these years; it emerges with some degree of disturbing clarity only at certain critical moments, such as the deadline for choosing a major area of study. If you're already working, then you might wonder what impact your present pursuit of higher education is going to have on your life. Will going to school help you to get a better job or bring you advancement in the job you now have? In what ways does going to college promise a fuller life? You need to structure the present so that it relates meaningfully to the future; this is one of the demands you now face.

In this book, we use the *developmental tasks* of this transitional period of life to organize the principal challenges you face.

Finding Support to Meet Developmental Challenges

In order to cope successfully with developmental tasks or challenges, you will need to learn to locate and make use of the sources of support that are available to you. By sources of support, we mean the people, the institutions, the practical information, and the skills that can help you meet developmental challenges successfully.

We will define and illustrate four developmental resources (sources of support) that will help you to face the kinds of challenges or demands to which we are referring: working knowledge, life skills, people, and institutions.

Working knowledge refers to the specific things you need to understand about yourself and your environment in order to cope successfully with a particular developmental challenge. Working knowledge does more than help you to understand something; it helps you to *do* something. One example of working knowledge is the information you need to plan effectively for a career choice: the phases of a systematic career-development process (see Chapter 10), the training and education requirements for particular careers, and the current predictions regarding employment possibilities in your areas of interest. Working knowledge is the practical "know-how" for living. One of the principal goals of this book is to provide the kinds of working knowledge that will help you to invest yourself more fully and effectively in development tasks such as establishing friendships, choosing an initial job or career, and forming and strengthening your personal values.

Life skills are the specific capabilities you need for certain kinds of accomplishments. One of the definitions of the term *skill* in *Webster's Collegiate Dictionary* is "a learned power of doing something competently." Skills, like working knowledge, are related to competence in carrying out the tasks of life. For instance, a certain set of interpersonal skills enables you to establish and deepen relationships with others. The ability to talk about yourself with some appropriate depth (self-disclosure), the ability to listen to others actively and respond with understanding (accurate empathy), the ability to challenge yourself and others caringly (confrontation), and the ability to discuss your relationships with others in face-to-face dialogue (immediacy) constitute the "skills base" for effective involvement with people in your life. We take a deeper look at the notion of competence in Chapter 3 and review the task of deepening relationships with others in Chapter 8. Throughout the book, we try to identify the kinds of life skills needed to carry out developmental tasks successfully.

People who care about you and are capable of both empathy (understanding your concerns from your standpoint) and challenge (helping you place demands on yourself in responsible ways) provide a third major source of support. These are individuals who encourage you to seize life—that is, to invest yourself more fully in your current developmental tasks—by the quality of their concern and involvement with you. During the transitional period that is the current development stage of your life, key sources of human support are often found in close friendships and in associations with particular teachers, advisers, and counselors. In many instances, parents and other family members also are significant sources of support and challenge.

Institutions of various kinds provide a great deal of support in complex societies such as ours. Churches, hospitals, governmental agencies, clubs, voluntary organizations, foundations, institutes, the professions, newspapers, libraries, and a host of other institutions provide a wide number of services. Many people feel isolated, because they don't know where to turn for support and help. They don't have a working knowledge of the kinds of institutions listed in this paragraph. There is a vast and growing self-help, or mutual-help, network in the United States today (Gartner & Riessman, 1977). Institutional support *is* available to those who need it.

Working knowledge, life skills, people, and institutions are the key resources you can mobilize in order to pursue developmental goals effectively. A major theme of this book is that it is within your power as an individual to seek out such resources. For example, if you are facing the task of making an initial career choice, the following sources of support might be available to you:

△ *Working knowledge:* a fairly extensive understanding of a variety of occupations (especially newer ones), an understanding of your own interests and aptitudes (measured by a variety of tests), an understanding of the education and training requirements for a particular job or career, employment predictions for the occupations you are considering, and knowledge gained from on-the-job experience. Are there others?

△ *Skills:* brainstorming, decision-making skills, job-search skills, interview behavior, and the skills called for by any given occupation (accounting skills for the business world, for example). Can you think of others?

△ *People:* faculty members, career counselors, older peers, persons in the occupations you are considering, and your parents. Are there others?

△ *Institutions:* the college career-counseling or guidance service, church-based vocational retreats, school-sponsored career weekends, and summer internships in various occupations. Are there others?

By contacting people, gathering information, investigating institutions and their programs, and developing skills, you can increase your chances of preparing yourself for and finding an occupation that satisfies your needs and wants.

Key Social Settings as Providers of Challenge and Support

Key social settings constitute the "where" of personal development. The support and challenge we've just discussed are found in these settings. During your transition into adulthood, your settings will probably consist of residence halls (or your home if you commute), friendship groups, classrooms, clubs, athletic teams, part-time work settings, and so forth. If their collective impact on you is a reasonable balance of challenge and support, your development is likely to proceed in a positive (but not always smooth) manner. Too much challenge is likely to leave you feeling anxious, depressed, and doubtful about your competence. (For instance, advanced math might prove to be beyond your capabilities.) Too little challenge can cause you to feel bored, frustrated, and uninvolved. (For instance, the fact that you choose not to join any kind of extracurricular activities at school might cause you to feel isolated.) Too little support might leave you feeling alone and lost, whereas too much support tends to be stifling—after all, it is *you* who must face these challenges. As we look at the major developmental tasks facing you during these transitional years, we'll ask you to reflect on the principal social settings of your life and the impact they have on your development—that is, the ways in which they contribute to or interfere with the challenging and supportive dimensions of each developmental task. Since the settings of your life are so important, we'll take time here to offer you a few tools that can be used to analyze these settings.

The Impact of the Settings of Your Life on Your Development

The fact that your development takes place in a wide variety of social settings (rather than in a vacuum) can be expressed in terms of the following formula:

$$HD = f(P \longleftrightarrow S).$$

In other words, your human development (*HD*) is a function of or is influenced by (*f*) the way you (*P*) interact with ($\longleftrightarrow$) the social settings or human systems (*S*) of your life. John Donne expressed the same fact in a poetic way when he said that "no man is an island." Each of us is part of the "continent"—that is, the mutually interacting systems of society that shape our lives in important ways. For instance, you are the person you are because of the family in which you were raised, the schools you've attended, the neighborhoods in which you've lived, and the jobs you've held. All of these are social settings in which developmental events, such as the formation of peer relationships and the development of cooperative social relationships, have taken place, for better or for worse. Such settings can influence developmental processes profoundly. Growing up in a ghetto, where personal safety is always a concern, differs from growing up in a suburb, where personal safety is taken for granted. Growing up in a family in which activities both inside and outside the home are carefully monitored and regulated differs from growing up in a family in which individual members are more or less on their own. Working in the summer as a caddy at a suburban country club differs profoundly from working as an oiler on an ore carrier sailing the Great Lakes, and both of these experiences are radically different from "hanging around the neighborhood" with nothing to do because there are no jobs to be found.

In *People in Systems* (Egan & Cowan, 1979), we presented a working model of human development based on the formula in the preceding paragraph. That model offers a way of analyzing the four levels of social settings or systems that influence development. We discuss these levels of systems in the following section.

The Four Levels of Social Systems

You live in a complicated world; it helps to have a framework that enables you to understand its complexity. We suggest that the social world in which you live has four basic levels, each of which has major effects on your development and on the opportunities that will be offered to you: (1) personal settings, (2) the network of personal settings, (3) large organizations and institutions, and (4) culture.

Level I: Personal Settings

Personal settings are the small, immediate systems of your everyday life. Examples of personal settings include your family, your workplace, your church group, your classrooms, and your group of friends. We refer to these personal settings as *systems*, because they are made up of individuals who interact with one another and affect one another's development in a variety of ways. Figure 1-1, adapted from Andrews (1974), is an example of this first level of human systems; it portrays the family as an interacting system.

In speaking of the family as a system, Andrews says:

> In a family of four . . . there exist six dyadic, reciprocal relationships possi-
> bilities. These tie each member of the family to every other member direct-
> ly or indirectly through another person to whom he is directly related. One
> might construct a physical model of this diagram by using paper clips to
> represent each family member and connecting rubber bands to represent
> the relationship vectors in the diagram. If the paper clips are each fastened
> down and the rubber bands drawn taut, the model will assume a stability
> that can be altered at any time. Plucking any of the rubber bands will
> reverberate the entire model. Similarly, any action or reaction pattern
> between any two family members will resonate throughout the entire
> family. Marital difficulties between parents will often manifest themselves
> in symptomatic behavior in one of the children. This "family resonance"
> phenomenon is the perpetuating mechanism of characteristic behavior
> within a family. Reinforcement of certain kinds of behavior is not unilater-
> al or even bilateral but multilateral . . . [p. 8].*

In small personal settings, such as the family and peer groups, the kinds of mutual influence that take place are fairly easy to grasp. As Andrews suggests, when parents are at odds with each other, their problems affect the well-being and development of their children, who might come to assume that marriage and intimacy are distressing and destructive. Later, as adolescents and young adults, these same children might face the dilemma of wanting and yet fearing the security and comforts of marital intimacy.

Interactions in personal settings, then, have important developmental consequences. The research of psychologist Douglas Heath (1977) regarding the effects

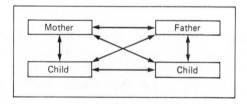

FIGURE 1-1.

*From *The Emotionally Disturbed Family and Some Gratifying Alternatives*, by E. Andrews. Copyright 1974 by Jason Aronson, Inc. Reprinted by permission.

of college and university life on the marriages and careers of a group of students illustrates these consequences in a simple but startling way. Heath found that students who performed well in terms of academic achievement were more likely to experience difficulties later on in nonacademic settings such as marriage and family life. In interpreting the meaning of these results, Heath suggests that colleges tend to stand in the way of the development of interpersonal maturity in their students. He maintains that this lack of maturity is a direct result of one major characteristic of the classroom experience—competition. Heath believes that a cooperative learning environment—one designed in such a way that students work together on learning tasks—is more likely to foster the ability to relate decently to others.

Research evidence and common sense suggest that, once you've left the classroom environment, you're likely to find that events in two key personal settings—your marriage (and the family to which your marriage might lead) and your work—will have a great impact on your development and your feelings of success and satisfaction as a person.

Level II: The Network of Personal Settings

In this transitional period, as well as in adulthood, you belong to several interacting personal systems, or settings, simultaneously. This level of the world of human systems is illustrated in Figure 1-2.

At this level, we find the collection of personal settings in which you live your life, as well as the interaction among those settings. Not only does a personal setting affect you as an individual member, but it often (directly or indirectly) affects the other personal settings of your life. If your family disapproves of the way in which you're arranging your life, they might have a direct impact on you and, through you, an indirect impact on your school, your extracurricular activities, and your intimate relationships. Your experiences in the classroom can affect your mood and your behavior with your family and friends. The effects of your relationship with a close friend can spill over into your life at work or in school.

One of the most difficult "balancing acts" you will be called upon to perform as an adult is one between your workplace and your family life. L. Richard Lessor (1971), a marriage counselor, captures this dilemma when he writes:

> When we wake up in the morning and are fresh we must go immediately to work. Then when the employer has wrung every bit of usefulness out of us, we are pushed onto a crowded bus or thrown into a tangled expressway and told to fight our way home. Once there, at the low point of our energy, we pick up with our marriage [p. 8].

The language is a bit dramatic, but the message is clear.

You don't have to wait until you finish college to experience Level-II realities. In any given day, you might go from your residence hall to classroom A, to a

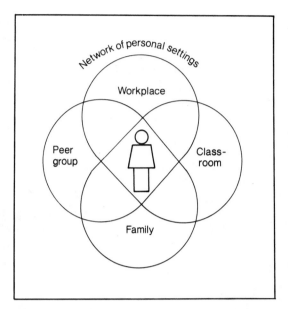

FIGURE 1-2. The network of personal settings.

peer or study group, to classroom B, to track practice, to a part-time job, to a quick visit with your family, and then back to your room and your roommate in the residence hall. You affect each of these settings, and they affect your development. If you have a fight with your roommate, you might go to your chemistry class in a very bad mood and learn very little. Because you finish your work for your English term paper, you might find that you haven't had enough time to study for your political science exam. On the other hand, if you spend a very relaxing weekend with friends, you might return to school on Monday ready for anything. You are a "linking pin" between these immediate settings. They affect you and, through you, they affect one another.

Figure 1-3 is a diagram of some of the systems that require balancing acts. Since this figure might not represent the realities of your own life, you should redraw the figure, including the systems that are relevant to your own experience. Then, in the space provided, write down in concrete terms two or three ways in which you have to balance the demands that are placed on you by these systems. For example, one student wrote:

> During vacation periods, especially the Christmas break, my intimate friend, my regular friends, and my family all expect to see a great deal of me. I find it difficult to parcel out my time. Also, I believe that I am more serious about studies than some of my friends. I find I am constantly forcing myself to decide between being with them and getting my work done.

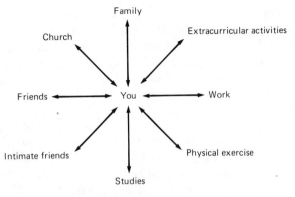

FIGURE 1-3.

Balancing Act #1

_____

_____

_____

_____

Balancing Act #2

_____

_____

_____

_____

Balancing Act #3

_____

_____

_____

_____

It shouldn't be assumed that belonging to a wide variety of systems, each with its own set of demands, is necessarily a negative experience. The resulting juggling acts might cause stress at times, but the overall experience can be quite positive. Having too many things to do can be exciting and fulfilling. The stress you experience is part of the price you pay.

This kind of ongoing pull between two or more key personal settings is an element of the second level of the social world with which you are now coping and with which you will continue to cope throughout your adult life. As you move along in life, the stakes can become higher and higher. The words of a young corporate manager in a firm with whom we have consulted capture the reality of this dilemma clearly:

> As I moved up with the firm, I began to notice that more and more of the families of my colleagues were breaking up. It's gotten to the point where no one is stunned when a marriage ends. I think that we've come to accept it as one of the risks of this type of work. If you want the rewards, you take the risks. More than one of my friends has left the firm to try to save his marriage.

Level III: Large Organizations and Institutions

The network of personal settings is not the end of your social world; in fact, it's just the beginning. Immediate settings are "nested" within two other levels: large organizations and institutions, and culture. Figure 1-4 illustrates the relationships that exist among the individual, the network of personal settings, and the large institutions of society.

Institutional systems, such as government, the economic system, the world of business corporations, and the mass media, don't affect you as directly and as

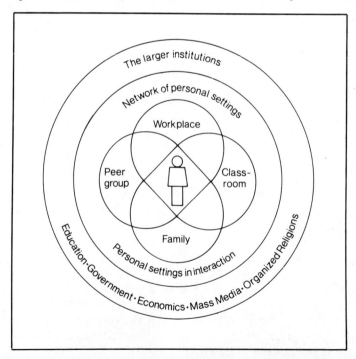

FIGURE 1-4. The large institutions of society.

immediately as the personal settings of your life, but they do influence you, your personal settings, and the entire network of these settings in important ways.

For example, although city government isn't one of the immediate settings of your life (unless you are employed by that government), it is one of the large institutions that affects you both directly and indirectly. When a city council votes to raise property taxes in order to provide better garbage-removal and sewage services, the families and neighborhoods in the city are affected in a number of ways. The rise in property taxes will mean that people will have less money to spend, but it also might result in a healthier and safer city environment. The improved services might provide jobs for a number of people, and these jobs will constitute good news for a number of families. The vote for improved services also might mean that the streets of the neighborhood will be torn up and that traffic and parking will be disrupted during the period of construction. In this example, the large institution of city government has both direct and indirect effects on individuals, personal settings, and neighborhoods.

A second and more serious example highlights the effects that our economic system has on the development of individuals and families. A report of the Carnegie Council on Children (Keniston, 1977) suggests that the most fundamental thing a society can do to foster the development of its children is to implement policies that make employment available to parents. The children of families who live with chronic and severe financial instability are often victims of developmental tragedies. The specific forms of these tragedies—crime, broken homes, delinquency, and educational failure—and the ways in which their effects spread throughout society illustrate the complex and interdependent relationships that make up the world of human systems.

On a more personal level, if your state decides to end tuition grants to students, you might have to leave school. If the state school system decides to open another medical school, you might have a better chance to become a doctor. If the economic system falters, you might lose your job or face bleak employment prospects when you leave school. If your church decides to ordain women to the ministry, you might want to switch from a regular college to a seminary.

Level IV: Culture

Individuals, personal systems and the networks they form, and the large organizations and institutions of society are all enveloped by the fourth level of systems—culture. Figure 1-5 illustrates the influence of culture.

Culture, the most pervasive level of our model, refers to the ways of thinking and feeling that shape individuals, organizations, and institutions. *Webster's Collegiate Dictionary* defines *culture* as "the customary beliefs, social forms, and material traits of a racial, religious, or social group."

At first glance, it might seem strange to refer to culture as a system, but the beliefs, social forms, and material traits of people have *systematic* effects on the ways in which they live. They could be called unwritten "blueprints" that dictate behavior. The way in which you grew up in your family was shaped in many

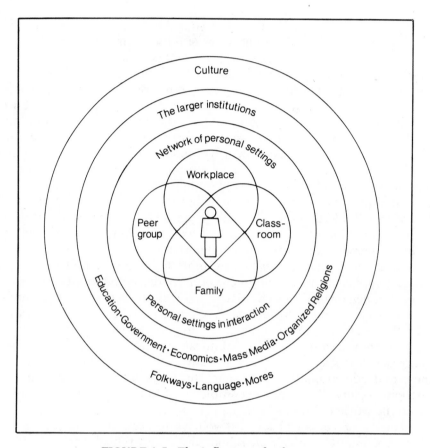

FIGURE 1-5. The influence of culture.

important respects by the blueprints of the society surrounding your family and by the blueprints drawn up within your family itself.

One way of thinking about the effects of culture on the social systems of which you are a member is this: culture provides "filters" for both people and systems as they look at the world. Culture teaches us what to look for and what to disregard. In the words of anthropologist Edwin Hall (1977):

> One of the functions of culture is to provide a highly selective screen between man and the outside world. In its many forms, culture therefore designates what we pay attention to and what we ignore. This screening function provides structure for the world [p. 85].

It isn't an exaggeration to say that your culture and the subcultures within it have taught you how to see; that is, they've provided a set of lenses through which you view the world.

Where do these "cultural glasses" come from? From the experiences you've had and the rules you've learned in your family, your schools, your church, your section of the country, and your country itself. For instance, colleges, collectively and individually, have their own set of norms and standards, their own blueprints for life. The vast majority of young people in our society go to high school, though a number of them leave before finishing; however, a much smaller percentage of young people go on to college. As a college student, you are a member of a more or less select group. The rules that apply to you differ somewhat from the rules found in high school and those that govern the behavior of people who haven't gone on to college. To say that you belong to a select group does not mean, of course, that your group is better than other groups, but it does mean that your group is different. For instance, college students aren't necessarily more mature than their counterparts who don't continue their schooling. If you were to study those who don't go on to college, you would find that they, too, have matured in a number of ways and that they face the same developmental tasks you do, though they deal with them differently. In some respects, they might mature more quickly than you do, since the hard realities of life (such as finding full-time work) force them into making decisions that you don't yet have to face.

Look at the following list and check the categories that apply to you.

_____ Two-year college
_____ Four-year college
_____ Working full-time
_____ Working part-time
_____ Married
_____ Male
_____ Female

The cultural blueprints for each of the possible combinations checked will be somewhat different. For instance, if you are single, male, unemployed, and attending a four-year college full-time, then your culture differs from that of a person who is married, female, working full-time, and attending a two-year college part-time. What is your combination? How would your blueprints differ from those of someone with a different combination?

Since you are reading this book, we assume that you're attending college and that the blueprints under which your particular college operates are affecting you. As we mentioned earlier, Heath (1977) suggests that the competition typical of much classroom experience (such as ranking people from top to bottom on the basis of grade-point average) is likely to be associated with eventual difficulties in marriage and family life, since marriage is a profoundly cooperative endeavor rather than a competitive one. Henry Giroux and Anthony Penna (1977) go even further, arguing that the *primary* effect of education is the socialization of students into their culture.

> Schools in every society cannot avoid . . . socializing youth into the prevailing culture. Schools, along with the family, church, trade unions, and other institutions, constitute the ideological apparatuses that pass on the dominant prevailing belief and value systems of a given society to each

successive generation. In accordance with the content, structure, and organization of schools the . . . configuration of the entire society is reproduced [p. 41].

The observations of Giroux and Penna apply to primary and secondary schools in an especial way, since younger students are more likely to assimilate experiences in a nonreflective way; however, assimilation and socialization occur in college as well.

Educational institutions, like all other institutions, both form and carry the culture of the society in which they are found. Competition is characteristic of North American culture as a whole. Some people argue that a primary (and typically hidden) goal is to turn students into competitors who will become contributors to an economic system that is based on and fosters competition. It is ironic that higher education, with its commitment to the "examined life," reinforces a kind of competitive behavior that could have a negative impact on an individual's development.

The point of this example is not to criticize any given culture, but rather to emphasize the all-pervasive character of culture. *Cultural indoctrination* doesn't appear on your college curriculum (nor did it appear on the curriculum in primary and secondary school), but it is certainly there, even though students, parents, teachers, and administrators might not reflect on it. We're seldom taught to reflect on and critique our culture. Instead, from birth to death we breathe in our culture like oxygen, and it works its way into the marrow of our lives.

A final comment regarding culture seems in order, since you're moving into a social and cultural world about which it has been said that the only constant reality is change. Culture is by no means an unchanging reality; it is a human creation, and it changes as people change, even though the change might be quite gradual. The women's movement is a clear example of significant change in cultural assumptions. If you are a woman, your life chances with respect to career probably differ in striking ways from those of your grandmother. Your culture is no longer as likely to dictate stereotyped career paths for you. If you are married, your relationship with your husband is probably on a much more equal footing. These changes have come about in part because individuals and groups have organized to pursue their belief that a person's sex should not rigidly determine his or her life chances.

In summary, we have suggested that there are four levels of the social world in which your development is taking place:

1. *personal settings*, such as the family, which constitute the immediate social contexts of life;
2. *the network of personal settings;* that is, the various ways in which these personal settings influence one another, especially through you as a linking pin;
3. *large institutions and organizations*, which affect you as an individual as well as your personal systems and the network they form; and
4. *culture*, which pervades and influences all levels of systems.

At first glance, it might seem as though you can do little to influence many of these systems. We hope this is not completely true. Some people, perhaps especially those who grow up in tougher neighborhoods, develop what has been called *street smarts*—that is, the practical working knowledge and skills they need to get along in a tough world. We hope that this book, together with your experiences and knowledge, will help you to begin to develop "system smarts"—that is, the kind of working knowledge and skills you need to examine, critique, invest yourself in, cooperate with, cope with, and even change the systems of your life.

Throughout this book, you will be asked to reflect not only on the developmental events of this transitional stage of your life but also on the settings in which these events take place. Ideally, you should develop a working knowledge of significant developmental processes, of the social and cultural settings that constitute the context of those processes, and of the important ways in which developmental tasks interact with those settings. These kinds of working knowledge, coupled with the life skills we will discuss in greater detail, provide, in our opinion, a basis for what might be called *developmental competence*. These skills represent some of the tools you need to assume greater self-direction with respect to the developmental tasks of life.

Self-Direction in Development: How This Book Can Help You

We've designed this book around four activities to be used with each topic discussed: (1) personal reflection, (2) systematic analysis, (3) structured group interaction, and (4) personal-action planning. These activities are designed to help you become more self-directed in your pursuit of developmental goals. Let us briefly explain what each of these activities involves.

1. Personal Reflection

At the beginning of each chapter (beginning with Chapter 3), you will find a number of questions and tasks that will help you to see where you stand with respect to a particular developmental task or challenge (establishing and deepening interpersonal relationships, for example). The questions and tasks are designed to help you identify and analyze the key dimensions of the developmental task in question and to pull these dimensions together into a coherent pattern. You will, in other words, be asking yourself questions such as: "Where do I stand right now on this particular developmental issue?" "What does my present behavior in the area look like?" "What am I accomplishing?" "At what cost?" Here are some examples of the kinds of questions and tasks that appear in this book.

△ What kind of support do you usually look for from other people?
△ Name three things you seem to do well.
△ List several adjectives that you think describe the important dimensions of yourself.

△ Pick out a relationship in your life that you would hate to lose. What is it that makes it so important to you?
△ What do you think you will be doing five years from now?
△ Write a one-sentence statement that reflects a personal value you hold.

These questions and exercises refer to a variety of developmental tasks. You need not answer them now. Later, they will be presented in a more systematic way.

2. Systematic Analysis

After you've responded to the reflection questions and exercises, you will be given a set of concepts derived from developmental theory and research. These are practical concepts designed to help you develop a working knowledge of specific developmental tasks. You will then be asked to return to what you discovered about yourself in the "personal reflection" part of this process and take a second, but now *systematic,* look at your behavior and accomplishments in this particular area using the concepts provided in the "systematic analysis" section. For instance, you will be given a systematic picture of the kinds of skills you need to develop and deepen interpersonal relationships. You will then be asked to take a second and more systematic view of how you actually relate to others from the vantage point of what you've learned about communication skills.

3. Structured Group Interaction

We've designed structured group activities that focus on each developmental area. Although this book can be used by individuals who don't have access to others who are interested in this type of exploration, ideally, the reader will find himself or herself in a learning community with others who can offer support and challenge along the way. We wish to emphasize the *social* character of human development. From birth through death, significant people in your life (parents, teachers, friends, colleagues, and so on) have profound effects on the person you become. The structured group exercises in phase three of our process are designed to encourage you to involve yourselves mutually in one another's learning. A good deal of research suggests that the climate of group support and interest can greatly enhance individual learning and growth.

4. Personal-Action Planning

In the fourth and final phase of this process, you will be encouraged to translate what you've learned in the first three phases into concrete decisions with respect to action programs related to your own development. Since a good deal of behavioral science research suggests that change is best accomplished through a series of small steps that lead to a larger goal, we present a straightforward and nontechnical process that you can use in creating a program for change and development in your own life. This process will be applied to each developmental challenge we consider. After you've worked through this book, you will be quite adept at using this process to formulate and execute your own life-planning process. This action-planning process is explained in Chapter 3.

The Values This Book Promotes

Two values of the authors are woven so completely into the fabric of this book that we think it important to call them to your attention at the outset. These values are *self-direction* and *mutuality*.

The value of *self-direction* reflects our belief that the knowledge and skills of the behavioral sciences can be made available to people so that they aren't dependent in any ongoing way on professionals. For us, a belief in self-direction is a call to initiative in your own life. This is not to suggest that all the factors affecting your development are under your control or purely psychological in nature. As we've already indicated, we're aware of the impact of social systems—the family, schools, government, religion, the economy—on your development. By emphasizing self-direction as a value, we mean to highlight our conviction that there is much you can do to enhance your own development, rather than wait for a teacher, counselor, psychologist, or other officially designated helper to come to your aid. Our intent is to translate behavioral science theory and research in a way that makes it possible for you to develop self-direction in your own life.

By *mutuality*, we mean the willingness of people to invest themselves in one another's lives in order to contribute to one another's growth and development. This value reflects our belief that human beings are the major source of influence on personal development. The term *mutuality*, as we are using it, refers to the following:

1. disclosing and sharing yourself with others in a game-free way when such disclosure is appropriate,
2. listening to others carefully and trying to understand their point of view,
3. challenging yourself and calling on others for help in this process,
4. challenging others caringly and responsibly when challenge seems appropriate,
5. engaging in nondefensive self-exploration when challenged, and
6. discussing with others the state of your relationship with them when this seems appropriate.

We believe that your capacity to establish relationships characterized by appropriate degrees of mutuality will greatly affect your own development as well as the development of those people who are important to you. The theme of mutuality in interpersonal living is the basis of the structured group activities that appear in Chapters 3 through 13.

A word of caution. By emphasizing mutuality, we don't mean to suggest that all the members of your group or class should become your intimate friends.

We *are* encouraging the kind of openness that fits in with the goals of this book. In this context, mutuality refers to people working to create a learning community rather than remaining highly individualistic members of a class. This book, then, suggests a kind of experiment in interpersonal living that perhaps doesn't characterize regular classroom experience. It is not an exercise in psychological nudity, or unwanted and inappropriate intimacy. On the other hand, it does call for a gradual development of trust, an appreciation of confidentiality, and an eventual willingness to take reasonable risks in discussing your own development and responding to others as they discuss theirs.

In Chapter 2, we look at the particular developmental tasks or challenges associated with the time of life in which you now find yourself—the transitional stage of moving beyond adolescence into adulthood.

2

Moving into Adulthood: The Developmental Challenges of the College Years

In this chapter, we look briefly at the structure of adult development, focusing on the challenges of the college years. Then, we provide an outline of the specific developmental tasks you will face during these years. Next, you are invited to complete self-reflection exercises that will help you to focus on your own developmental concerns and to take part in a structured group interaction in order to learn how other students are experiencing this important time of life.

The Pattern of Adult Development

We can understand the moving-into-adulthood years by placing them in context—that is, by developing an appreciation of how they build on previous development and provide preparation for life's next stage. You've already moved through a number of developmental periods and worked through a variety of developmental challenges. Take a moment to read through Table 2-1, which outlines life stages and the accomplishments (tasks) to be achieved at each stage. This table deals with the past, the present, and the future—that is, the stages you've already moved through, the stage you are in, and the stages toward which you are moving. It also indicates the settings in which developmental events take place and some of the resources that key social settings provide. Don't try to memorize the chart; instead, read through it briefly and note how life gradually places more and more complex demands on you. One of the functions of this chapter is to spell out the implications of this chart.

TABLE 2-1. A map of adult development.

Life Stage	Key Systems	Developmental Tasks	Developmental Resources
Infancy (birth–2)	Family —nuclear —extended	Social attachment Sense of continued existence of non-self Sensorimotor intelligence and primitive causality Maturation of motor functions	Security Basic need fulfillment Stability
Early childhood (2–4)	Family —nuclear —extended	Self-control Language development Fantasy and play Self-locomotion	Basic human support Human interaction Sensory stimulation Protected environment Limit setting
Middle childhood (5–7)	Family Neighbor- hood School	Gender identity Early moral development Concrete mental operations Group play	Basic human support Appropriate models Explanation of rule setting Consistency in rule enforcement Peer-group interaction

TABLE 2-1 *(continued)*

Life Stage	Key Systems	Developmental Tasks	Developmental Resources
Late childhood (8–12)	Family Neighbor- hood School Peer group	Cooperative social relations Self-evaluation Skill learning Team membership	Basic human support Cooperative learning environment Cooperative recreational environment Effective skills teaching —learning to learn —basic interpersonal relationships Feedback on self and performance
Early adolescence (13–17)	Family Peer group School	Physical maturation Formal mental operations Peer-group membership Initial sexual intimacy	Basic human support Physiological information Cognitive problem-solving and decision-making skills Relationship-building skills Knowledge of sex roles and their cultural sources Opportunities for independent moral judgment
Late adolescence (18–22)	Peer group School or work setting Family Surrounding community	Independent living Initial career decisions Internalized morality Initial sustained intimacy Relativistic thinking	Basic human support Knowledge and skills for: —financial independence —self-exploration —making decisions —deepening relationships —dealing with pluralism Responsibility for choices and consequences
Early adulthood (23–30)	New family Work setting Friendship network Surrounding community	Family living Initial parenting Career development Life-style management Capacity for commitment	Basic human support Knowledge and skills for: —family financial planning and management —interpersonal negotiating and conflict resolution —parenting —role discrimination and integration

Levinson and Adult Development

Daniel Levinson and his associates (1978) have discovered a sequence of developmental periods that they believe apply in a broad way to the development of adults in our society. Their research suggests that, during your adult life, you're likely to experience three major "eras," each beginning with an important transitional period. Table 2-2 illustrates these eras.

TABLE 2-2. Levinson's adult-development periods.

Era	Length of Era	Transitional Period Preceding Era
Early adulthood	age 22–40	age 17–22
Middle adulthood	age 45–60	age 40–45
Late adulthood	age 65–death	age 60–65

Levinson and his associates have formulated useful "cognitive maps," based on the ways in which people actually live their lives. These maps help individuals to form an orderly overview of the major developmental events that unfold as life progresses. If you are between the ages of 17 and 22, you haven't yet entered the era of early adulthood. To use Levinson's term, you're in a *transitional period*; you're leaving adolescence and moving into adulthood.

A Time of Transition

Levinson and his colleagues refer to the transitional periods (ages 17–22, 40–45, and 60–65) as *developmental bridges*. This image clearly describes the experience of the college years. It suggests that you're leaving a particular piece of solid ground and moving to another. Your old life is gradually being left behind, but the one that will replace it hasn't yet emerged. You are, in a very real sense, on a bridge that links adolescence with adult life. Another image we might use to describe this transitional period is a ferry boat. You've left dry land, and you're beginning to see dry land on the horizon. But sometimes the sea is quite rough. You are in transition.

Since transitional periods stand between the stable eras of the life cycle, they involve the termination or transformation of what went before and the creation of what's ahead. You are, no doubt, already quite aware of this. For example, your relationship with your family is clearly in a process of change—a process that may not always be comfortable for you or for them. At times, it may seem that your parents are completely supportive of your budding adult autonomy; at other times, they may seem to be trying to keep you under their control. In all likelihood, your parents experience a similar kind of confusion with respect to what you want from them. The seas can get rough for both you and your parents, but the degree of roughness differs greatly from person to person and from family to family. We believe that the working knowledge of human development that you will acquire by working through this book will help you see that much of the conflict that arises in the process of redefining your relationship with your family is due to the nature of development during a transitional period rather than a lack of love, trust, or respect either on your part or on the part of your family.

The Characteristics of a Transitional Period

What are some of the characteristics of a transitional period and how do they affect you? The following list of characteristics is adapted from Levinson (1978).

1. Boundary Zone

A transitional period is a boundary zone between two more or less defined or structured periods of life; therefore, during this moving-into-adulthood period, you might feel that you're neither fish nor fowl. Perhaps at times you feel suspended between the past and the future. Your roles aren't as clearly defined as they used to be. Boy or man? Girl or woman? You struggle to find out which you really are. At times, you might feel very young, and at other times, you might feel quite old. For some people, these feelings are quite intense; for others, they are mild enough most of the time to seem almost nonexistent.

2. A Time of Termination or Modification

During a transitional period, you terminate or modify your relationships with important *people*, such as your parents and your peers, and with important *institutions*, such as your school and your church. Although transitions lead to growth and development, they are times of uprooting, separation, and loss. Those who study the process of dying have discovered that certain strong feelings often accompany a time of loss. During this current transitional period, you might experience the following: denial, anger, bargaining, depression, and acceptance.

Denial. You might want to ignore the fact that you are in a transitional period—that the time has come to begin to move out of adolescence and face adult responsibilities. This kind of unwillingness can take a number of forms. For instance, you might feel that the study habits you had in high school are sufficient for college. You might deny that college is making greater demands on you.

Anger. Perhaps the new demands life is placing on you cause you to feel anger. This anger can crop up anywhere (and unexpectedly). You shout at your parents or your friends. You become angry with yourself. You find that school, teachers, and courses make you angry. At times, you might feel like ditching the whole thing.

Bargaining. You want yourself and others to allow you to remain an adolescent, at least in certain ways, for just a little longer. You put off decisions about a major or about working out finances for next semester or next year. You'd like to buy just a little more time before you're forced to face adult responsibilities.

Depression. This is not an uncommon emotion during the college years. A few people your age find this time so dark and bitter that they commit suicide. They can't seem to find the resources they need; they can't see the light at the end of the tunnel. This extreme is rare; much less severe levels of depression are most common.

Acceptance. You will acquire the ability to accept, without excessive regret, both natural developmental losses (including, later on in life, the loss of hair or of smooth skin) and developmental challenges, together with the turmoil they generate.

Of course, the difference between a transitional period and dying is that a transitional period is not just the end of something—you are dying to one stage of life but are being reborn into another. *The point is that the kinds of feelings described here are quite normal during a transitional period.* It's not a question of whether you experience these feelings or not, but rather of how you handle them. Learning how to accept the losses that are associated with a transitional period and seeing them as signs of a full adult life that is about to begin are important but sometimes painful tasks. Termination and modification can involve uncertainty and confusion; it's difficult to know what you should reject and what you should keep from the past. Again, there are wide individual differences here. You might experience some of these feelings intensely, or you might scarcely notice them.

3. Questioning

A transitional period is one during which you question the world and your place in it. You question your values and the ways in which you put them into practice. You question your present way of doing things. For instance, you might question the way in which you always seem to give in to authority figures. Or you might question the dogmatic way in which religion has been presented to you. You begin searching for different ways of seeing yourself, your world, and yourself in the world. You consider ways in which you would like to change—maybe you shouldn't be so compliant, or maybe you should become more serious about studying, or maybe you need to seek out new friends.

4. Experimentation

Questioning leads naturally to experimenting with new or different ways of doing things. For instance, you might decide to become much more assertive in pursuing relationships with members of the opposite sex. Or you might decide to choose electives that interest you (even though they don't fit into the overall plan of studies that your parents or advisers favor). You might begin to choose friends who differ from the people you associated with in high school. Doing things differently is a way of breaking out of the old mold and giving yourself a wider variety of experiences on which you can base decisions about your future. As Levinson noted, during a transition period, the neglected parts of the self seek expression; this naturally leads to experimentation.

Erik Erikson (1959) uses the term *psychosocial moratorium* to describe the period of experimentation. Ideally, society offers you "time off" from ordinary role expectations so that you can experiment with new roles, new values, and new belief systems. Some high school students take a year or two off before going on to college. Some college students take a year or two off in the middle of their college years. Some of them work, some travel, and others join the Peace Corps or some other voluntary agency. In these kinds of cases, the moratorium is more or less well defined. Many students don't actually take time off for work or travel; instead, they pursue the tasks of the moratorium while remaining "on the job," as it were.

It's easy to see that a transitional period is a time of legitimate experimentation; however, some people find it difficult to free themselves enough to engage in reasonable experimentation. They find it difficult to distinguish between legitimate developmental experimentation and a disregard of norms and standards learned at home, at church, and in school.

5. Initiation of New Patterns

Experimentation during a transitional phase helps you to move toward *commitment* to choices in areas such as love, marriage, and career. These choices form the basis for the period of young adulthood toward which you are moving. After testing some preliminary choices relating to adult living, you will be ready to say something like "At least for now, I'll do whatever is necessary to prepare myself for a career in clinical or counseling psychology," or "At least for now, I'll develop a close relationship without immediately choosing to marry," or "At least for now, I'll take whatever job I can get. Once I begin supporting myself, I can take a look at other options." As a result of these initial choices and commitments, a new life structure will begin to emerge during the transitional period, and you'll begin to consolidate your initial adult identity. You'll begin to picture yourself more and more as a member of the world of young adults.

6. Transitional Periods Come to an End

As Levinson notes, you'll know that this transitional period is ending when the tasks of questioning, exploring, and experimenting lose their urgency and you begin to make commitments in critical areas of life—when you begin to move beyond the "boundary zone" and create a life within the adult world. As we shall see, not everyone moves out of this transitional period into young adulthood with the finality suggested here. Some people don't want to leave adolescence or don't want to give up the advantages of the moratorium. In certain areas of life, they hang onto this transitional period.

You've probably thought from time to time about the temporary nature of the college years; they don't go on forever. If you're already working, you're well aware of this fact. If you're a full-time student, serious choices concerning career, marriage and family life, and the kind of life-style you'll follow await you in a relatively short period of time; however, until you approach the end of this transitional period (age 22 or 23), you can put off those choices in many ways—you can do some "bargaining." You might not have to sign an employment contract, enter law school, marry, or decide whether to live in an urban, suburban, or rural

Form 2-1

Current Life Concerns Assessment

1. *Brainstorming*

2. *Clustering*

Theme: _____   Theme: _____   Theme: _____

Items

Theme: _____   Theme: _____   Theme: _____

Items

3. *Items rated 4 or 5*

setting right this minute. At the same time, you need to choose a major course of study, work out your involvement in important relationships, and perhaps deal with your growing awareness that the pattern of your day-to-day life for the next decade will be the result of the experiences you're having and the choices you're making (or not making) right now.

Personal-Reflection Exercise: An Assessment of Current Life Concerns

1. Find a quiet place in which you can work for about 20 minutes. Using the "brainstorming" section of Form 2-1, write down anything that comes to your mind in response to the following question: What concerns, decisions, problems, or worries do you find on your mind at this point in your life? Relax, close your eyes, and pay attention to whatever thoughts or feelings come into your mind in response to this question. When something has registered, jot down a few words or a short sentence that conveys your concern. For example: "car payments," "no major yet," "fight with mom," "I need a summer job," "religion," "my relationships with members of the opposite sex," "the hassle of full-time work and part-time school," and so on. When you've finished, your list should include most of the things that are of concern to you at this point in your life. Put the list aside for awhile. Review it later and make any necessary additions.

2. Go back through your list, and, using the "clustering" section of the form, see whether the items you listed in the brainstorming section can be divided into categories and labeled ("concerns about studies," for example). One student who worked on this form came up with the following clusters:

Family	*Social life*	*Career*
—home or apartment living	—fight with Ken	—disagreement with adviser
—Dad might lose his job.	—I'm not doing much dating.	—flunking finance course
—kid brother is into drugs.	—my part-time job versus friendships	—applying for law school

See if you can find categories that seem to help your concerns hang together in some way. Items may appear in more than one cluster. For instance, "home or apartment living" might be a social-life issue as well as a family issue for some individuals.

3. Go back through your items in the brainstorming section and pick out the ones that seem most pressing, most important, to you. Rank all the items in that section by assigning a number between 1 and 5 to each item (5 = very pressing or important, 3 = moderately important, and 1 = not very pressing). When you've finished ranking all the items, make a list of all concerns that are rated 5 or 4 on the scale.

Once you've determined what your top concerns are—that is, those rated 4 or 5—write them on a 3 × 5 card. These cards will then be collected and read; this will give you some idea of the range of concerns expressed and indicate the concerns you share with other students.

4. After the cards have been read, discuss people's reactions to what they've heard.

The Developmental Tasks of Moving into Adulthood: An Overview

As we've indicated, an important function of this book is to provide working knowledge—information that assists you in dealing effectively with the life concerns currently facing you. A great deal of research has focused on the moving-into-adulthood years. Patterns of development have been identified. We would like to share with you some of the highlights of this research as a way of helping you to develop a working knowledge of the challenges you face. We will start with an overview of ten developmental tasks of moving into adulthood. The next ten chapters are designed to help you reflect in a systematic way on where you stand with respect to these tasks.

The research of Arthur Chickering (Chickering, 1969; Chickering & McCormick, 1973), among others, has yielded a useful framework that can be used in describing some of the demands of transitional years. We've structured the next ten chapters to follow Chickering's model with some modifications and additions. Here, then, is an overview of the ten developmental tasks of moving into adulthood: (1) becoming competent, (2) achieving autonomy, (3) developing and implementing values, (4) forming an identity, (5) integrating sexuality into life, (6) making friends and developing intimacy, (7) loving and making a commitment to another person, (8) making initial job or career choices, (9) becoming an active community member and citizen, and (10) learning how to use leisure time.

1. Becoming Competent

All of us engage in developmental tasks throughout the entire life-span, and most of us want to carry out these tasks *competently*. In one sense, competence refers to the development of the kinds of working knowledge and skills needed to carry out developmental tasks and the actual use of the knowledge and skills to complete those tasks. In other words, competence involves not only abilities and behaviors, but accomplishments as well. Chickering talks about intellectual competence, physical competence, and social competence. We include the abilities needed in these areas *and* the accomplishments achieved when these abilities are used. Your *sense* of competence is the degree of confidence you have in your ability to get things done. Your *actual* competence refers to your ability to get them done. Your self-esteem needn't rest on your being better than others, but it *does* rest in part on both your sense of competence and your actual competence. In this book, we stress competence in accomplishing developmental tasks.

2. Achieving Autonomy

Autonomy refers to a mature type of independence. You've achieved autonomy when you can answer the following questions in the affirmative.

△ Am I capable of living from day to day without a need for constant approval and affection from others?

△ Can I carry out the routine activities of daily life and cope with problems that come up *on my own*—that is, without continually seeking help from others?

△ When I want or need something, do I do what needs to be done without waiting for someone to take care of it for me or for something to "just happen"?

△ Can I ask others for help when I need it without becoming dependent on them?

△ Do I recognize that my needs and wants have to be considered in relationship to the needs and wants of the other people in my life— parents, friends, teachers—and society as a whole? Do I recognize the need for *interdependence*?

3. Developing and Implementing Values

During the early years of life, you're provided with a set of values by your family, school, church, community, and country. Many of these values aren't discussed directly, but you assimilate them simply by being a member of these basic social settings. You now face the challenge of choosing a set of personal values that gives meaning and direction to your life. These values are subject, of course, to the influence of parents, teachers, ministers, friends, national leaders, authors, and the media. Still, you are faced with the task of selecting and integrating a set of personal values based on these different influences.

At times you will have to reconcile seemingly competing values. This process of reconciliation relates to many different areas of life:

△ academic performance versus personal and social development

△ self-centered sexual behavior versus sex at the service of deep commitment

△ personal needs and wants versus the needs and wants of others

△ choosing a career to make money versus choosing a career for personal satisfaction

△ the demands of family versus personal demands

△ competition versus the pursuit of personal standards of excellence in academic settings

△ continuity versus change in religious beliefs

△ immediate gratification versus deferred gratification of needs and wants

As we shall see, what William Perry (1970) calls the *committed individual* is one who has come to terms with the bewildering diversity of value perspectives and has chosen a set of values—values that seem sound and make ethical sense to the individual in question.

4. Forming an Identity

One working definition of *identity* is "a stable sense of who you are that is confirmed by the people in your life who are important to you." This definition makes two important points about your sense of identity: it deals with the way in which you think and feel about yourself *and* it takes into consideration the way in which the important people in your life see you and treat you. In other words, your personal sense of identity has both a *psychological* and a *social* component. The years of moving into adulthood tend to be filled with questions relating to identity:

△ Who am I?
△ Where am I going in life?
△ Are my values really me?
△ Can I honestly be the person that "he" or "she" or "they" want me to be?
△ Why do I sometimes feel like a different person when I go back home to visit?

Erik Erikson (1950, 1959, 1968, 1974) has written extensively over the past three decades, focusing on what identity is in North American society. Most authors who write about identity incorporate much of what Erikson has found. In an earlier version of their text, Newman and Newman (1975) describe identity as "eventual commitment to a personal integration of values, goals, and abilities" (p. 219). As we shall see, identity is an integrating concept. It has much to do with how you see yourself as a unique, separate person with past identifications and future possibilities—a person who maintains many relationships with people, organizations, institutions, and culture.

5. Integrating Sexuality into Life

Sex is an important kind of intimacy; however, the fact that, for so many people, it is such a strong force increases the difficulty they have in integrating it with the rest of life. It does not help to live in a society that has been described as "adolescent" in its approach to sex (for instance, in its blatant use of sex to promote consumerism). During the moving-into-adulthood years, you are challenged to develop values with respect to sexuality and sexual expression and to integrate these with other values. If sex is not to be a disruptive force, it must be integrated with the other forms of intimacy that enrich interpersonal living—it must serve and not control interpersonal relationships. Some people try to "solve" the problem of sex by overemphasizing it, in which case sex can become their demanding taskmaster. Others try to minimize the importance of sex, thereby losing the warmth and contact that is provided by an integrated sexuality.

Chapter 7, which focuses on sexuality, neither teaches nor reviews the basic facts of life. It is meant to help you review your current sexual identity and life-style so that you can make the kinds of decisions that will help you to integrate sex with other developmental challenges—especially the challenges of friendship and marriage.

6. Making Friends and Developing Intimacy

During the years of moving into adulthood, the ways in which you relate to other people might undergo important changes. For instance, as your emotions deepen and become more complex, you become more and more capable of experiencing and expressing different kinds of intimacy. Once you're relatively secure in your own identity, it's possible for you to allow and even value the differences you find between yourself and others. Individuals who are still trying to establish their own identities are likely to prefer to be with others who think and feel as they do, whereas individuals who have achieved some measure of stable identity are more likely to accept others for what they are—they're more likely to value individual differences rather than minimize or ignore them.

This growth in the ability to relate to others has been described by Chickering (1969):

> Relationships shift toward greater trust, independence, and individuality. They are less symbiotic; the support provided is more simple and strong, more implicit, more taken for granted, more to be relied on. These friendships and loves survive the development of differences and episodes of disagreement. They persist through times of separation and noncommunication [p. 15].

Such relationships can add a dimension of richness and "connectedness" to your life that is beyond value. We will examine friendship and the different kinds of intimacy associated with it in Chapter 8.

7. Loving and Making a Commitment to Another Person

Even though there is a great deal of talk today about the disintegration of marriage and the family, the vast majority of adults in our society marry and have families. It is also true that more and more people are deferring marriage and allowing themselves greater freedom in experimenting with intimate relationships. Due to the rapidity of technological and social change we are witnessing in society today, it may be very difficult to establish a stable marriage; however, many people *do* achieve stable marriages. You may or may not marry during your moving-into-adulthood years, but this transitional period is certainly one in which you can lay the foundation for whatever kinds of deeper commitments you want in your life. You might ask yourself questions such as: "What are the competencies in terms of working knowledge and skills that I need for marriage and deeper commitment? Do I have them? Where can I get them?" Success in your deepest commitments to others is not just a function of good will. Choosing a marriage partner is one of the most rewarding of the developmental challenges; it is also one of the most difficult.

8. Making Initial Job or Career Choices

Since approximately one third of your life before retirement will be spent at work, the effort you put into preparing yourself for a job, occupation, or career is obviously important. As Levinson and his associates (1978) point out, you experience a dilemma with respect to career at this time in your life:

> One of the great paradoxes of human development is that we are required to make crucial choices before we have the knowledge, judgment, and self understanding to choose wisely. Yet, if we put off these choices until we feel truly ready, the delay may produce other and greater costs. This is especially true of the two great choices of early adulthood: occupation and marriage [p. 102].*

What can you do during these transitional years to resolve the dilemma Levinson describes? If you are a pre-med student and have a reasonable hope of being accepted into a medical school, you might well be committing yourself to a lifelong career choice. But most people your age don't have that kind of clarity or expectation of success. If you have no idea which occupation you would like to enter, your experience is hardly an uncommon one. Perhaps the best thing you can do right now is develop a broad range of competencies that could relate to any number of different occupations.

9. Becoming an Active Community Member and Citizen

The developmental challenge of becoming an active community member and citizen receives relatively little treatment in the moving-into-adulthood literature; it is considered only at later stages. However, we believe that the best predictor of future behavior is present behavior. Although this developmental challenge might not be central now, it cannot be dismissed or completely deferred. You live in a world that has grown quite small. You know this world more intimately than any of your forebears, because television, radio, newspapers, and magazines place it before you day in and day out. The media deal mainly with dramatic news, and, for the most part, dramatic news is bad news—scandals in local and national government, the disintegration of our cities, disasters, the ener-

*From *The Seasons of a Man's Life*, by Daniel J. Levinson. Copyright © 1978 by Daniel J. Levinson. This and all other quotations from this source are reprinted by permission of Alfred A. Knopf, Inc.

gy crisis, the depletion of our natural resources, the destruction of the environment, political "danger spots" throughout the world, war, and a whole litany of despair.

In the face of all of this, you might ask yourself "What can I do to make this world just a little better for myself and my children?"Some people simply avoid the question, while others answer it naively or cynically. Through the decisions you make during the moving-into-adulthood years, you are laying the foundations of the way in which you will answer this question. An old song refers to building a comfortable nest somewhere out in the West and letting "the rest of the world go by." This is one answer to the question we've posed. On the other hand, some people have answered this question, at least initially, by spending some time in the Peace Corps or by finding other ways of getting a better picture of the world in which they live and of determining just how they want to relate to it. As you can see, the kinds of values you develop will greatly influence both your initial and your ultimate answer—what can you do to make this world just a little better for yourself and your children?

10. Learning How to Use Leisure Time

You live in a society that affords a great deal of leisure time, and it may be that the amount of leisure time you can expect will increase in the years to come. The question is "How am I to use my free time?" You cannot answer this question fully without clarifying your values. What do you want to get out of life? By attempting to answer this question, you're beginning to formulate criteria for your use of leisure time. When we examine the ways in which people actually spend their leisure hours, we find striking differences. We find some people sitting almost continuously in front of their television sets. Others are out investing themselves in political campaigns, volunteer work, and sky diving. From the perspective of this book, the important point here is that, during these transitional years, you're developing the patterns of leisure pursuits that will characterize your adult life. If you want your leisure pursuits to be *productive* in some sense of that term, you will probably have to start "producing" now. Obviously, there is no "best" pattern. If you want to develop self-enhancing leisure patterns, now is the time to do something about it. If, like many people, you prefer to let your leisure life "just happen," then there is little you need to do. The material in Chapter 12 will help you to think systematically about your leisure time and its use.

The Formulation of Your Dream

You probably have some hopes, desires, longings, expectations, and plans with respect to the developmental tasks, or challenges, we've discussed here. For instance, you might expect to marry within the next five or ten years and establish a family. Or your hopes might be focused on your sense of identity—you hope to be able to "pull yourself together" more effectively than you have up to this point, and you hope that you'll feel better about yourself than you do now. Levinson and his associates (1978) call this group of hopes and expectations your *Dream*, and they suggest that one important developmental task that starts in the moving-into-adulthood period and continues in adult life is "forming and living out the dream":

> In everyday language, we say that someone "succeeded beyond his wildest dreams," or that he "dreamed of a world he could never have." These are neither night dreams or casual daydreams. A "dream" of this kind is more formed than a pure fantasy, yet less articulated than a fully thought-out plan. It is the central issue in Martin Luther King's historic "I have a dream" speech. It is the meaning Delmore Schwartz intended with the title of his story "In Dreams Begin Responsibilities." . . .
>
> In its primordial form, the Dream is a vague sense of self-in-the-adult-world. It has the quality of a vision, an imagined possibility that generates excitement and vitality. At the start it is poorly articulated and only tenuously connected to reality, although it may contain concrete images, such as winning the Nobel Prize or making the all-star team. It may take a dramatic form as in the myth of the hero: the great artist, business tycoon, athletic or intellectual superstar performing magnificent feats and receiving special honors. It may take mundane forms that are yet inspiring and sustaining: the excellent craftsman, the husband-father (wife-mother) in a certain kind of family, the highly respected member of one's community [p. 91].

We do not list the formulation of your dream as the eleventh developmental task, because it relates to elements in the ten tasks that have been described.

Following Levinson, we can discuss what a Dream is like (characteristics), where it comes from (source), and what you can do about it (process).

Characteristics of the Dream

The Dream has the following characteristics:

△ It concerns *the adult world*. It includes projections of what you might like to be and do in the adult world. For instance, you might see yourself as a head mechanic in a large automobile repair shop or as the owner of a shop yourself.

△ It includes *imagined possibilities* that generate excitement and vitality. These possibilities can motivate you to strive for their realization. For example, you see yourself teaching in high school, and you like what you see.

△ It's *neither pure fantasy nor pure reality;* it's somewhere in between. For instance, you see yourself as a full partner in a large accounting firm. The eventual reality might be that you are a senior accountant in such a firm.

△ It relates *not only to occupation but to any or all dimensions of your developmental tasks and life-style*. You see yourself as rich, or as a person of great integrity, who puts important religious values into practice. Or you might see yourself as a person who has a great deal of control over the lives of others, or as a very independent and self-sufficient person. Your Dream might be simple and refer to a single theme, or it might be quite complex and include many themes.

△ It refers to the *good life* in some way. It often includes elements of ideal involvement with work, family, and community.

The Source of the Dream

Your Dream has a combination of sources. Your Dream comes in part from yourself. You are a person with certain life goals (however clear or murky they might be), longings, strivings, competencies, abilities, talents (realized or unrealized), motives, values, fears, hopes, and anxieties. In short, all those things that go into your personality makeup can also contribute to your Dream. For instance, if you have musical talent and great manual dexterity, these characteristics can contribute to your Dream of being a musician. If you are shy and have misgivings about yourself, your Dream will probably differ from that of a very outgoing person. Your dream might include an occupation that doesn't require a great deal of contact with other people. It might also include a marriage that doesn't include a great deal of socializing outside the home.

Your Dream also comes from your interactions with significant others. Special people in your life can contribute in significant ways to your Dream. For instance, your grandmother is a fine, caring human being who can be of service to others without losing her own identity. She is a strong yet compassionate woman. People admire her. Without saying directly to yourself "In some ways, I want to be like her," you identify with her and incorporate parts of her style into the Dream of the kind of person you would like to be. Or your uncle is rich and ruthless. He likes you and thinks you have what it takes to follow in his footsteps. You admire him and incorporate elements of his life into your Dream.

Finally, your Dream comes from your interactions in the social settings of your life, both past and present. Elements of your Dream come from and are related to your family, social class, schools, church, peers, and relatives. If you live in a ghetto and are relatively poor, your Dream might focus on getting out of the ghetto and "making it" in society, or it might focus on doing something about those who are born with social disadvantages.

Implementation of the Dream

There are, broadly speaking, three phases to the implementation of your Dream: (1) defining the Dream, (2) obtaining needed support and training, and (3) translating the Dream into reality.

1. Defining the Dream. When a Dream begins, it is ill-defined and fragile. Even though you begin to formulate your Dream during high school, it still needs greater definition. Various people and institutions can help you in defining your Dream. Some people, for instance, have vague feelings that they would like to help others and that they would like to live a comfortable life. Eventually, helping others takes the form of becoming a social worker, and the comfortable life includes marrying someone who is also earning a living in some helping profession, such as nursing, and deferring children until enough money is saved to buy a house.

2. Obtaining needed support and training. As your Dream becomes more clearly defined, you need to find the resources that will enable you to transform elements of the Dream into reality. For example, if your dream involves working in business, you could take business courses and work part-time in the accounting department of a firm where you might meet people who could help you to clarify your goals and teach you how to involve yourself effectively in the business world. By doing this, you could obtain some of the training and support you need.

3. Translating the Dream into reality. Once you've obtained training and searched out sources of support, you're ready for the actual execution of the Dream. This is often a very gradual process. As Levinson and his associates point out, translating the dream into reality involves creating, experimenting with, and slowly actualizing a new "self-in-the-world." For instance, you might first take a job you don't like with a firm that doesn't appeal to you. But at least it's a job in an area that interests you. You can begin to use the working knowledge and skills you've developed. Once you get established in this job and get the "feel" of it, you can plan to move on.

Mentors and Models

There are two special "people" resources that can help you to define, discover resources for, and implement various aspects of your Dream: mentors and models. Levinson and his associates focus a great deal of attention on this resource. In fact, they go so far as to suggest that one of your developmental tasks is to find mentors in key developmental areas. First, let us explain what they mean by the term *mentor.* According to Levinson and his associates, a mentor has certain characteristics and exercises certain functions.

Characteristics of a Mentor

A mentor is older than his or her protégé—too old to be a peer and too young to be seen as a parent. And yet, a mentor is a mixture of parent and peer—a person who has greater experience than his or her protégé and also expertise in some area of life. A mentor is both responsible and successful with respect to one or more areas of life. For instance, Joan Kaul, 26, is married and has two young children. Betty Tricot, 37, also is married and has three children. Joan and Betty are friends, but there is a tacit understanding that Betty, at least on occasions, acts as a mentor toward Joan. She has had more experience than Joan, and she has a successful marriage. When it comes to relating to her husband, raising children, and managing a household, Betty has a great deal of expertise. Joan isn't a dependent person, but she counts on Betty's "wisdom" (especially because Betty doesn't force it down her throat).

Functions of a Mentor

Mentors can provide support and challenge in a number of different ways. First of all, they can act as models, or exemplars, for others. This doesn't necessarily mean that they place themselves in this role. Since they have experience, expertise, and success, others naturally see them as exemplars. They can engage in teacher/trainer functions, helping their protégés to develop expertise. Mentors often act as sponsors, helping others to enter a system or to find advancement in it. This type of sponsorship is seen quite often in the business world, politics, and in certain church circles. Mentors can act as hosts or guides for those entering new occupations or for those undertaking a developmental task, such as marriage, for the first time. In this role, mentors can initiate newcomers into the values, customs, norms, standards, and rules of a system, especially when these are unwritten. In a business, in a new neighborhood, or in a prison, mentors can teach newcomers "the ropes." Mentors are, in some ways, task-related friends. They model competent behavior, share their experience, and provide counsel, or advice.

As we have seen, mentors aren't limited to the business world; they can be artists, teachers, family men and women, ministers, professional people, plumbers, or prisoners. The mentor/protégé relationship is usually transitional. In the example we cited, as Joan develops her own expertise in family life and management, she no longer needs Betty as a mentor. If Betty clings to that role, then the relationship can become troubled; however, if she can relinquish the role of mentor, then she and Joan will be able to become good friends. The mentor/protégé relationship isn't an all-or-nothing relationship. There can be elements of the mentoring process in many different kinds of relationships. The point that Levinson makes is that mentors can be quite influential in helping people to initiate, define, and execute their Dreams. The mentor/protégé relationship can be flawed but still be useful to both parties. For instance, a manager who is helping a younger worker to advance in the company might enjoy this relationship and yet fear that the protégé is eventually going to outshine her. Or the person being sponsored might resent his sponsor, because he sees the person as parent, even though the sponsor is not acting in a parental way.

A Mentor Exercise

Perhaps you've never thought about the process of "mentoring." Or perhaps it sounds foreign to your experience, at least up to this point. But take a few minutes to think of people older than yourself who, in some way or other, might fulfill the role of mentor. You needn't discover a full-fledged mentor; any relationship that has a mentor/protégé quality will do. If anyone comes to mind, describe the way in which the two of you relate. Remember that the relationship can involve any of the developmental-task areas we've examined. Describe your feelings regarding this relationship.

If you can find no mentor/protégé relationship in your life, describe briefly what you think about mentoring and how you would feel about developing such a relationship.

Models

Although not all of us have mentors, we all (consciously or unconsciously) have models—all of us see people doing things we would like to be able to do. Imitation, which is *not* limited to childhood, is one of the most powerful sources of learning (Bandura, 1969, 1977). All around you, people carry out developmental tasks, or combinations of tasks, quite well. We suggest that it might be very useful to take a more reflective look at such people and see what you might learn from them. We don't suggest that you pick a hero and try to imitate him or her in any slavish way. Your models can be quite ordinary people who are carrying out ordinary tasks competently. You can imitate them in a way that makes you what you want to be and not merely a kind of second-hand imitation of them. Models can be one of your best "people" resources.

An Exercise Relating to Models

You might hesitate to examine your life with regard to the models you have, precisely because you are at a time of life during which the development of greater autonomy is an important task; however, the fact that you have models in various developmental areas or with respect to a certain kind of life-style doesn't signify that you are a dependent person. Having models is a part of full living.

A. Developmental-Task Models

1. Pick three developmental-task areas that interest you.

2. Comb through your experience and see whether you can identify someone who is doing well in each of those developmental areas. For instance, you might respect your older sister or brother for the way in which he or she worked for greater independence without either surrendering principles or inflicting unnecessary pain on your parents.

3. Describe the way in which you might imitate such a person while still remaining yourself.

4. Share with one of your fellow students the one developmental-task area in which you learned the most.

B. Life-Style Model

1. Think of a person older than yourself whose general life-style you like or admire—someone who approximates your Dream for the future.

2. Write a brief explanation of what it is about that person that appeals to you.

3. Indicate what you would have to do to imitate that person (again, while being yourself).

In order to take the three steps involved in the development of your Dream—defining your Dream, obtaining support and training, and translating your Dream into reality—you'll have to overcome certain obstacles. Some people move in directions that are opposed to the Dream because they are pushed that way by parents or other significant adults or because the resources for fulfilling the Dream—money, talent, or opportunity—are lacking. Others fail to pursue their Dream because of passivity or guilt or some other internal obstacle. For instance, a young woman considers entering the business world, but fails to prepare herself because she fears that others will think she isn't "feminine," or because she feels she's not "tough enough" for a male-dominated world, or because she has religious scruples about making money. Very often, a Dream is difficult to accomplish. Years of struggle are required to overcome obstacles and to fashion a Dream step by step. People who don't pursue their Dreams end up feeling empty, guilty, or unfulfilled. If a Dream dies, a person's sense of aliveness and purpose might die with it.

Instead of dealing with the Dream as a separate task, we will ask you to try to identify the components of your Dream as you consider each of the ten developmental tasks, or challenges. As we've already noted, your Dream might focus on one developmental area, such as career or family life, or it might be a more generalized Dream that refers to a particular kind of life-style that appeals to you. In Chapter 13, where we deal with life-style as an integrating concept, we deal once again with the idea of the Dream.

An Initial Look at Your Dream

1. After reviewing the descriptions of the nine developmental tasks, write down three or four elements of your Dream that you think are fairly well-defined right now. Picture yourself five or ten years from now and write a brief scenario of how your life will look then, at least according to your Dream.

2. Write down two or three ways in which you think your Dream is indistinct or ill-defined. For instance, one student wrote:

> I want to be very independent, and yet I want to have some very close friends I can be with and count on when I want. This sounds a

Form 2-2

Rating Developmental Tasks

Current Developmental Task	Rating	Importance to You		
	1 2 3 4 5 6 7 8 9 10 (Low)　(Moderate)　(High)	Increasing	Same	Decreasing
Competence				
Autonomy				
Values				
Identity				
Sexuality				
Friendship, Intimacy				
Love/Marriage/Family				
Job, Career				
Society, Community				
Leisure Time				

bit confusing and maybe even contradictory. I need to work out more what I really want.

3. Find a student with whom you can share an element of your Dream that is fairly clear and a part of it that isn't well defined. Try to help each other clarify your Dreams.

Discovering Developmental Priorities

This exercise is intended to help you identify the developmental tasks that seem most important to you right now (perhaps because they relate immediately to some phase of your Dream). Use Form 2-2 to rank each of the developmental tasks that are described in this chapter according to their importance to you at present. You are *not* being asked to line them up in the order of their importance. You can rank all of them as "highly important" or none of them as "important." Also, indicate whether each particular task is changing in its degree of importance or remaining the same.

Make a copy of this form after you've completed it and give it to your instructor without putting your name on it. Your instructor will tabulate the responses, indicating the range of ratings and the group average. You can then compare your ratings with the group average. In discussing the meaning of these ratings, remember that there is no single pattern to which everyone should conform.

Systematic Analysis: A Developmental-Task Inventory

Return to the first exercise in this chapter (the Assessment of Current Life Concerns) and do the following:

1. Take the items in your brainstorming list and place them in the developmental-challenge categories outlined here. If you think that any given concern should be put into more than one category, do so.

One student's list looked, in part, like this:

Competence	*Autonomy*	*Values*
—I feel awkward in a crowd.	—I follow the crowd a lot.	—I drink because it seems the thing to do.
—I'm flunking biochemistry.	—I still live at home.	—I have fights with Dad over his ways versus mine.
—Don't know how to fix my car; it's costing too much.		

Identity	*Sexuality*	*Friendship, Intimacy*
—I melt into a crowd. —I'm not sure at all what others think of me.	—I'm still pretty sexually self-centered.	—Not making new friends at school. —I feel lonely a lot.

Love, Commitment	*Job, Career*	*Community/Citizen Involvement*
—I can't understand guys who say they want to get married. —I'm not sure if any girl likes me.	—School seems to be a dead end. —Dad's a salesman; it seems terribly dull. —I don't know much about possible jobs.	—I belong to no clubs or organizations on campus.

Use of Leisure Time

—I waste a lot
of time.
—I get angry for
watching so much
TV.
—I'm good at sports
but have not joined
intramurals.

This student's list might not relate to your experience at all; therefore, use Form 2-3 to make your own list.

    2. Circle the concerns that you've rated 4 or 5.
    3. Add any concerns that have occurred to you as you read the brief descriptions of the developmental challenges of these transitional years.
    4. Use what you've learned about yourself as the basis of the group-sharing exercise outlined later in this chapter.

You've now taken a systematic look at the range of your developmental concerns and have pinpointed the ones that seem most important, or pressing, to you. You can't solve problems simply by looking at them, but getting a clear idea of your needs, concerns, issues, or problems is the first step—and an important one—in doing something about them. Soon, we will ask you to share some of your concerns and problems with other members of your group.
    Many of your concerns and problems are most likely developmental issues

Form 2-3

Developmental-Task Inventory

Competence

_____

_____

_____

_____

_____

Autonomy

_____

_____

_____

_____

_____

Values

_____

_____

_____

_____

_____

Identity

_____

_____

_____

_____

_____

Sexuality

_____

_____

_____

_____

_____

Friendship, Intimacy

_____

_____

_____

_____

_____

Love, Commitment

_____

_____

_____

_____

_____

Job, Career

_____

_____

_____

_____

_____

*Community/Citizen
Involvement*

_____

_____

_____

_____

_____

Use of Leisure Time

_____

_____

_____

_____

_____

that are quite normal and natural at this time in your life. A good deal of the "messed up" feelings you might experience from time to time are due to the fact that you are on a transitional "bridge." Once you realize that there is nothing terribly wrong with you, that you are experiencing the normal challenges and turmoil of moving through a transitional period, you can begin to determine just how you want to face each developmental task. Ideally, to face developmental challenges, whether they're called problems, concerns, or tasks, you need a combination of the following:

△ *a working knowledge* of the developmental task in question;
△ *a systematic way of facing problems* or concerns and of elaborating realistic goals and programs;
△ *skills* related to this task and to the programs you design;
△ *self-challenge*—that is, seeing yourself as an "agent" rather than a "patient" with respect to the major challenges of life;
△ *human challenge*, in terms of people who help you to place demands on yourself;
△ *human support*, in terms of people who provide you with understanding and help you to acquire the resources you need;
△ *institutional challenge*—that is, social settings such as school or work that place reasonable demands on you; and
△ *institutional support*—that is, social settings that provide the resources you need to meet the demands placed on you.

Structured Group Interaction: Developmental Tasks

You can learn a good deal about your own development by coming to understand what others are experiencing in the course of their development. This group exercise, and the others that follow in subsequent chapters, are designed to make appropriate sharing an ongoing part of your learning in this course. If you are using this book on your own, you might want to discuss what you are learning about yourself with a friend or a group of friends.

1. Share one of the important things you've learned from this chapter, either from your reading or from the exercises you've done, with a group of students. Every person should have an opportunity to speak. The purpose of this exercise is to share your feelings, not to embarrass yourself; therefore, choose a topic that is important to you, but one which you feel you want to share with others. If you don't understand someone else's statements, feel free to ask him or her to clarify them. At this point, *do not* challenge or disagree with others' reactions. Try to understand what others are saying by putting yourself in their shoes, especially if their experience seems quite different from yours.

2. In the second step of this exercise, each member of the group should indicate one or two developmental tasks that seem most important at the present time and give a couple of reasons why. Try to be as concrete as possible. Again, when others are speaking, your task is to try to understand what they are saying from their point of view.

3. Finally, share some of the resources you feel are available to you to help you accomplish your most important developmental tasks to your satisfaction. To help yourself complete this step, review the principal sources of developmental support outlined in the section immediately preceding this exercise and in Chapter 1.

Summary

In this chapter, we've given you an overview of the nature of human development during the current transitional period of your life and of the specific challenges or tasks confronting you. We've invited you to reflect on your current life concerns and then to consider them again in the light of the developmental-task framework. Finally, we encouraged you to share the results of your analysis with the members of your learning group. We concluded by indicating that Dreams, mentors, and models are developmental resources.

In Chapter 3, we focus on the developmental task of competence.

What Do I Do Well?
Competence and Development

What Do I Do Well? Competence and Development

51

Chapters 3, 4, and 5 deal successively with the developmental tasks we call competence, autonomy, and values. We start with these tasks, because the issues associated with them pervade all other developmental tasks. For instance, you not only want to begin to fashion a career, but you want to do it successfully. You want it to be *your* career choice and not someone else's, and you see your job or career as instrumental in your pursuit of values that make sense to you. Or you would like to develop a fuller social life, and you want to do so with social intelligence, avoiding both crippling dependency and isolating individualism. You realize that your values guide you in your choice of friends and the structuring of your social life.

We begin by discussing competence, because most people would like to carry out all developmental tasks competently, including the tasks that relate to autonomy and values. In this chapter, then, we look at competence as a key developmental task facing you during the years of moving into adulthood. We begin by helping you to reflect in an overall way on what you feel you do competently and on what you don't do as competently as you would like. Then we examine some current theories and research concerning competence, focusing on practical implications for you. Next, we ask you to reflect on yourself in a systematic way, using the information provided in the practical-theory-and-research section. Then you are asked to take part in a structured group interaction with a focus on competence. Finally, we encourage you to complete an action plan dealing with competence in some area of life.

Gerald Grant (1979) begins an article on competence-based education with a rather remarkable story gleaned from the New York Times (November 13, 1976):

A few years ago the Philadelphia Welfare Department denied a mother custody of her baby on grounds of incompetence. It was an unusual case: The father was absent and the mother was a lifelong quadriplegic whose shrunken limbs were virtually useless. The Welfare Department asserted she was unable to care for her daughter, then five months old, even with daytime household help. But the mother went to court to prove her competence. As spectators stood in awe, she changed the child's diaper before the judge, using her lips and tongue. The judge awarded her full custody of her daughter, commended her courage, and commented, "You have proven that the physical endowments we possess are only a part of the spectrum of resources that human beings possess" [p. 1].

In this book, we focus on "full spectrum" competence. As Grant notes, *competence* is a much used, but often ambiguous, term: "Competence is something all Americans admire, even if, when pressed, they are not quite sure what it means or whether they or society possesses it in adequate amounts" [p. 2]. We hope that this chapter will help give greater definition to this term and that this book will provide a working knowledge of what we might call *developmental competence*.

Personal-Reflection Exercise: Things I Do Well—and Things I Don't Do Well

Using Form 3-1, draw up a list of things that you currently do well and things that you don't do well. One student, Barbara, came up with the following responses.

Things I Do Well—and Things I Don't Do Well

+	−
—playing the piano	—talking freely on dates
—making friends	—learning foreign languages
—taking essay exams	—dancing
—playing basketball	—giving class presentations
—being a big sister	—standing up to my Dad
—doing math	—taking multiple choice tests
—making pottery	—working on my car
—helping others	—thinking about a job or career
—organizing my time in some systematic way	—being intimate with males
—getting good grades in science courses	

This list might not reflect your experience at all. Use Form 3-1 to draw up your own list.

Form 3-1

Things I Do Well—and Things I Don't Do Well

+	−

What Do I Do Well? Competence and Development

53

List three things you feel you do best on a 3×5 card, and list three areas in which you feel most incompetent on another card. Your instructor will collect and read the lists. Once you've assessed the range of competencies and incompetencies in your group, have an open discussion on competency and incompetency. Do you feel that people in our society are becoming more competent, less competent, or staying at the same level of competence in their jobs and in the other tasks of life? Explain your answer.

Competence: Definition and Basic Elements

Behavioral Competence

Competence refers to the ability to engage effectively in the kinds of concrete behaviors that lead to valued goals and accomplishments. The "valuing" agent might be you yourself, the people around you, society in general, or any combination of these. For instance, if you were a competent volunteer tutor working with disadvantaged children, your competence would be valued by you, the children you tutored, their parents, the schools they attended, and society in general. To be fully competent in some area means not only that you have acquired certain kinds of *working knowledge* and *skills* that relate to particular goals; it also means that you actually use this knowledge and these skills to achieve your goals and that you have the necessary motivation, or drive. Note, then, that competence relates only to behaviors that lead to valued accomplishments and attainments. For instance, Carla learns how to type (a skill), learns the format used in term papers and themes at her college (working knowledge), and uses this knowledge and skill not only to do her own papers but also to earn money by typing papers for other students. Her accomplishments, which she and others value, are a sign of her motivation and drive.

On the other hand, Carlos knows how to persuade others, organize programs, and get things done; but he never engages in activities that call for this kind of knowledge and skill. When he is asked to participate in activities such as the student government, he says that he isn't interested in them. He has great potential for competence in the organizational and "political" areas of life, but he doesn't actually use his knowledge and skills. He isn't competent in our sense of the term, because he doesn't use his knowledge and skills to achieve accomplishments. Behavior is not enough; it must be goal-achieving or accomplishment-oriented behavior. The kinds of accomplishments involved will depend on the values involved. Establishing a loving relationship with a friend is just as much an accomplishment as getting a high-paying job.

A Sense of Competence

Some people feel incompetent, even though they achieve goals in some areas of life. For instance, Joan receives good grades in her math courses, but she still feels incompetent: "I still feel like a nitwit in math. I know that I get things right, but I'm still not sure what I'm doing. I fly blind." On the other hand, although some people are not competent in a particular area of life—that is, they do not achieve substantial goals in that area—they *feel* competent in that area. For instance, Paul has run for a variety of school government offices but has never been elected, nor has he ever been chosen for any significant position by incumbents; yet he says "I feel that I am a good politician. I always get good grades in political science courses. I think my career lies in politics."

A sense of competence is the subjective feeling that tells you you can achieve goals in one or more areas of life. For instance, many students who go into examinations feel that they can do well in them; that is, they go into the exams with a basic sense of competence. The distinction between *feeling* competent and *being* competent is an important one, since it isn't unusual for people to overestimate their knowledge, their skills, and their ability to accomplish goals. Your level of self-esteem is directly related to your personal sense of competence.

In writing about the sources of self-esteem, Silverberg (1952) makes this observation:

> Throughout life, self-esteem has two important sources: an inner source, the degree of effectiveness of one's own activity; and an external source, the opinions of others about one's self. Both are important, but the former is the steadier and more dependable one. Unhappy and insecure is the man who, lacking an adequate inner source for self-esteem, must depend for this almost wholly upon external sources [p. 29].

Silverberg's comment calls your attention to the fact that your personal sense of competence (and, therefore, of your self-esteem) has its roots in your self-evaluation and the ways in which others evaluate you. Both forms of evaluation should be based on actual accomplishments rather than fantasies.

David Riesman (1979) believes that the United States faces a crisis of competence.

> Indeed, in comparison with earlier American feelings of exalted or almost omnipotent competence vis-a-vis the rest of the world, we have discovered that many countries can make both technological and social inventions superior to ours; they can make more efficient automobiles, reduce infant mortality and general morbidity, and, as in the notable case of Japan, manage such crises as the oil embargo with greater social cohesion and compliance of citizens [p. 23].*

Riesman claims that, paradoxically, the drive for competence seems to be slacking off in our society, even though, as the society becomes more complex, it demands higher levels of competence.

*From "Society's Demand for Competence," by D. Riesman. In G. Grant (Ed.), *On Competence: A Critical Analysis of Competence-Based Reforms in Education*. Copyright 1979 by Jossey-Bass, Inc. This and all other quotations from this source are reprinted by permission.

What Do I Do Well? Competence and Development

55

Perhaps the most immediately plausible explanation for this concern over competence is that levels of competence once thought at least tolerable for a society moving at a slower pace are quite inadequate for a society whose internal management is growing steadily more complicated. Consider, too, the amount of knowledge that individuals must master to conduct themselves competently and to have the self-confidence that comes from believing themselves competent.

Today, in fact, belief in one's own competence is no longer enough, and a demand for demonstrated competence now motivates much of education [p. 19].

Riesman's remarks apply not only to job or career but also to the developmental tasks under discussion here.

A subtle shift occurred among these innovators in the kind of competence they valued. It came to be a competence that was not "strictly academic," and it was to include the ability to make one's way in the nonacademic world, in the civic and occupational world, and in the world of one's own personal horizons. It was still traditionally American in its individualism, but the qualities defined as competence and thus sought for, nurtured, and rewarded were not traditionally competitive: They were rather the qualities of caring, of cooperation, of inventiveness, and—in the case of professional programs—of being able to provide superior professional services that were more concerned with individual clients than with the institutional frameworks in which the services were delivered. . . . What is requisite . . . is *humane* competence [pp. 32, 33–34].

He suggests that humane competence includes such things as "the ability of individuals to endure frustration, subdue narcissism, and accept as well as exercise authority."

Realistic Goals

Since competence and the feeling of competence are related to accomplishments, the kinds of goals you set formally, through planning, or informally, without planning or reflecting, are very important. Tom has moderate athletic ability. If his goal is to play tennis well enough to make it an enjoyable sport and an excellent means of obtaining both exercise and recreation, then his goal is quite realistic. He plays tennis with people who equal him in talent. Sometimes he wins, and sometimes he loses; but he always enjoys the struggle. However, if his goal is to make the college tennis team or to be among its top five players, then he might be bound for failure, because his ability is not commensurate with his goals. It's one thing to set your goals realistically high and force yourself to "stretch" to reach them. In such a case, achievement of your goals or even near achievement can be very rewarding. It's quite another thing to set goals (or to let other people set goals for you) that are unrealistically high.

Ella's case is quite different from Tom's. She is a very bright student who chooses a physical education major, not because she likes athletics and physical conditioning programs, but mainly because it is one of the easiest majors in her college. She glides through the program practically without having to make any demands on herself. Some of her friends envy her, because she doesn't have much work to do, but she becomes more and more dissatisfied with herself and with what she's doing. Although it's true that she is competent in the sense that she achieves all the goals required by the program, achievement is simply too easy for her. Her goals are unrealistically low. She develops no sense of competence, because there is no striving involved. She has talent that is unused and therefore "left over" after she does the work called for in her program. The message seems to be clear. Learning how to set realistic goals and how to reevaluate them as you work toward them can do much to help you become competent and develop a sense of competence.

Gary suffers from goal overload. He's working full time, going to school practically full time, and trying to make a go of his recent marriage. Although he is an average student, he finds that he's doing below-average work because of the many demands on his time and energy. Perhaps a more talented student could handle such demands, but Gary cannot. Since the work he is doing is merely a job and not something he's interested in, he finds himself giving less attention to it than it requires. His supervisor is dissatisfied with him. Even though he cares a great deal about his wife, he doesn't have the time and energy he needs to give himself to their relationship. Misunderstandings and fights leave him even less prepared to face school and work. Gary is not accomplishing his goals in any of these areas of life. This isn't because he's incompetent in the sense that he lacks the basic skills needed for success. He needs to set priorities among his goals; for instance, he might cut down on the number of hours he's taking in school. This would mean that he would spend more months in school and put up with a frustrating job longer than he would like. Gary needs goal-setting and program-development skills and the ability to live with a reasonable degree of frustration.

Working Knowledge and Life Skills

Since competence refers directly to accomplished goals, it refers indirectly to the kinds of working knowledge and skills needed to execute programs that lead to goals. We have indicated that one of the functions of this book is to help you acquire a working knowledge of the developmental tasks facing you at this time in your life. Obviously, other kinds of tasks demand different kinds of working knowledge. Moreover, a wide variety of skills are needed to accomplish developmental and other life goals—so many that it's impossible to enumerate them all; however, we can divide basic competencies into three broad categories. Although different labels are sometimes used by different writers, three general subdivisions of competence emerge: intellectual, physical/manual, and social/emotional.

Intellectual competence refers to your ability to use your mind to reflect, learn, choose, and solve problems. The specific skills related to intellectual competence—reading, writing, reasoning, dealing with numbers, and so forth—

What Do I Do Well? Competence and Development

57

have been and will continue to be the focus of much of your formal educational experience.

Physical/manual competence refers to your ability to use your body skillfully in the pursuit of desired goals. Coordination in the use of limbs, eye/hand coordination, and other basic motor skills are included in this category. The average person takes these skills for granted until deprived of them through sickness, aging, or an accident.

Social/emotional competence refers to your ability to relate decently and effectively to other people. The argument has been made that your social competence is one of the most basic sources of your self-esteem. For instance, White (1958) says:

> The degree to which a sense of interpersonal competence is attained is of high significance for the ultimate pattern of personality. In adult life the feeling of being able to have some effect on people, to get them to listen, provide some of the things we need, do some of the things we want, receive some of the love and help we want to give, provides a substantial foundation for security and self-respect [p. 225].

Some people talk about *social intelligence* rather than *social competence* (Walker & Foley, 1973), though we prefer the latter term. Social intelligence refers to the ability *to know* what is called for by a social situation, along with the ability *to respond* appropriately. For instance, you find out that your roommate has just had a fight with her boyfriend. She seems to be steaming mad, but she's not saying anything. You tactfully try to find out if she'd like to talk about it; if she does, you listen and try to respond appropriately. If she doesn't, you let it drop for the time being, tactfully indicating that, if she does want to talk about it later, you'd be glad to listen when you're free. In this chapter, we list the kinds of skills needed for such interactions.

Your ability to reach out and "connect with" other people—from coworkers to intimate friends and spouses—is a powerful determinant of your subjective feelings of worth. We return to the topic of feelings of self-worth in Chapter 6, which deals with the development of a sense of personal identity.

Another way of viewing competence is to outline basic "packages" of skills needed to carry out the normal tasks of life effectively. These may be called "life skills" (Egan & Cowan, 1979, Chapters 3 and 8). A brief description of seven basic "packages" will both broaden your understanding of the term *competence* and give you the opportunity to do a little self-assessment. It will soon become obvious that these categories are interdependent. For instance, full sexual expression requires both physical and interpersonal skills. The competent use of interpersonal skills requires intellectual skills. You, as a person, are the central and integrating reality. In real life, the skills outlined in the following paragraphs are not as distinct as they appear here; they are dimensions of yourself.

Skills relating to physical development and expression. These are the kinds of skills you need in order to develop "body" competence. They range from basic coordination and motor skills to the ability to use your body as a vehicle of artistic expression (through dance, for example). Skills relating to physical fitness (including skills that relate to nutrition), personal health care, sexual expression, grooming, art, and athletics are included in this package. Although some attention might have been paid to these physical and manual skills in your elementary and secondary education, it's likely that little time was devoted to them. As a consequence, many of you reach the years of moving into adulthood with the basic physical skills you need to survive, move around, work, and play, but without task-related or enjoyment-related skills. One of the frequently voiced criticisms of our educational system is that it tends to stress intellectual development to the detriment of other areas of competence, leaving people to develop such competencies randomly, if at all. The current resurgence of interest in running and other forms of physical conditioning reflects a growing awareness of how our society has tended to underestimate the importance of "body" competence. If you arrive at the conclusion that such one-sidedness characterizes you in some way, it's possible for you to initiate specific steps to correct this imbalance. What skills would you include in this package? What skills are most important to you at this time of your life?

Skills relating to intellectual development. In this package we include not only such basic skills as reading and writing but also higher-order skills, such as learning how to learn. You've been engaging in the process of learning ever since you were born, and you've engaged in formal, school-related learning for many years; however, it may be that no one has ever talked to you about the important process of learning how to learn. Most of us could become better learners, but there are few people who are able to teach us the skills needed to do so (see Shepherd, 1979, on college study skills). As Toffler (1970) notes in his controversial book entitled *Future Shock,* the world you live in is characterized by rapid change. Information becomes obsolete quickly; in order to keep pace with a changing world, you need to have a capacity for new learning. In such a world, learning-how-to-learn skills are critical. Another higher-order skill is the ability to translate theoretical knowledge into working knowledge—that is, the ability to make the intellectual transition from theory to practice, from academic knowledge to practical knowledge. Knowledge can certainly be savored for its own sake, but you can also make it work for you. Ideally, theories help us not only to understand the world about us and within us but also to predict and control these worlds. How good are you at making your knowledge work for you in some way? Give an example or two.

Value-clarification skills. The issue of values is treated extensively in Chapter 5. Suffice it to say here that the ability to get a clear picture of your own values, the values of those with whom you are involved, and the values of the groups, organizations, and institutions of which you are a member is a skill that can be learned. Most of us learn how to do this to some extent, but most of us could be far better at it (see Simon, 1974; Smith, 1977).

Self-management skills. These are the kinds of skills you need to make your own way in life (Williams & Long, 1979); therefore, they are intimately related to the task of achieving autonomy. Included in this package are the ability to set value-related goals, and the ability to develop, implement, and evaluate programs designed to implement these goals. Beginning with B. F. Skinner's pioneering work (1953), psychologists have elaborated the principles underlying behavior and behavioral change. The ability to apply the principles to your own life is an important element in what has been termed *self-directed behavior* (Watson & Tharp, 1977). For instance, the principle of reinforcement states that people tend to repeat behaviors that are rewarded and discard behaviors that go unrewarded or are associated with punishment. Therefore, in striving for goals, it is essential that you see to it that attaining goals is a rewarding process. What kind of self-manager do you see yourself to be? Cite one of your strengths and one of your weaknesses in this area.

Interpersonal-relationship skills. For purposes of greater clarity, the skills of relating interpersonally can be broken down into four categories:

- △   the skills of self-presentation,
- △   the skills of attending and listening to others,
- △   the skills of responding to others, and
- △   the skills of challenging others responsibly.

The skills of self-presentation enable you to share your opinions, feelings, values, needs, and so forth with others in a direct way. The skills of attending and listening help you to orient yourself toward others actively. The skills of responding build on attending and listening skills and involve your ability to communicate to others an accurate understanding of what they say and the feelings they express. The skills of challenging others responsibly enable you to confront other people constructively, when necessary, with information or feedback that you think they might find useful. Systematic procedures have been developed to train people in these sets of skills (Egan, 1976, 1977). In what ways are you satisfied with your interpersonal abilities and style? In what ways are you unsatisfied?

The skills of small-group involvement. Much of the relating you do takes place in small groups such as your family, peer groups, work teams, discussion groups, committees, and the like. At first glance, group participation seems easy, requiring only the skills we've already mentioned. Your experience, however, might tell you a different story. Being an active and effective group member involves such skills as the ability to clarify the goals of a group, to mobilize and use the resources of a group to achieve personal and group goals, to promote collaboration instead of competition, to help manage conflict, and to involve oneself in the dialogues of others in a helpful rather than a distracting way. What are the small-group settings of your life? What kind of group participant are you? What do you do well when you participate in a group? What might you do better?

Skills relating to involvement in large organizations and institutions. Many movies and novels that deal with prison life focus on a new inmate who has to "learn the system." This includes such things as:

△ learning who has power,
△ learning the norms, standards, and customs that constitute the internal culture of the system,
△ learning how to get ahead by determining which behaviors are rewarded and which are punished,
△ learning how to find resources to cope with the system when it hinders the pursuit of personal goals,
△ learning how to form coalitions in order to change the system.

Can you think of other skills that the new inmate must learn in order to survive or get ahead in such a system? When you read the finished list of skills, it should become apparent that such skills relate not only to prisons but also to involvement in all kinds of systems. Some students fail to develop as fully as they might while they are in school, because they never really learn how to "work the system" in the ways outlined above. How good are you at understanding the social settings of your life, including school, and getting them to work for you? What do you do well in this regard? What might you do better?

These, then, are some of the basic life skills needed for full investment in human development. At this point, the interactive nature of these skills should be apparent. For instance, the development of system-involvement skills will be hampered in the case of the person who has failed to develop adequate interpersonal skills.

The Role of the Environment

As we've already pointed out, working knowledge and skills are useless if you fail to set realistic goals for yourself. It helps to ask yourself questions such as: Does the environment support the goals I am setting? Does it provide the working knowledge, skills, and other resources I need to reach these goals? Failure to ask such questions can lead to frustration. One student we knew wanted to take a directed-study course in the form of an unpaid internship in the department of urban planning in a large city in the Midwest. She was majoring in urban studies and felt that she would get more out of practical experience than another theoretical course. She had gathered a great deal of information about cities and the ways in which they work, and she wanted a chance to translate theoretical knowledge into practical working knowledge. She had acquired a relatively high proficiency in many of the life skills outlined earlier in this chapter. So she felt, and rightly so, that she was ready for a practicum or internship experience. She persuaded her adviser to agree to her program and found someone in the department of urban planning who would support her. She refused to face the fact that both these parties were lukewarm in their commitment to her goals. She was given run-of-the-mill tasks to do in the city agency and received little if any supervision

What Do I Do Well? Competence and Development

61

on site or from her adviser. She felt betrayed. She had counted heavily on her own enthusiasm and had failed to assess the kind of institutional support available to her. Competence involves accomplishments, not just skills and enthusiasm; environmental opportunity must be taken into consideration. In what ways does your environment help you to reach some of your major goals? What are the major environmental obstacles facing you right now?

The Demand for Multiple Competencies

One of the dilemmas of the moving-into-adulthood years (indeed, of life in general) is that you are constantly faced with demands to behave competently in all of the areas we have mentioned: intellectual, physical/manual, and social/emotional. For example, social/emotional demands and intellectual demands must be met simultaneously. In their study of depression among college students, Beck and Young (1978) relate the following story about a young man who experienced real difficulty in managing these simultaneous demands for competence.

> Carl knew that he wanted to become a doctor, and wanted to guarantee his admission to medical school as soon as possible. . . . [He] decided before starting college that if he was going to compete successfully, he would have to devote all his time studying. By the end of his first week at college, he was spending virtually every waking hour at classes, in the library, or shut in his room alone. Carl knew many of the other students in his dormitory by name, but felt that he could not spare too much time for socializing because he might lose his "competitive edge." He decided not to continue with his tennis because he simply could not spare the time required for team practice every afternoon.
>
> When Carl received a 'C' on his chemistry midterm exam, he felt his world crumbling. He believed that he had lost any chance for admission to medical school and that, to make matters worse, nobody else really cared what happened to him. Carl soon developed a severe depression [p. 45].*

Carl attempted to cope with demands by focusing solely on intellectual competence. When he received a setback in that area, he had little to fall back on, since he had decided to set aside social and physical activities in order to concentrate on his studies. Such an imbalance, though not unusual, can be costly in terms of an overall sense of satisfaction and effectiveness. We've already mentioned the results of Douglas Heath's research dealing with overemphasis on intellectual pursuits during the college years. Students who stress intellectual accomplishments at the expense of social/emotional and physical pursuits may pay a heavy

*From "College Blues," by A. T. Beck and J. E. Young, *Psychology Today*, 1978, *12*(4), 80–92. Copyright © 1978 Ziff-Davis Publishing Company. Reprinted by permission.

price later on in life in terms of social/emotional adjustment. This should serve as a warning of the costs that might be involved in sacrificing everything for academic accomplishments during the college years. One definition of a *well-rounded person* is one who achieves a workable balance of intellectual, physical/manual, and social/emotional competence.

Overcoming the Psychopathology of the Average

Abraham Maslow (1968), in reflecting the thinking of a long line of psychologists, suggests that most people set goals that are too low or fail to develop the kinds of working knowledge and skills we've been discussing here. He calls this condition the *psychopathology of the average*—a condition he sees as so pervasive among us that, for the most part, we don't even notice it. Ella, the young woman who decided to major in physical education because it happened to be one of the easiest majors at her school, is a striking example of the psychopathology of the average, since her abilities obviously exceed the goals she sets for herself. The kinds of competences described here serve as an antidote to the psychopathology of the average; ultimately, however, you must decide for yourself what kinds of goals and competencies are realistic for you. There is obviously some middle ground between pushing yourself to achieve high goals in every area of life and always settling for less.

A Brief Planning and Problem-Solving Model

Since competence involves the ability to plan ahead and to solve both intellectual and practical problems, we present here a brief model that relates to both planning and problem solving. This systematic model, based solely on common sense, is, in our opinion, one of the most useful and yet, paradoxically, most underused models known to humankind. Research has shown that most people "muddle through" planning and problem solving, rather than develop a systematic approach. As a result, people are, in practice, much less competent than they should be. We believe that the model we present is one of the most important "instruments" of competence that you might use.

This is both a planning and a problem-solving model. When you hear the word *problem*, your instinct might be to substitute the term *emotional problem*, as in the sentence "She really has a problem!" We use the term in a much more neutral sense. It refers here to any obstacle standing in the way of the achievement of a valued goal. The model we are about to describe also will be used to help structure the personal-action programs found at the end of each chapter. This model has four steps:

1. Defining and clarifying the need, want, problem, or issue.

2. Setting goals that help you meet the need or want, face the issue, or solve the problem once it has been clarified.
3. Developing step-by-step programs to achieve each goal or subgoal.
4. Implementing and evaluating programs.

Now a word about each of these steps.

1. Defining and Clarifying the Need, Want, Problem, or Issue

John Dewey, who has had a great impact on the way in which education has been fashioned in the United States, said that a question well asked is half answered. In the same way, an issue, need, or problem that is explored, defined, and clarified in a behavioral way is much further along the road to solution than one that remains vague and general. If you say "I have a need to do something with my life," your need is too vague; however, if you say "I love to write, and my instructors all tell me that I write very well. I'd like to find a job where I can use this talent," you are stating your need in a way that leads to further action. Or, if you say "I'm having trouble with my parents," your problem, stated in such general terms, will be difficult to solve; however, if you say "My parents don't want me to go away to college, because I'm an only child and they say they need me for company and to help with the chores around the house," then you're stating the problem much more clearly and behaviorally. We will provide exercises in each of the following chapters that will enable you to identify your developmental needs and clarify the problems you might have in completing developmental tasks.

2. Setting Goals

The more clearly the problem is defined, the easier it is to see what might be done to solve it. A goal is an achievement, accomplishment, or end state that meets a need or solves a defined problem. For instance, you might say that one of your problems is loneliness. You describe loneliness as having no close individual friends and not belonging to any group either inside or outside school. Your goal, then, is the other side of the problem "coin." In this example, your goal would be to establish a relationship with at least one person in whom you could confide and to join a group either at school or in the neighborhood. Goals state *what* you want to do to handle your need or problem, not necessarily *how* you are going to do it. Goals are useful to the degree that they are clear, concrete, specific, behavioral, realistic or achievable, capable of being measured or at least verified in some way, and related adequately to a specific problem or need. Moreover, you'll find it useful to work out a time frame for the accomplishment of each goal. "I should try to relate to people better somehow" is an example of a goal that lacks most of these characteristics and, therefore, serves as a poor solution to the problem of loneliness. However, if a person says "I will attend the social sponsored by the Campus Ministry Association next weekend," this is probably a good intermediate goal, because it has all the qualities outlined above. By attending the social, you will not automatically solve the problem of loneliness, but this could well be a step in the right direction.

3. Developing Step-by-Step Programs to Achieve Each Goal or Subgoal

Programs are step-by-step procedures used to achieve goals or subgoals. Programs are usually useful to the degree that each step is clear, attainable, and coordinated with the other steps—that is, one step follows logically from the text. There are two kinds of programs: full programs and subprograms.

Full programs. A full program includes all the steps and all the subgoals leading up to the achievement of the principal goal or goals (accomplishments) that satisfy the presenting need or problem. In our example, the accomplishment is "relationships established," together with "strong feelings of loneliness eliminated." The full program includes all steps and all subgoals that lead to this accomplishment.

Subprograms. A subprogram includes all the steps leading up to an intermediate goal or accomplishment. In our example, the intermediate goal is attendance at the Campus Ministry Association social. It is a subgoal, because it is a step toward the defined accomplishments—"relationships established" and "loneliness eliminated." The subprogram includes whatever steps must be taken in order to attend the social; for instance, make sure the time is free, buy the ticket, arrange for transportation, and the like.

There are two basic steps involved in program development: making a list of possible programs, and choosing the best combination of programs.

Making a list of possible programs. Very often, there is more than one way to achieve a goal. For instance, if you want a close friend, you can advertise for one in the local paper, wait until someone asks you, or attend social gatherings where there is some probability that you might meet someone with whom you are compatible. The first two of these "programs" would probably prove ineffective. In trying to work out a program, it is often useful to brainstorm—that is, to list as many ways of achieving a goal as possible. For instance, let's say that you drink too much and, fearing that you are becoming an alcoholic, you decide to stop drinking. Before reading any further, write down all the ways (programs) you can think of that might help a person to accomplish the goal "drinking stopped."

In order to stop drinking, you could stop "cold turkey" on sheer will power or decide to cut down gradually. You could join Alcoholics Anonymous, move to a locale that prohibits the sale of alcoholic beverages, stay away from places that serve liquor, associate with people who don't drink, make a solemn promise to someone you care about that you will stop drinking, take Antabuse (a drug that causes nausea when its user drinks alcohol), see a counselor, or take a course on alcoholism. What other possibilities are there?

Choosing the best combination of programs. The next step is to choose the program or combination of programs that best suits you—that is, your style, your access to resources, your preferences, your level of motivation, and so forth. In our example, this combination might involve joining Alcoholics Anonymous in addition to taking Antabuse. Programs that are tailored to individual situations are more likely to work than programs chosen because they seem good in themselves. "Yes, it's a good program, but is it good for me?"

4. Implementing and Evaluating Programs

The final stage of problem solving involves two steps: implementing plans or programs and evaluating the whole process.

Implementing plans or programs. This means carrying out the steps of your program according to the time frame established for each step. Programs often seem easy during the planning stages, but once initial enthusiasm has waned, they can seem much more difficult, if not impossible. Can you remember any program you began more or less enthusiastically and then abandoned? Have a brief classroom discussion on failed programs. There are certain key questions to be asked at the implementation stage of the planning or problem-solving process:

△ Are the steps of the program clear?
△ Is any step so big or complicated that it should be divided into smaller steps?
△ Do I have the resources I need to accomplish each step?
△ Where do I find the challenge and support I need to stick with this program?
△ What rewards can I expect along the way?
△ What do I do when the going gets rough?

Four students who had rented an apartment near the university asked us to help them with some problems they were experiencing. They liked one another, but, when they decided on this living arrangement, they didn't even think about the possibility of conflict. When conflict appeared, as it inevitably will when four people rub elbows in relatively close quarters, the students didn't know how to handle it.

Evaluating the whole process. There are three major areas of evaluation that the planner or problem solver should consider: program evaluation, goal evaluation, and need or problem evaluation.

Program evaluation. Are you involving yourself in the program on a day-to-day basis, working with the kind of persistence the program demands? For instance, the person who wants to stop drinking checks to see that he or she is attending AA meetings, avoiding bars, engaging in alternative recreational pursuits, and, in general, fulfilling the day-to-day requirements of the program that was developed.

Goal evaluation. Did the completion of the program lead to achievement of the goal? In our example, goal achievement means that the person actually stops drinking. If the program doesn't lead to the desired accomplishment, then a new or reworked program is needed.

Need or problem evaluation. Did achievement of the goal solve the problem or handle the need? For instance, Teresa wants a part-time job that will be interesting (or at least won't be boring) and will provide her with enough money to pay for school and incidental expenses. She does what is necessary to search for a job (the program), but after she gets a job (the goal), she finds that it's very boring and that what she earns doesn't cover her expenses (the need). She begins looking for a new job, because her needs aren't being met.

You might not achieve your goals and satisfy your needs perfectly the first time you attempt to do so. If you don't, then you must decide whether you should lower your expectations, modify your goals, or try once more, fortified perhaps by partial success and by the learnings you've picked up in the planning/problem-solving process.

Much more could be said about the problem-solving process; books have been written about it (Carkhuff, 1973, 1974; Watson & Tharp, 1977; Williams & Long, 1979). However, this outline of the process will be sufficient for our purposes. You will become more familiar with the process as you use it in each chapter.

Systematic Self-Assessment: Personal Competence

1. Refer to the initial exercise in this chapter, and use Form 3-2 to arrange the lists of things you do well or fail to do well according to the three areas of competence: intellectual (*I*), physical/manual (*P*), and social/emotional (*S*). If any task demands more than one type of competence, list that task under the competence you think is central and, in parentheses, indicate the other kinds of competencies involved. For instance, Eva placed "being captain of the volleyball team" under physical/manual competence—she believes that she was chosen for that position because she is the best player on the team. She also realizes that social competence is critical in that position, so she wrote *S* in parentheses following "being captain of the volleyball team."

2. Review the items you've listed in each of the three categories, adding items to each of them as they occur to you. Try to include whatever you consider to be a *valued accomplishment* in your life. Also, review the material in this chapter concerning life skills. You might find hints there regarding the areas in which you feel competent or less than competent.

3. Review your revised list. What *patterns* do you observe? In what areas do most of your accomplishments fall? Does one area appear to be much stronger or weaker than the others? Do most of your accomplishments require a variety of competencies? Using the three competency areas to organize your thoughts, write a brief summary of your current assessment of personal competence. In writing this summary, remember that competence isn't related to raw skills or talent but rather to the *accomplishment of valued goals* in various areas of life. One student, Rob,

What Do I Do Well? Competence and Development

67

who had completed this self-assessment, wrote the following brief summary.

> Several things hit me as I looked at the things I'd listed as pluses and minuses. I spend lots of time and energy on books and athletics, so, in the intellectual and physical areas, I feel OK about my abilities. I carry a $B+$ average. But more than that, I feel that I'm becoming an educated person. And that's an accomplishment I prize. But the social, that's another story. I guess I've spent so much time studying and trying to do well in athletics that I've neglected friendships with both boys and girls. To be honest, I think I've even started to avoid people a bit. I never thought of relating to others as a sort of competence—something I could learn. I just labeled myself as shy and I've been trying to live with it.

Rob's assessment yields a very practical insight regarding competence in his life. His experience might be completely different from your own; therefore, you should complete your own summary in Form 3-3.

Form 3-2

Things I Do Well—and Things I Don't Do Well

Intellectual

Physical/Manual

Social/Emotional

Form 3-3

Personal-Competence Assessment: A Summary

Key Settings and Competence: An Assessment

As we noted in Chapters 1 and 2, personal development is the result of challenge and support in the key settings of life. The development of competence is no exception to this rule. The various settings of your life—family, residence hall, classroom, teams, friendship groups, clubs, workplace, and so forth—are the places in which your personal competence is or is not enhanced. It's useful for you to know how to dig out competence-enhancing resources from any given setting. It's also useful to realize the ways in which a setting can limit the development of a competency or prevent its development altogether. We invite you to reflect on whether the settings of your life are, in fact, providing the challenge and support you need to develop competence in each of the three areas we've discussed.

1. List one or two goals you are presently striving for in each of the three areas of competence. We will give examples from students we have known; however, they are only examples. You might not agree with the values implied in these goals. If they don't apply to your experience and, therefore, do not stimulate your thinking, disregard them and write examples from your own experience that are consonant with your values.

A. *Intellectual accomplishments*

Examples:

△　Maintaining a *B+* average for two semesters.
△　Writing two short stories this term.
△　Reading at least one good novel a month this year.
△　Learning to speak Spanish.

Intellectual accomplishment #1. _____

_____

_____

Intellectual accomplishment #2. _____

_____

_____

B. *Physical/manual accomplishments*

Examples:

△　Losing 15 pounds and keeping it off this year.
△　Running two miles in under 18 minutes at least four times per week this semester.

△ Learning to do five simple maintenance procedures for my car by the end of the term.

△ Using my time in ceramics class to make at least two pieces of pottery that I'd be glad to either display myself or give to someone I like.

Physical/manual accomplishment #1. _____

_____

_____

Physical/manual accomplishment #2. _____

_____

_____

C. *Social/emotional accomplishments*

Examples:

△ Reducing my fear of speaking in public; speaking up in each of my classes at least twice a week.

△ Cutting down on gossip; eliminating gossip I think could harm another person's name.

△ Inviting my parents to talk reasonably with me about my homosexual orientation.

△ Getting at least two people I like to go to bed with me this term.

Social/emotional accomplishment #1. _____

_____

_____

Social/emotional accomplishment #2. _____

_____

_____

2. For each accomplishment you list, indicate at least one concrete way in which a key setting is providing you with challenge and support and one way in which a key setting is standing in the way of your achievement of your goal. One setting can provide support *and* put obstacles in your way. For instance, Sid had this to say about his English literature class.

Helping. The teacher is smart and extremely enthusiastic. This class is small and her enthusiasm is infectious. There is a lot of discussion. She helps us to relate literature to our lives. I find that I use what I learn there to get a better vision of my entire life and the world around me.

Hindering. However, she demands so much work in terms of reading assignments and written reports that sometimes I feel so snowed that I want to quit. I forget how good the content is.

Sid feels intellectually enhanced in this course, but, at times, he feels the price is too high.

Another example is offered by the young man who was trying to reduce his fear of speaking in public. He said that his speech/communication class was very supportive. The instructor was quite familiar with problems such as his and knew how to shape the class into a kind of supportive learning community. On the other hand, when the young man was with a group of his friends, some of them would make fun of his speech defects. They were just having "good fun," but he felt hurt when they did this, and he tended to withdraw.

The student who was trying to lose 15 pounds found her gym class and a weight-loss group sponsored by Student Development Services most helpful. The members of her family had an adverse effect on her program, because most of them were overweight and were doing nothing about it. Whenever she was home, she fell back into her old habits.

Indicate the ways in which a key system is facilitating the attainment of each of your goals and the ways in which the same system or a different one is standing in the way of attainment.

Intellectual accomplishment #1

Helping. _____

_____

_____

Hindering. _____

_____

_____

Intellectual accomplishment #2

Helping. _____

_____

_____

Hindering. _____

_____

_____

Physical/manual accomplishment #1

Helping. _____

_____

_____

Hindering. _____

_____

_____

Physical/manual accomplishment #2

Helping. _____

_____

_____

Hindering. _____

_____

_____

Social/emotional accomplishment #1

Helping. _____

_____

_____

Hindering. _____

_____

_____

Social/emotional accomplishment #2

Helping. _____

_____

_____

Hindering. _____

_____

_____

3. Once you've discovered the ways in which key social settings are standing in the way of goals you would like to accomplish, these obstacles can be seen as problems and become grist for the problem-solving process

described earlier in this chapter. List two ways in which the social settings of your life stand in the way of goals that you would especially like to attain. Later in the chapter, you will be asked to do something about these obstacles.

Structured Group Interaction: Competence

1. In a small group, share one personal learning regarding a specific area of competence from the reading and exercises in this chapter. Early in the life of the group, you might be reluctant to share anything that you think is too personal. This is certainly a normal reaction; therefore, if this part of the structure of the class is to become helpful, you and the other members of your group need to develop trust. Two things are enormously helpful in developing trust in a group. Trust among members of a group is facilitated when:

△ group members provide understanding and support for one another, and
△ individual group members are willing to take *reasonable risks* in sharing themselves.

One student had this to share:

> I've discovered that I'm afraid to be too different from my friends, even if this means putting aside things I'd really like to do. For instance, no one in the group I hang around with has the same kind of interests as I do. I like to read both fiction and nonfiction; but most of them read only when they have to do an assignment. I like popular music, but I also am getting to like classical music a lot. None of them likes it at all. I'm not putting them down or suggesting that they have to meet my "high standards." But I also need people with whom I can share my interests. I think I've begun splitting my socializing time between two groups.

This student's intellectual and emotional competence, which were enhanced by his interest in literature and classical music, weren't fostered by his primary group; he decided to add another social setting to his life to help him achieve his goals.

2. Review the section in which life skills are described (pp. 56–60). What do you consider your strongest and your weakest skills at present? Share this information with the other members of your group. For instance, one person, in talking about interpersonal skills, had this to say: "I'm good at listening to others [a responding skill], but I have a very tough time letting them know what's going on with me [a self-presentation skill]. I'm still afraid that people will not like me if they know too much about

What Do I Do Well? Competence and Development

75

me." After you share what you have to say about yourself, give others a chance to respond to you. Group members should make sure that they have an accurate understanding of what another person is saying before they offer comments.

Action Plan: Competence

Now that you've examined yourself with respect to competence in various areas of life, shared yourself with others, and listened to what others have had to say about themselves, you are in a position to do some systematic planning and problem solving. Review the problem-solving process presented earlier in this chapter, and then take the following steps. In this chapter, you aren't being asked to carry out a full-scale program; you're being asked to familiarize yourself with the planning/problem-solving process.

1. Need or Problem Clarification and Definition

At this point, you should be able to express one or more needs (wants) or problems (obstacles) in the area of competence. For example, one student put her problem this way:

> I have some problems in the social area. I find, for instance, that I'm always letting other people have their way. I almost never assert my opinions in class, in the residence hall, or with my friends. Whenever I do say what I feel, I get very apologetic about it.

This student feels that she wants to be much more assertive in her dealings with others. Another student wrote:

> I guess I've badly neglected physical competence. I am overweight. I can't play any sports without getting winded right away. I can't even walk far without getting winded. I don't want to become a marathon runner, but I do want to be a person in fairly good physical shape.

On a separate sheet of paper, list some of the needs, wants, and problems (obstacles) that have suggested themselves to you as you've worked through this chapter. Then pick the one you would like to work with and describe it in greater detail. Remember that, the more clearly you describe your need or problem, the easier it will be to do something about it.

2. Goal Setting

Write a brief description of one or more goals you would like to accomplish that are related to your specific problem or need in the area of competence. If you describe your need or problem clearly, then your goal or goals also will be clear. Express your goals as concretely as possible. Review the instructions on goal setting found at the end of the preceding chapter. The student who wanted to improve her assertiveness wrote down this goal:

> At least once a day, I want to express a personal opinion or want in one of the following settings—my clique, the dorm, my psychology class—and do so without apologizing for myself.

The student with problems in the area of physical fitness came up with the following goal.

> By the end of next month, I want to be able to run 1½ miles in 13 minutes or less. That gives me 53 days to achieve this goal.

Of course, this student had goals that were related to other kinds of exercising and loss of weight.

Review the need, want, or problem you described in Step 1. Write one or more goals that, if achieved, would satisfy the need or solve the problem. If you are having a hard time coming up with goals, this probably means that you haven't sufficiently clarified your need or problem.

Goals. _____

_____

_____

_____

3. Development of Step-by-Step Programs

The next step in the planning/problem-solving process is to formulate step-by-step programs for each goal. A program outlines the things you are going to do to achieve a goal. The student who was interested in becoming more socially assertive came up with the following program:

△ Read a good recent book on responsible assertiveness. Ask a psychology prof for suggestions.

△ Attend the six-session workshop on social assertiveness sponsored by the student development center. Use this experience to further clarify assertiveness goals and to learn the skills. Use this opportunity to rehearse the kinds of assertive behaviors I would like to engage in.

△ Pay attention to Ann's assertive style—she's well liked, but she also sticks up for her own rights. She's a good model.

△ Try out assertive behavior in one or two situations and evaluate the results.

Choose one goal from Step 2. On a separate sheet of paper, do the following:

a. Do some brainstorming; that is, write down as many ways of accomplishing that goal as possible. Let your imagination roam freely; don't criticize any of the possibilities you come up with, no matter how crazy they might seem.

b. After you've completed your list, take a more critical look at what you've written. Place an *x* in front of the possibilities that make most sense to you—that is, those that fit your situation, style, motivation, and resources. You are beginning to formulate a coherent program.

4. Helpful Settings

The next step is to list the settings, and the resources within those settings, that will provide support and challenge for you in the pursuit of the goals you've set through the programs you've outlined. The student who was trying to get into better physical shape listed the following settings:

△ The physical education department of the college had drawn up a number of different physical fitness programs. Testing programs were offered for those who were about to begin such programs, and consultation services were provided throughout the programs.

△ The local community had a running club. It provided companionship in running and some rewarding social events.

△ A national weight-reduction organization had a local chapter that offered systematic and safe weight-reduction programs.

Take a look at the program steps you've marked with an *x*. Then, for two or three of these steps, list one or two helpful settings and some of the resources within these settings.

Step: _____

_____

_____

Setting and resources: _____

_____

_____

_____

_____

Step: _____

_____

_____

Setting and resources: _____

_____

_____

_____

_____

_____

Step: _____

_____

_____

Setting and resources: _____

_____

_____

_____

_____

5. Implementation

Take another look at the steps in your program. Choose one particular step and answer the following questions:

△   What makes this step easy?
△   What makes this step difficult? What are the obstacles?

The student who wanted to become more assertive said this:

> There are some pluses and minuses in attending the six-session workshop offered by the student development center. I am already so busy that I think that it would be easy for me to say "I can't make the session this evening." If I start to do that, I know that I'll give up the whole thing. So I have to monitor my tendency to find excuses. On the other hand, the six sessions are a highly structured program, and I've heard from others that the people who run it are very competent.

Choose one or two steps in your program and indicate what will make it easy for you to do that step and what obstacles you think you might run into.

Step: _____

What Do I Do Well? Competence and Development

79

_____

_____

What will make it easy: _____

_____

_____

_____

_____

_____

What will make it difficult: _____

_____

_____

_____

_____

_____

Step: _____

_____

_____

What will make it easy: _____

_____

_____

_____

_____

_____

What will make it difficult: _____

_____

_____

_____

_____

_____

There is, of course, a difference between foreseeing obstacles and making them up. You can deal with foreseen difficulties by using the problem-solving process you are engaged in here.

6. Evaluation

Even before you begin a program, you can determine how you will monitor your participation and evaluate the program. To do this, you can ask yourself questions such as:

△ How will I know that I am succeeding?
△ What sources of feedback will I have, other than myself?
△ What will I do if I see that the program is not working for me?

The student who was interested in developing assertiveness had this to say about evaluation:

> Feedback will be very important to me. I have to find out whether I still sound compliant or whether I go too far and become aggressive. So I need the views of people I can trust. I know that the staff of the student development center will tell me how I am doing. Getting feedback will be harder when I begin trying to be more assertive in real situations. I think I can count on a couple of people. They are not close friends, but I'm with them in a variety of situations, and I trust them.

Take a look at the steps of your tentative program and provide brief answers to the following questions:

How will I know I am succeeding (criteria)? _____

_____

_____

_____

_____

What are some possible sources of feedback, other than myself? _____

_____

_____

_____

_____

This exercise is intended to familiarize you with the steps of the planning/problem-solving process. At the end of each of the next eight chapters, we offer some suggestions for action programs based on this process.

What Do I Do Well? Competence and Development

81

Summary

In this chapter, we focused on competence and its three major subdivisions: intellectual, physical/manual, and social/emotional. We invited you to reflect on your personal competence in each of these areas and to engage in a discussion of competence with the members of your learning group. Finally, you were asked to select a target competence area for action, identify settings that are likely to be helpful to you in pursuing competence-related goals, and devise a set of action steps.

In the next chapter, we turn our attention to the task of developing autonomy.

CHAPTER

Can I Make It on My Own?
Developing Autonomy

The next developmental task to be considered is the development of autonomy—your capacity to attain reasonable self-sufficiency. In this chapter, you will be asked to complete a self-reflection exercise. Then, the developmental challenge of becoming autonomous—that is, of moving toward mature interdependence—will be examined. This examination will include a discussion of four major dimensions of personal autonomy: (1) the need for approval, (2) the ability to cope independently, (3) the capacity for self-initiated planning and problem-solving, and (4) awareness of how one's own needs relate to the needs of others and the ability to integrate those needs. You will be asked to evaluate the ways in which the key settings of your life are presently contributing to your development of autonomy. You will then be asked to do a systematic self-assessment, take part in a structured group interaction, and complete a personal-action plan regarding autonomy in your life.

We begin with an exercise in self-assessment in the area of independent living.

Self-Assessment Exercise: Personal Autonomy in Your Life

You are being asked here to rate yourself on your ability to act independently in various areas of life. Using the scales described here, place an X at the point that most accurately describes your current behavior. You may put more than one mark on a scale; this would indicate that, in that particular area, you feel and act both dependently and independently at times. Give at least three concrete examples from your own experience that illustrate the rating you give yourself. (Even if you put more than one X on a scale, you needn't give more than three examples.) In the following scale, note that an X in the "moderately dependent" slot would most likely mean that you also feel "slightly" or "moderately independent" with respect to the situation you are considering. Where are you to put the Xs? A rating of 2 or 3 means that your predominant *feeling* is one of dependence, even though you are exercising some degree of independence. A rating of 4 or 5 means that your predominant *feeling* is one of independence, even though, in certain ways, you are dependent.

The following example, drawn from the experience of one of our students, will help to clarify these instructions.

Area: Family Living

1	2	3
.__X__.	._____.	.__X__.
highly dependent	moderately dependent	slightly dependent

4	5	6
.——— .	.——— .	. X .
slightly independent	moderately independent	highly independent

Since this student placed an *X* under 1 (highly dependent), 3 (slightly dependent), and 6 (highly independent), he needed to give examples for each. He did so as follows:

Rating ___1___ Example:

"All my money comes from my parents. I don't have any other source of income." This student is dependent, and *feels* quite dependent, in this area.

Rating ___3___ Example:

"Sometimes—not all the time—I still accompany the family to other people's houses for dinner, even when I would rather not go. I don't go, even when they want me to, if I have something else to do that I consider very important." He still feels slightly dependent, even though he does exercise a fair degree of independence at times. If he had rated this area 4, he would have implied that he feels some degree of independence, even though he realizes that some dependency is a reality here.

Rating ___6___ Example:

"At school, I have made all decisions with respect to choice of courses and major myself. I did not ask my parents for their advice before I made the decisions, nor did I expect to hear any criticism afterwards. If they asked, I let them know what I had done." This student acts and feels very independent.

Now, using Form 4-1, rate your own level of independence in each of the suggested areas.

Form 4-1

Area: Family Living

1	2	3
._____.	._____.	._____.
highly dependent	moderately dependent	slightly dependent

4	5	6
._____.	._____.	._____.
slightly independent	moderately independent	highly independent

Rating _____ Example:

_____

_____

_____

_____

Rating _____ Example:

_____

_____

_____

_____

Rating _____ Example:

_____

_____

_____

_____

Area: School—Classroom and Related Activities

1	2	3
.———.	.———.	.———.
highly dependent	moderately dependent	slightly dependent

4	5	6
.———.	.———.	.———.
slightly independent	moderately independent	highly independent

Rating ——— Example:

_____

_____

_____

_____

Rating ——— Example:

_____

_____

_____

_____

Rating ——— Example:

_____

_____

_____

_____

Area: School—Extracurricular Activities

1	2	3
. ——— .	. ——— .	. ——— .
highly dependent	moderately dependent	slightly dependent

4	5	6
. ——— .	. ——— .	. ——— .
slightly independent	moderately independent	highly independent

Rating ——— Example:

_____

_____

_____

_____

Rating ——— Example:

_____

_____

_____

_____

Rating ——— Example:

_____

_____

_____

_____

Area: My Peer Group

1	2	3
. ———— .	. ———— .	. ———— .
highly dependent	moderately dependent	slightly dependent

4	5	6
. ———— .	. ———— .	. ———— .
slightly independent	moderately independent	highly independent

Rating ———— Example:

_____

_____

_____

_____

Rating ———— Example:

_____

_____

_____

_____

Rating ———— Example:

_____

_____

_____

_____

Area: Closest Friend

1	2	3
. ——— .	. ——— .	. ——— .
highly dependent	moderately dependent	slightly dependent

4	5	6
. ——— .	. ——— .	. ——— .
slightly independent	moderately independent	highly independent

Rating _____ Example:

_____

_____

_____

_____

Rating _____ Example:

_____

_____

_____

_____

Rating _____ Example:

_____

_____

_____

_____

Area: Work

1	2	3
.———.	.———.	.———.
highly dependent	moderately dependent	slightly dependent

4	5	6
.———.	.———.	.———.
slightly independent	moderately independent	highly independent

Rating ——— Example:

_____

_____

_____

_____

Rating ——— Example:

_____

_____

_____

_____

Rating ——— Example:

_____

_____

_____

_____

Area: Church

1	2	3
.———.	.———.	.———.
highly dependent	moderately dependent	slightly dependent

4	5	6
.———.	.———.	.———.
slightly independent	moderately independent	highly independent

Rating _____ Example:

_____

_____

_____

_____

Rating _____ Example:

_____

_____

_____

_____

Rating _____ Example:

_____

_____

_____

_____

Area: Use of Leisure

1	2	3
.———.	.———.	.———.
highly dependent	moderately dependent	slightly dependent

4	5	6
.———.	.———.	.———.
slightly independent	moderately independent	highly independent

Rating _____ Example:

_____

_____

_____

_____

Rating _____ Example:

_____

_____

_____

_____

Rating _____ Example:

_____

_____

_____

_____

Any Area Not Covered

Name area: _____

1	2	3
._____.	._____.	._____.
highly dependent	moderately dependent	slightly dependent

4	5	6
._____.	._____.	._____.
slightly independent	moderately independent	highly independent

Rating _____ Example:

_____

_____

_____

_____

Rating _____ Example:

_____

_____

_____

_____

Rating _____ Example:

_____

_____

_____

_____

What Is Autonomy?

One way of understanding autonomy is to contrast what it *isn't* with what it *is*. As a newborn infant, you relied totally on your immediate family for day-to-day survival. Without their almost constant care, you wouldn't have been able to survive. You were completely dependent. On the other hand, the hermit who lives on a deserted island, who is completely self-reliant and able to live from day to day with little or no human contact, is an example of a person who is extremely independent.

Autonomy can be seen as a mature form of *interdependence*. Although autonomous people are quite capable of functioning adequately in day-to-day life, they recognize their need for others. Consequently, autonomous people do not need continuous support and reassurance, and yet they are able to reach out to others when they need assistance. On the other hand, they also are respectful of others' needs—including their need to be autonomous and their need for reasonable assistance.

Autonomy can be thought of as having four important dimensions: the need for approval, the ability to cope independently, the capacity for self-initiated planning and problem solving, and the awareness of how one's own needs relate to the needs of others, including parents, friends, teachers, classmates, and society as a whole. Let's look at each of these dimensions separately, and consider some examples.

The need for approval. This refers to the extent to which you need others' positive reactions to you and your behavior. People who have an extremely high need for approval find it difficult to feel good about anything unless others indicate their positive evaluation of their behavior, directly or indirectly. David, a college sophomore, described his need for approval in this way:

> It seems like no matter what I do, I'm watching to see if others like it. Sometimes I get so worried about it that I can't concentrate on what I'm supposed to be doing. The more important the thing, the more I look around to see what they think. I'm just beginning to realize how this ties me up.

This tendency to look outside oneself immediately and exclusively for evaluation has been called *other-directedness* (Riesman, Denney, & Glazer, 1969). Other-directed people always have their antennae extended, trying to see how others are reacting to them.

Persons with a comparatively low need for approval are likely to focus on the particular tasks in which they are engaged rather than on the reactions of others to their activities. We don't mean to suggest that such individuals have no interest in what others think of their efforts, but rather that they are not so concerned that their confidence in their ability to work independently and effectively suffers. Jenny, an upperclass student, described her feelings about the approval of others in these words:

> Sure I care about what others think of me. Doesn't everybody? But, if something that's important to me has to be done, then I do it. I wouldn't hurt my friends' feelings on purpose, but I sometimes have to make choices that they don't like.

Jenny's integrity doesn't allow her to overvalue the approval of others.

The ability to cope independently. This refers to the degree to which you can accomplish the tasks of day-to-day living without seeking help from others. Again, it is helpful to think in terms of two extremes. People who lack this ability can't seem to do anything without someone's assistance—roommate, teacher, friend, or parent. Such individuals haven't yet developed a belief in their ability to manage life's demands on their own; they tend to put great pressure on the other people in their lives. Sid describes a former roommate who "used up" people's goodwill in this manner.

> Russ would go through friendships in a two or three month period —from love to hate. People always liked his initial openness about himself, his worries, and so on, but they couldn't handle his constantly talking about himself and his constant desire to be with them. He had an especially difficult time with women. I hung in there for a year but decided that was enough for me.

At the other extreme, we find people who never turn to anyone for help, regardless of the seriousness of the issue. Their ability to cope with everything that comes along seems to be a point of honor. Marc, remembering his freshman year, described his behavior in this way:

> In our family, independence—standing on your own two feet—was very highly prized. I guess that's where I learned not to expect help from others. As I think about it now, though, I see that I've hurt myself at times by carrying it too far. Like that economics midterm. A good study group offered to include me, but I was too proud to accept their offer. I'm pretty sure that cost me an *A* in the course.

Autonomous people accomplish most of what needs to be done without assistance from others, but they are willing to seek or accept help whenever necessary. They don't feel guilty or self-reproachful when they find that they need to ask others for assistance. Autonomous people also are capable of *collaborative* behavior. Highly independent people sometimes lose their efficiency when they are forced to work with others.

Anita worked as a part-time secretary in the office of the dean of students. She worked on her own and was considered quite efficient. In the middle of the semester, the office started a project that demanded that she work cooperatively with two other people. All of a sudden, her efficiency decreased. She vacillated between being completely dependent—asking others to explain even simple instructions, doing less than her share of the work, asking a lot of questions, calling in sick, and the like—and being overly independent, ignoring others and getting whatever work she could get done on her own. Both kinds of behavior interfered with Anita's efficiency. Finally, she was transferred to another office, where she could work on her own.

Anita's brand of independence interfered with her ability to collaborate with others and, therefore, set limits on the quality of her work.

Self-initiated planning and problem solving. We've already reviewed planning and problem solving in Chapter 3. The key word in our discussion here is *initiative.* People who have initiative act rather than react; that is, they act, when possible, before events force them to act. People who lack initiative just hope that good things will happen and that problems will go away. Such persons fail to develop the abilities or seek out the resources needed to plan ahead or cope with problems.

One student, Constanza, used the planning/problem-solving process in the following way.

a. She realized that, because she was working full time while going to school full time, she was ineffective both at work and at school.

b. She set a goal of financial aid—"financial aid secured"—in terms of "accomplishment" language. Financial aid would enable her to continue as a full-time student with a reasonable part-time job.

c. She found that she could achieve her goal by:

—taking out a student loan,
—obtaining scholarship money either from the state, the school, or a combination of both, and
—finding a part-time job with a better hourly rate than she was getting in her full-time job.

d. She pursued this action program and came up with the following evaluation:

—I got a federal loan and some scholarship money from a Latino fund at school. I got a part-time job, but the pay is only slightly better per hour than the full-time one.

—I have reached my goal, because I find that I can still go to school full time and live on what I earn at the job.

—I am making slightly better grades at school, and the combination of school and work doesn't draw all my energy away. I even have some time for reasonable social life, though I can't do things that require money. All in all, I'd say that the process has been reasonably successful.

Constanza showed a great deal of autonomy in solving her problem, because she showed a great deal of initiative. She didn't wait for others to solve her problems. She needed help, but she reached out for it herself.

When you take the initiative, you shouldn't ignore individuals or settings that are potential sources of help in the planning/problem-solving process. Every college offers resources to assist you in dealing with developmental challenges —faculty members, counselors of various types (such as academic, career, personal, social, and residence hall counselors), and peer advisers. Other people in your life—parents, ministers, former teachers, friends—also are potential sources of assistance. Seeking out such people when you need them is one indication of your level of autonomy. Constanza talked with her school adviser, a loan officer, the director of the Latino club, and an adviser in the student employment office (among others) as she went about the task of solving her problem. The point is that she took charge of the process and sought the kind of help she needed.

We stress the fact that self-initiated behavior is as important in planning as it is in problem solving. You can initiate new behaviors in different areas of your life—studies, social life, extracurricular activities, family relations, career choice, and so forth. You don't have to be "in trouble" in an area before you decide to initiate a new behavior. In fact, you can often prevent trouble by acting promptly on concerns that seem to have the potential to become problems.

Ron, a senior, talked about initiating in this way:

It occurred to me not long after I arrived here that, with 15,000 students around, no one was going to be watching over me to see how I was doing. I'd really have to have a huge problem before anyone would notice. I made it a point to seek out my adviser, get to know her, and stay in touch. Last week, she wrote me a great letter of recommendation for a job.

The capacity to initiate—to become an agent of self-directed change in your own life—is a primary indicator of personal autonomy.

Awareness of the relationship between your needs and those of others and the ability to integrate those needs. This is another important dimension of autonomy. Chickering (1969) sums up this awareness in the following words:

One realizes that parents cannot be dispensed with except at the price of continuing pain for all; that he cannot be supported indefinitely without working for it; that he cannot receive the benefits of a social structure without contributing to it; that loving and being loved are necessarily complementary [p. 13].

Autonomy, then, refers to a sometimes complicated balance between self-direction and sensitivity to the needs of others, not total independence and lack of regard for the feelings and opinions of others. This balance is never permanently achieved—it remains a lifetime task; however, you can take major steps toward achieving such a balance during the years of moving into adulthood.

> Conrad worked full time, and his wife, Jessica, worked part time so that he could go to school. But Jessica was interested (at least eventually) in a career, and this would mean more school for her. Conrad, however, working from a set of values he had assimilated at home and had not challenged, only partially listened to Jessica's needs. He assumed that his education and job needs were primary, since he was to be the principal breadwinner. After a great deal of bickering between the two, Jessica announced that she was going back to school the following year and that they would have to come up with some kind of arrangements for financial survival.

Obviously, marriage is one of those arrangements in which awareness of another's needs and the ability to give and take are extremely important.

In *The Culture of Narcissism*, Christopher Lasch (1978) suggests that we live in a national culture that so overemphasizes individualism that we find it difficult to reconcile personal needs with either the needs of others or with the needs of society as a whole. Ellen, a recent college graduate, talked about her awareness of the importance of balancing her needs and those of others:

> For the first half of college, my motto was "Do your own thing." One day, a friend of mine confronted me with how much my thoughtlessness and egotism had hurt him. I could see the pain in his eyes. I'd never realized that what I wanted could be so at odds with a friend's needs.

Obviously, whether or not you try to balance your needs and wants with the needs and wants of others (and the way in which you attempt this balance) depends on your values; therefore, the task of developing autonomy is intimately related to the task of establishing a set of working values.

Systematic Self-Assessment Exercise: Dimensions of Autonomy

Need for Approval

This refers to the extent to which you need others' positive reactions to you and your behavior. Using the following form, rate yourself with regard to the need for approval. You can put more than one X on the scale, but for each *X*, give one or two examples of your behavior that illustrate the rating.

High Need		Medium Need		Low Need
1	2	3	4	5

Rating _____ Example:

_____

_____

_____

_____

Rating _____ Example:

_____

_____

_____

_____

Rating _____ Example:

_____

_____

_____

_____

Independent Coping

This refers to the degree to which you can accomplish the tasks of day-to-day living without seeking help from others.

High Independence		Moderate Independence		Low Independence
1	2	3	4	5

Rating _____ Example:

_____

_____

_____

_____

Rating _____ Example:

_____

_____

_____

_____

Rating _____ Example:

_____

_____

_____

_____

Self-Initiated Planning and Problem Solving

This refers to the degree to which you take charge of and direct planning and problem-solving processes in coping with your needs and problems.

Low Initiative   Moderate Initiative   High Initiative

1   2   3   4   5

Rating _____ Example:

_____

_____

_____

_____

Rating _____ Example:

_____

_____

_____

_____

Rating _____ Example:

_____

_____

_____

_____

Balancing My Needs with the Needs of Others

    This refers to your ability to balance your wants and needs with the wants and needs of others.

Self-Centered		Balanced		Other-Centered
1	2	3	4	5

Rating _____ Example:

_____

_____

_____

_____

Rating _____ Example:

_____

_____

_____

_____

Rating _____ Example:

_____

_____

_____

_____

An Exercise in Assessing the Impact of Key Individuals and Social Settings on Autonomy

    As we noted in Chapters 1 and 2, there are certain key individuals and environments that play a major role, both positively and negatively, in development during the moving-into-adulthood period. This exercise asks you to look at the ways in which two key individuals (for instance, your mother or father, a friend, a teacher, a mentor or model of some kind, someone from your church, and so forth) and two key social settings of your life (for instance, family, residence hall or other living situation, friendship groups, classrooms, clubs, athletic teams, prayer groups, and so forth) affect your growth, for better or worse, toward autonomy. In this exercise, we are interested in the impact these individuals and settings have on the four dimensions of autonomy we've considered: the need for approval, the ability to cope independently, self-initiated planning and problem solving, and awareness of the relationship between your needs and those of others and the ability to integrate those needs.

1. Pick out two individuals and two life settings that currently have considerable influence on your development. You might choose, for example:

△ My father, my best friend; the honors program, the family of a close friend of mine.
△ A student in chemistry lab, a drug pusher; an English classroom, the church I attend.
△ My faculty adviser, my fiance; the center for student development, a group of high school friends I still hang around with.

Enter the individuals and social settings you choose in the blanks at the left side of the forms provided on the following pages.

2. Next, rate these individuals and settings in terms of their impact on the four dimensions of autonomy. Do this evaluation by placing an *X* in the appropriate space.

3. Finally, jot down at least one example that illustrates the basis for each of the evaluations you make. One student's form looked like this:

Need for Approval

Person or Setting	*Encourages me to rely on the approval of others*					*Encourages me to rely on self-evaluation*	
	1	2	3	4	5	6	7
father						X	
drug pusher	X						
church			X				
tennis team							X

Concrete Examples:

Father (6). Once I entered college, Dad considered me pretty much a man. For instance, he even encourages me to consider from time to time whether I want to stay in college or get a job and become more independent sooner.

Drug pusher (1). This guy can twist me around his finger. I buy grass from him, and I have almost let him talk me into doing a little amateur pushing myself.

Church (3). I really like the social activities of the Young People's Club. I'm one of the officers. They let us organize our own events, but the minister, I feel, is always right behind me looking over my back, making sure I do the "right" thing.

Tennis team (7). Our squad is so large that the coach uses a system of individualized goals and practice routines. We evaluate our own progress from day to day.

Form 4-2

Need for Approval

Person or Setting	Encourages me to rely on the approval of others				Encourages me to rely on self-evaluation		
	1	2	3	4	5	6	7
_____	___	___	___	___	___	___	___
_____	___	___	___	___	___	___	___
_____	___	___	___	___	___	___	___
_____	___	___	___	___	___	___	___

Example 1:

_____

_____

_____

_____

Example 2:

_____

_____

_____

_____

Example 3:

_____

_____

_____

_____

Example 4:

_____

_____

_____

_____

Form 4-3

Independent Coping

Person or Setting	Encourages me to stand on my own					Encourages me to lean on others	
	1	2	3	4	5	6	7
_____	___	___	___	___	___	___	___
_____	___	___	___	___	___	___	___
_____	___	___	___	___	___	___	___
_____	___	___	___	___	___	___	___

Example 1:

_____

_____

_____

_____

Example 2:

_____

_____

_____

_____

Example 3:

_____

_____

_____

_____

Example 4:

_____

_____

_____

_____

Form 4-4

Taking Initiative in Planning and Problem Solving

Person or Setting	*Encourages me to wait for help to arrive or for the problem to go away*				*Encourages me to seek out assistance actively*		
	1	2	3	4	5	6	7
___	___	___	___	___	___	___	___
___	___	___	___	___	___	___	___
___	___	___	___	___	___	___	___
___	___	___	___	___	___	___	___

Example 1:

_____

_____

_____

_____

Example 2:

_____

_____

_____

_____

Example 3:

_____

_____

_____

_____

Example 4:

_____

_____

_____

_____

Form 4-5

Balancing My Needs with the Needs of Others

Person or Setting	Encourages me to focus on my needs		Balance		Encourages me to prefer the needs of others		
	1	2	3	4	5	6	7
_____	___	___	___	___	___	___	___
_____	___	___	___	___	___	___	___
_____	___	___	___	___	___	___	___
_____	___	___	___	___	___	___	___

Example 1:

_____

_____

_____

_____

Example 2:

_____

_____

_____

_____

Example 3:

_____

_____

_____

_____

Example 4:

_____

_____

_____

_____

Phases in the Development of Autonomy

As Lessor (1971) and others have noted, there are phases, or stages, in the development of autonomy. You are likely to encounter four such phases along the road toward autonomy: dependence, counterdependence, independence, and interdependence.

Dependence

As we have seen, dependence is the state of the human infant—total reliance on others for physical survival and psychological well-being. In the absence of virtually constant nurturing by others, the survival of the infant is seriously threatened. On the other hand, excessive dependence later on in life usually indicates that something is wrong, either with the individual who persists in being dependent or with the social settings that encourage or demand dependence.

> Tony seemed to be having a hard time getting started in life. He did not work hard at college, grew to hate it, and finally left during his third year. He moved back home and drifted from job to job. He would spend periods of up to six months without work. He expected to be supported by his parents and they in turn, even though they had misgivings about his passivity, paid his bills, got him a used car, and even went out looking for jobs for him. When relatives and friends suggested to them that they were doing neither themselves nor Tony a favor, they would listen agonizingly; but they felt incapable of changing the pattern that had been established. Almost predictably, Tony did not get any better. If anything, he seemed to grow even more dependent. For instance, he failed to pay the insurance premium on his car—a fact that went unnoticed until he had a minor accident.

During crises, people often become more dependent than usual; this is a comparatively normal coping strategy. This kind of *regression*, if we want to use that term, can be, in the words of one social scientist, "in the service of the ego" (Kris, 1952). If, for instance, Tony had been making it on his own and then had had an accident or some other kind of setback, a temporary period of greater dependence on his parents or others could help him to pull his own resources together once more.

Counterdependence

Counterdependence involves radical swings between needing direction and support from no one and desperately needing guidance and reassurance. Such changes in mood are often a predictable part of adolescence, with its dramatic physical and psychological changes. As Lessor notes: "At one end of the pendulum is 'I don't need you at all'; at the other end is, 'I need you desperately—now!'" Such swings between dependence and independence are fairly normal during adolescence. Adolescents use counterdependence as a way of testing the limits with individual adults in a variety of social settings. Counterdependence is, in many ways, the other side of the dependency coin. Testing limits is useful to the degree that it helps the individual to move beyond dependency; however, when counterdependence becomes part of a personality structure, it is no longer functional; that is, it is no longer a step along the road to developmental maturity.

> Candice, a woman in her early 20s, was, predictably, "against" almost everything. She was an attractive and intelligent person, but she had a way of rejecting almost any kind of compliment. It was almost impossible for her to work with others on any kind of project, because her immediate response usually was that it was poorly designed, that it was not going to work, that it was relatively meaningless, and so forth. Wherever she went, people soon learned that Candice was the kind of person who had to be "dealt with." She refused any feedback designed to make her aware of her behavior and its implications. It goes without saying that, in terms of work and social life, she became more and more isolated. She attributed this isolation to envy on the part of others.

Candice is counterdependent with a vengeance. If she were to examine her behavior, she would probably find that much of her counterdependence is a cover for her feelings of dependency. Usually it isn't easy to live with a counterdependent person. This includes the counterdependent adolescent; however, in the adolescent's case, counterdependence is a transitory phase.

Independence

When you are able to function on your own from day to day and no longer look to others to provide the resources you need to cope with the demands of life or to constantly reassure you that you are OK, you have achieved independence. To quote Lessor once again: "Independence signifies an awareness of inner resources as well as the resources of the world. When a person says 'I can do it myself' without sticking his tongue out, he is comfortably independent rather than hostilely counterdependent." Independent people don't disregard others, nor do they lean on them. Independence implies a legitimate striving for personal power.

Many people pride themselves on being independent. In a recent television program concerning an investigation into sheltered workshops for the blind, a young man was asked how he felt about his wages. (The issue was the fact that many blind people working in these workshops were not being paid the minimum wage.) He answered that he was earning money and that that was better than not earning money and depending on others or the state for survival. For him, the issue of independence was first; the issue of a just wage was second.

In our complex society it's impossible to attain absolute or complete independence. The way in which you live your life is made possible by an interlocking web of services that allows you to meet your basic needs for food, shelter, clothing, transportation, sanitation, energy, and the like. We are made aware of the magnitude of such services only when they are suspended in some way—a blackout, an oil embargo, a truckers' strike, or frost in Brazil's coffee growing regions.

Interdependence

Interdependence is the mark of individuals who, although confident of their ability to function on their own, allow themselves to need and be needed by others. This is not, however, the desperate need of dependence on another person ("I can't live without you"); it is an awareness of a mutual need for support and challenge. The word *need* can be used in two radically different ways: although it conveys a sense of being dependent, it refers also to a certain fullness of life. A person can convey dependence by saying "I need you"; however, that same phrase can refer to a relationship that provides life with a certain fullness. In the second case, need can be very strong without being desperate. In Lessor's words, interdependence is characterized by the desire for "comfortable sharing." We wish to form meaningful relationships with others, not because we are unhappy with ourselves, but because we wish to share a self that we esteem with others whom we also esteem. Interdependence moves beyond mere independence and implies that striving for personal power is not enough. "Being with" is not only necessary; it is also an important social/emotional value.

On reflection, you will probably see that you zigzag among all four of these phases in your movement toward autonomy; this is quite normal. The dependence-counterdependence-independence-interdependence cycle involves issues that will come up again and again throughout your life. Like other developmental tasks, autonomy is not something that is taken care of once and for all early in life.

An Exercise in Assessing the Steps toward Autonomy

Dependence

Give one example of a way in which you are or have recently been *nongrowthfully* dependent. For instance, one student wrote "I'm ashamed to say that I still take my laundry home for washing."

_____

_____

_____

_____

Give one example in which you believe that a present or recent period of dependence has been *of some benefit* to you. One student wrote "When I lost my job and failed an exam in the same week, I let my girl friend take care of me for a while. I felt dependent, but it felt good."

_____

_____
_____
_____

Counterdependence

Give one example of a way in which you have been or are now *non-growthfully* counterdependent. One student wrote "I can't seem to stand anyone in authority. I get surly around anyone who has control over me. I don't distinguish between people who are exercising legitimate authority for my benefit and those who are manipulating me in some way. Last week I yelled at a teacher who is a really fine person. I just forgot myself."

_____
_____
_____

Give one example of counterdependence that has *contributed in some way to your development*. One student wrote "I have refused any help in math—from teachers, friends, tutors. I know I have the ability, but I get lazy and act stupid. To remedy this, I'm avoiding even legitimate help for a while."

_____
_____
_____

Independence

Give an example of a way in which you have chosen to be independent —a way that *hasn't worked out for you*. One student wrote "I decided to live in an apartment by myself this semester. It hasn't worked out—I'm too lonely."

_____
_____
_____

Give an example of a way in which you have chosen to be independent —a way that *has contributed to your development*. One student wrote "I have begun to drink much less this semester. I don't let people talk me into more at parties, and I spend a lot less time in the local dives with the guys. I feel better about it."

_____

_____

_____

_____

Interdependence

Give an example of a way in which you have experimented with inter-dependence, but without much success. One student wrote "I tried to work out a curriculum for the fall with my parents. I wanted their advice and all that. But they kept pushing me in ways I didn't want to go. Finally, I gave up and did it my way."

_____

_____

_____

_____

Give an example of a way in which you have experimented successfully with interdependence. One student wrote "I felt that my most intimate friend was calling the shots most of the time. He'd decide where to go, what to do, when and how intimate we were going to be. Or at least that's the way it seemed to me. It's not that he's such a controlling person; it's that I've been so wishy-washy. Recently, I began to assert myself much more. I make my needs and wants known, but I don't push them off on him. We've talked about it, and both of us like it better this way."

_____

_____

_____

_____

Structured Group Interaction: Autonomy

The purpose of this structured group interaction is to assist you and the other members of your group to share insights and questions regarding autonomy—questions that have come from your individual reading and the exercises you have done in this chapter.

1. Share your understanding of what autonomy means to you, in your own words. You may ask for clarification of another person's definition, but do not challenge or disagree; try to understand the definition as the other person means it.

2. Next, share something that you learned in assessing the ways in which particular individuals or social settings in your life affect your development of autonomy. You might choose to share an example of an individual and a setting that are hindering your autonomy and an individual and a setting that are enhancing it.

3. Tell the group which dimension of autonomy you rated most positively, and why. After each member has done this, go around again and share the dimension that you rated most negatively and your reason for doing so.

4. Share one of your findings about yourself with respect to one of the four dimensions of autonomy—the need for approval, the ability to cope independently, the capacity for self-initiated planning and problem solving, and the awareness of how one's own needs relate to the needs of others. If possible, give one or two examples of how autonomy has affected your classroom behavior. Other members of your group can give feedback to the speaker to indicate whether or not they agree with his or her evaluation, and why. Remember that your comments should relate to behavior that has taken place in the group.

5. Finally, make a statement about yourself with respect to the stages of the development of autonomy, from dependence, through counterdependence and independence, to interdependence. Give your overall impression of how you are handling this developmental challenge.

Personal-Action Plan: An Exercise in Planning/Problem Solving—Autonomy

Establishing Goals

Up to this point, the work you have done in this chapter relates to the first step in the planning/problem-solving process we reviewed earlier; that is, you have been clarifying your needs and defining the problems you have in the area of autonomy. You will now be asked to apply the remaining planning/problem-solving steps to what you have learned about yourself in the area of autonomy.

Use what you have learned about yourself from the exercises and the sharing you have done to determine the goals you would like to achieve in the area of autonomy. Ask yourself what you would like to accomplish in the area of autonomy. One student responded by considering the four dimensions of autonomy. She came up with the following possible goals:

Goals in the area of need for approval:

I'd like to cut down on the need for approval I have in the clique I hang around with. I find myself doing things I don't want to do just because they do them.

I'd like to lessen the number of times I tell my more intimate friends I disapprove of what they are doing.

Goals in the area of independent coping:

I'd like to study for and pass a test without using the notes taken in class by two fraternity brothers of mine whom I count on all of the time.

I'd like to earn some of my spending money instead of counting on parents and other relatives who give me gifts.

Goals in the area of self-initiated planning and problem solving:

I'd like to straighten my relationship with Patty, instead of letting it drag on in a kind of limbo, expecting *her* to do something about it.

I'd like to take an honest look at my use of drugs and make some hard decisions about what I want to put into my body and what I want my mind to be like.

Goals in the area of balancing my needs with the needs of others:

I'd like to set up some working rules between my roommate and myself about how our room is to be used, instead of trying to work around his schedule and his activities.

I'd like to replan the semester-break trip with Fred. I railroaded him into a trip he does not really want to take.

These goals might not relate to *your* experience. You aren't likely to embark on a program unless you own the goals and think the payoff is sufficient to warrant the work involved.

Another way by which you can determine the goals you would like to accomplish is to return to the first self-assessment exercise in this chapter and perform one more operation with it. You've already rated yourself as to how you see yourself in various areas. Now, using an *O* instead of an *X*, indicate *where you would like to see yourself* in each area; the results of this operation will indicate what your goals are in the area of autonomy.

1. See if you can come up with six or eight goals that relate to what you have discovered about yourself in the area of autonomy:

_____

_____

_____

_____

_____

_____

_____

_____

2. Next, review these goals after at least six hours (but no more than 48) have passed. Add any new goals that have occurred to you during that time. Sometimes, more realistic goals present themselves as you move through the activities of everyday life.

3. Now review your goals and choose two or three that seem most important to you. Choose goals that:

△ make sense to you, offer you a payoff, and lead to accomplishments you value;
△ are concrete and specific rather than vague and general;
△ are related in significant ways to what you have learned about yourself in the area of autonomy;
△ can be accomplished with the resources you have at hand;
△ you are willing to work for; and
△ have a specific time frame for completion.

Choose only those goals you value. If you have no significant needs, wants, or problems in the area of autonomy, it is senseless to manufacture a change program for the sake of a classroom exercise. One of the students we knew (we'll call him Ned) had this to say: "A lot of the time, I drink heavily and take drugs. I do it because I want to belong. I'm a follower in more ways than I want to admit. My goal is to stay drug and alcohol free for the next month. I just want to be my own person for a month. I don't care who thinks what."

Check to see if this goal meets the requirements we've outlined. Does it? Would you want to change it in any way?

4. Describe one of your goals in the area of autonomy as concretely and specifically as possible.

_____

_____

_____

_____

_____

5. Check to see whether your goal fulfills the requirements of an effective goal.

Programs

Remember that a program is a step-by-step series of behaviors or actions that leads to the accomplishment of a goal; therefore, each goal you choose needs a program.

The program Ned came up with included the following steps:

> I'll get rid of the drugs in my room.
>
> I'll plan two or three things to do each week that will prevent me from just wandering around and drinking and smoking grass because there's nothing else to do.

Do you think that Ned's program is adequate? Review the requirements for effective programs in Chapter 3, and then see whether you have any suggestions for improving Ned's program.

1. Draw up a program for each goal you've chosen; that is, outline a concrete, step-by-step action plan that will help you to reach your goal. Also, draw up a timetable for implementation of steps.

_____

_____

_____

_____

_____

_____

_____

_____

_____

_____

2. Repeat this process for each goal you've chosen.

Execution of a Program

The next step is to implement the program according to the timetable that has been established. Here are some hints for this phase of the process.

1. If one step seems too big when you start to act, break it down into smaller steps that are easier to accomplish. (One student rehearsed with an adviser before she told her parents about her decision to live with her boyfriend.) Do you want to revise the steps of your program in any way?

_____

_____

_____

_____

2. We usually continue a program as long as it is rewarding. Make sure that you build reinforcements, or rewards, into this step-by-step process. What rewards do you think Ned could set up for himself? Indicate what payoff you expect to experience as you move through the steps of your program.

_____

_____

_____

_____

_____

3. Try to foresee obstacles and think of how you will handle them when they arise. What obstacles do you think Ned might run into? List the obstacles you think you might face in carrying out your program.

_____

_____

_____

_____

4. Think of sources of support and challenge both in terms of individuals and social settings in your environment that you can call on whenever your program becomes difficult. One student arranged sessions with a tutor in order to get through a difficult statistics course that was essential to the completion of a psychology major. Do you have any suggestions for Ned? List important sources of support and challenge for your own program.

_____

_____

_____

_____

_____

5. Don't be afraid to rethink a goal or a program; this is not giving up. The things you learn about yourself and your environment as you attempt to execute a program should be channeled into the planning/problem-solving process. One student thought that she wasn't doing well in a computer sciences program because she wasn't really applying herself. She set up a step-by-step study program based on the principles we've been discussing, but she found that, when she really applied herself, she only did slightly better. She learned that the computer sciences program wasn't really for her. After discussing this with friends and an adviser, she decided to change her major to something more appealing and more suitable.

Evaluation

As you move through and complete your program, you need to evaluate your participation in the program, the program's effectiveness, and your overall goal.

1. First, you should determine how well you are participating in the program. This kind of evaluation has to be done throughout the program. Ask yourself questions such as:

△ Am I doing each step of the program?
△ Am I doing each step well?
△ Do I search out the resources I need to do each step?
△ Do I make sure that the program remains rewarding rather than neutral or punishing?

2. Once you've moved through the program, ask yourself whether it has achieved the defined goal. If the program you are engaged in is not moving you toward your goal, the program should be modified. Ned found out that his program was much more difficult in practice than it seemed on paper. He had to modify it several times, but he actually did stop using drugs and alcohol for one month.

3. Finally, ask yourself whether the achievement of this goal has taken care of the problem or need that initiated the problem-solving process. For instance, at the end of the month, Ned felt very good about himself. He felt free again. He saw more clearly that the issue was autonomy, not alcohol or drug abuse. He felt that he could now make his own decisions about alcohol and drugs without constantly looking over his shoulder to see what everyone else was doing.

Summary

In this chapter, we focused on the development of autonomy by outlining the elements of autonomy as well as the stages people typically pass on the way to interdependence. We asked you to assess yourself in various ways and to reflect on how the key settings of your life affect your approach to autonomy. We encouraged you to continue to share the results of your exploration with the members of your group and to develop an initial action plan in the area of autonomy.

In the chapter that follows, we turn our attention to another important task—the clarification and development of values.

What Do I Believe in?
Values and Development

In this chapter, we turn our attention to the question of values and moral, or ethical, development. We begin by asking you to reflect on a moral dilemma that we present and to state your personal position regarding that dilemma. We then present practical information derived from theory and research concerning moral development and ask that you use the information to reflect on yourself in a systematic manner. Finally, you will take part in a structured group interaction and an exercise to help you focus on ethical issues and directions in your life.

Self-Assessment Exercise: The R.A.'s Dilemma

A resident advisor in a college dormitory is approached by a student who says she needs advice regarding a serious problem. She demands that the R.A. promise to tell no one about what she has to say. The R.A. gives her word that the conversation will be kept in confidence. The student then tells the R.A. that she has become addicted to barbiturates and has no way of supporting her habit, except by selling pills to other students in the dormitories. The dealer who supplies her is now threatening to expose her, unless she agrees to increase her selling activity. The R.A. must decide what action to take.

Instructions: In the space provided, answer each of the questions regarding the resident advisor's dilemma.

1. What would you do if you were the resident advisor? _____

_____

_____

_____

_____

_____

2. Explain the specific reasons for your answer to question 1. _____

_____

_____

_____

_____

_____

Moral Development: Steps along the Way

The area of moral development has attracted the attention of many talented investigators in recent years. Their work has produced various models of moral development and the process by which it occurs. In our effort to describe the current state of knowledge in this area, we will draw from the work of two such investigators and their colleagues. Lawrence Kohlberg (1969) and William Perry (1970) have introduced models of moral and ethical development that suggest that there are stages in the process of developing moral maturity. Table 5-1 displays a series of five stages of moral development that incorporates concepts from the models of Kohlberg and Perry.

TABLE 5-1. Stages of moral development.

Stage	Basis for Moral Judgment
I Self-Centered	Will the consequences of my action be pleasant or painful for me? Can someone powerful make me do such-and-such?
II Other-Centered	Will the consequences of my action maintain and demonstrate my loyalty to the significant groups to which I belong: my family, friends, nation, and culture?
III Questioning	There are so many different views on what goodness, truth, beauty, religion, and so on really are: how can I trust any of them? So, does this act make sense or feel good to *me*?
IV Relativistic	How would that particular act be judged by this set of standards? What about this other set of standards?
V Committed	By the standards of my *chosen* values, is this act moral or not?

In Stage I, individuals make moral judgments by assessing the consequences of their actions (whether they will be painful or pleasurable) or by assessing whether someone has the authority to demand or sanction particular actions. Stage-I moral judgments are illustrated by two students' responses to the R.A.'s dilemma presented here.

What Do I Believe in? Values and Development

123

△ If I were the R.A., I'd tell my boss about the situation so I wouldn't have to worry about it. It would drive me crazy to keep it to myself.

△ I don't think I'd keep the woman's secret. What if the police found out that I knew? I could go to jail as an accessory.

In attempting to understand levels of moral development, remember that assessment isn't based on what people say they would do in a particular situation, but rather on their *motives* for choosing a particular action. In the first student response, the reason given for the choice is that the individual wants to avoid worry. This is a clear example of a moral judgment based on personal comfort—a Stage-I response. The second response, also a Stage-I response, illustrates that the individual didn't want to risk the sanction of powerful people—in this case, the police.

Here are some examples of Stage-II moral judgments:

△ I would keep the person's situation secret. Being a snitch has never been O.K. in my family.

△ We have laws against drugs and I'm no lawbreaker. I'd have to turn her in.

These responses are justified on the basis of norms or standards held by groups to which the speakers belong—family "rules" and the laws of the state or the nation.

Moral judgment undergoes a major shift during Stage III, when individuals ask serious questions regarding the standards and values that were "given" to them by family, religion, nation, and culture. This personal crisis of faith, this questioning of the tenets held by authorities, involves a shift from a noncritical acceptance of family, religious, national, and cultural "rules" ("Of course drug abuse is wrong") to a period in which all rules are open to question. This is not to say that, during this stage, people necessarily engage in behaviors that violate established rules. The challenging is very often of a cognitive or verbal nature and is carried out mentally or in discussion with others. Stage III of moral development is often referred to as a moratorium—a "time-out," at least cognitively. During this stage, people begin to select and reject rules for life. Here are some examples of Stage-III moral judgments:

△ I couldn't say what I'd do just from reading the story. It would depend on whether I felt I could trust the person or not. If I thought she was playing me for a sucker, I'd notify school authorities; if not, I'd keep quiet and try to help.

△ The cops waste too much time on individual drug users already. Whether a person buys and uses drugs or not is her own business. I'd stay out of it.

△ That kid has to make up her own mind about what to do. I probably wouldn't have listened to her story in the first place. It's a private matter. I guess I wouldn't be much of an R.A.

These are Stage-III responses; they reject external rules and justify positions in a way that stresses the individual's freedom to choose. People at this level of moral development tend to feel that moral judgments are based on what they think, feel, or believe.

During Stage IV of moral development, individuals come to the realization that it is possible to refer to standards of value beyond their own personal feelings. They are aware that the quality of an action is determined not only by what they think but also by the particular set of values they use in making decisions. Therefore, a decision that makes perfect sense (is "good") from the standpoint of economic self-interest ("good" from that perspective) could be in direct contradiction to a particular set of values ("bad" from that perspective). Individuals who have reached Stage IV realize that moral judgments are relative to the particular standards by which they are made—that they aren't absolute ("for all people in all places at all times"). Here are some examples of Stage-IV moral judgments:

△ What the R.A. should do depends on what concerns her most. If the law is most important to her, she should probably talk the woman into telling some authority, or tell someone herself. If she's mainly concerned with keeping her promise, then she can't tell anyone. She'll have to convince the person to do something herself or else keep quiet.

△ If the R.A. believes that confidentiality is an obligation of her role as a counselor, I think she'd have to honor her promise not to tell anyone.

△ I think what she decides will depend on whose welfare she puts more weight on. If she's only worried about the girl with the drug problem, she probably will keep the secret; if her primary concern is with others in the dorm who might get into using downers through the woman, then she'll probably have to say something.

Each of these responses indicates an awareness on the speaker's part that the morality of the R.A.'s action should be judged against the standard by which it is made. If standards conflict or change, so do the judgments of the morality of the R.A.'s decision.

In Stage V of moral development, individuals are aware that moral judgments vary with different standards; they have also begun to choose a set of standards by which to judge their own behavior. This stage, which Perry calls *commitment*, involves what is often referred to as an existential choice, or a leap of faith. In Stage V, individuals are no longer content with relativistic moral judgments; they have begun to shape a set of standards for living to which they will hold themselves personally accountable. The key element here is personal responsibility. The following are examples of Stage-V moral judgments of the R.A.'s dilemma:

△ If I were the R.A. and had given my word, I don't think I could break it. It seems to me that the best thing would be to try to persuade the

What Do I Believe in? Values and Development

125

> student to seek help and maybe go with her to the authorities if she were willing.
> △ I would hate to break my promise to the student, but, if she wouldn't do anything on her own, I'd probably have to say something. I think it would be wrong to risk the welfare of others in the dorm to protect one person.

Moral judgments at this level are *not* made for reasons of:

△ personal comfort or fear (Stage I),
△ what others would say (Stage II),
△ doubt about the existence of valid moral standards (Stage III), or
△ relativistic "perspective-hopping" (Stage IV).

They are made on the basis of personally selected standards used by individuals to assess the morality of particular acts.

Values: Ideal and Real

A value has been defined by Simon, Howe, and Kirschenbaum (1972) as something that a particular person:

△ prizes, even in public, when appropriate;
△ chooses freely from alternatives, after considering the consequences of those alternatives; and
△ acts on rather than just thinks about.

For instance, if treating others decently is a value for you, then you engage in behaviors, or courses of action, that reflect this value; you don't merely think about the fact that you should treat others with decency.

Values are related to behaviors, goals, and life-styles. In other words, your values constitute the ways in which you commit yourself to your own life, to others, and to the world. Values are of extreme importance, because they govern the ways in which you act. Your values are a significant part of your identity—the person you see yourself to be.

The research of Rokeach (1973) suggests that most of us have two sets of values: an idealized set, which is made up of *notional values,* and a practical set, which is made up of *real values.* For instance, if you think that helping others in time of need is one of your values, but, in reflecting on your behavior, you find that you are always too busy or that some other activity is always more important, then helping others in need is, for you, a notional value rather than a real value. (It's a "good idea" that seldom, if ever, gets to see the light of day.) The results of Rokeach's research indicate that practical values determine actual behavior, whereas notional values are those that individuals endorse as the ideals by which they (and others) should live.

Is a gap between notional values and real values inevitable? In the sense that few of us constantly act in ways that are completely consistent with our deepest concepts of what is right, some discrepancy is clearly to be expected. On the other hand, Rokeach found that, in many cases, individuals who become aware of the fact that they have opinions, interests, feelings, beliefs, and attitudes (notional values) that have not yet become real values often begin to translate notional values into behavior. One of our main intents in writing this chapter is to encourage you to move toward greater consistency between notional values and real values—between what you believe and what you do in your day-to-day life.

Moral development—the level of moral judgment and the degree of integration of values with actual behavior—is, like autonomy and competence, one of the basic psychological foundations on which the effective pursuit of life's concrete challenges is based. Your ability to participate in friendship, love, marriage, family, and career, and your involvement in your community, your country, and, in Marshall McLuhan's words the "global village" that the world is becoming are directly related to your moral development.

Values, Goals, and Programs

In Chapter 3, we reviewed the importance of goals and programs to life-planning and problem-solving processes. However, setting and achieving goals makes sense only if you *value* those goals; therefore, your ability to clarify your values and relate them to your goals is very important. For instance, one student, Dismas, tried for some time to do well as a psychology major. Finally, he shared his growing misgivings with his adviser. After talking with her, he found that he was in psychology because two of his best friends were in it and because it was the most popular undergraduate major at the school—*not* because he personally valued the successful completion of the requirements for a psychology major or because he had intended to go on to graduate school in psychology. He actually disliked psychology. He used his time with his adviser to review his interests and values and to establish a different goal.

Programs, as we have seen, are the means by which you achieve your goals. Since there is often a variety of different routes to any given goal, it is up to you to choose the program or combination of programs that best suits you. In order to do this, you need to be able to discern the values that are embedded in different programs, and you need a working knowledge of your own values. For instance, Christine realized that there were a number of different ways in which she could present legitimate gripes to her roommate. She could:

△ move out,
△ present them to her in writing,

△ blow up and let out all the anger and ill feelings she had been saving up for weeks,

△ have somebody else do it for her,

△ present her gripes apologetically, and hint that she had probably offended her roommate in various ways,

△ tell her casually and gradually (over a period of days or weeks) what is bothering her,

△ tell her roommate that she wants to talk to her soon about some things that are bothering her. Arrange a time, and, at the meeting, describe without apology the behavior that bothers her, state her own reasonable needs as clearly as possible, and offer to negotiate.

Christine rejected all but the last program, because the others violated values that relate either to her own self-respect or her desire to respect her roommate. You need to clarify your values in order to make any significant decision in your life.

Dreams, Models, and Mentors I

1. Indicate some of the important values you want to include in your Dream. Be as concrete and specific as possible.

_____

_____

_____

_____

_____

_____

2. Choose two or three of these values and indicate people who serve as models of these values for you. Indicate the ways in which these people employ these values in their lives.

_____

_____

_____

_____

_____

_____

3. Can you think of anyone who is capable of becoming a mentor for you in the area of values? Explain why.

_____

_____

_____

_____

_____

_____

Religion, Values, and Moral Development

Traditionally, religion has dealt with the question of values and has fostered a number of different approaches to moral development. You may or may not maintain a formal affiliation with a particular religious group. Even if you don't, you might still feel that you are religious in a sense of that term and that you have some concern regarding issues that traditionally have been called *religious*. For instance, you might place importance on belief in God, interest in religious writings, respect for religious heroes (contemporary or historical), questions concerning communities of believers (whether they are called churches, brotherhoods, sisterhoods, or congregations), and a concern for such questions as the origin of the universe, the meaning of life, and the mystery of death and its aftermath. If you do maintain an affiliation with a formal religious group, you might find that the stages of moral development outlined earlier in this chapter are relevant to your participation in your church group. For instance, you might find yourself following the norms and values of your particular group more or less without question, you might be questioning your church or religion in a variety of ways, or you might think that one religion is as good (or as bad) as another. Perhaps you've given up some of your religious practices, or maybe you are pursuing some dimensions of religious life quite intensely. Some people view a questioning of one's beliefs as a cross of faith, but we interpret such questioning as a transitional stage of development, with all the characteristics of such a stage reflected in the moral, ethical, and religious dimensions of life. Perhaps it might be useful to review the characteristics of transitional stages of development as they were outlined in Chapter 2 and see how they relate to your present religious concerns. These characteristics include the notions of boundary zone, termination or modification of relationships, questioning, experimenting, and initiating new forms of behavior.

Five Models of Churches and Religious Communities

Avery Dulles (1974) provides a schema that may be helpful in rethinking religious issues in your life. In his schema, Dulles talks about five models of

What Do I Believe in? Values and Development

129

churches and religious commitments, each of which portrays a dimension of religious experience. Dulles' five models are: (1) the institutional, (2) the herald, or prophet, (3) the servant, (4) the mystical community, and (5) the sacramental.

The institutional model. Perhaps this is what you first think of when you think of a church or a religious congregation—the Catholic Church, the Methodist Church, Orthodox Judaism, or Islam, together with their creeds and dogmas, their structure, their authority figures, their buildings, central headquarters, politics, and the like. Those who limit their consideration of religion to institutions maintain a rather narrow view of religion.

The herald, or prophet, model. This is the church or religious community insofar as it proclaims its message—its religious writings and traditions—to the surrounding community or to the entire world. The church or religious community hopes that its message will inspire people to believe in certain values and live better lives. The message, at least indirectly, serves as a standard by which society, its morals, and its institutions can be critiqued.

The servant model. This is the congregation that is acutely aware of human needs and desires to minister to those needs concretely in a variety of settings. This type of organization appeals to some people in the moving-into-adulthood transition, because it's compatible with the Dream they are fashioning. Any given church can either restrict its ministry to its own members or be open to ministering to anyone in need.

The mystical-community model. This is church in the sense of a small group of people who concentrate on their inner lives, or what is called in religious terms the *life of the spirit*. Their focus is on the God within—the God that pervades human life. This model appeals to some people in the moving-into-adulthood stage. They find support in small groups, and this approach to religion is emotionally enriching and helps them come to terms with their developing awareness of self.

The sacramental model. This is church in the sense of a community of like-minded people—that is, people who share the same religious vision and goals and who see the church as a sign of authentic hope. They find both belonging and meaning in religious community. They celebrate the mysteries of religion in public liturgies that serve, in part, their need for ritual expression.

Dulles suggests that the institutional model cannot be primary, because it exists to serve one or more of the other models. Otherwise, these models complement one another, each one emphasizing a different dimension of religious experience. Some churches and individuals take one of the last four models as the primary model and weave the others into one model.

As we have suggested, for some people, religion is meaningless; for others, it is a part of life that can be compartmentalized; for still others, religion pervades every aspect and dimension of life. Dulles' models can be used to obtain a picture of religion that includes more than the institutional church and, for those who like, can be used as a tool for rethinking some of the basic questions of life.

Dreams, Models, and Mentors II

1. What are the significant ways, if any, in which religion fits into your Dream?

_____

_____

_____

_____

_____

2. What models—either peers or people older than yourself—appeal to you? Describe several people who are carrying out developmental tasks in the area of religion in ways that appeal to you. What is it about them, concretely, that makes them appeal to you?

_____

_____

_____

_____

_____

_____

_____

3. Can you think of any mentors in this area of life whose experience you would like to share or whose counsel you would like to have?

_____

_____

_____

_____

_____

What Do I Believe in? Values and Development

131

Systematic Self-Assessment: Level of Moral Judgment

1. Refer to your response to the R.A.'s dilemma and the stages of moral judgment. In the space provided, indicate the stage of development your response reflects and why. Remember that you can make this judgment only by knowing *why* you said that you would take one particular course of action rather than another. In your answer, then, it is important that you focus your analysis on Step 2 of the personal-reflection exercise at the beginning of this chapter.

Here are some examples of students' efforts to assess their responses to the R.A.'s dilemma.

Step: 3

Reasons: I put 3 down, because my answer was that she should do whatever fit her conscience—no one or no rules could help her.

Step: 2

Reasons: I think my response was a 2, because I said the most important consideration was what the law said. What kind of a world would we have if people decided whether the law was right or not? I rate it a 2, because it seems to focus on group standards.

Step: 4

Reasons: My response was a Step 4. I said the R.A. would have to decide whether her most important obligation was to the student, to other students, or to the law. On that basis, she'd decide what to do.

Now, assess the level of moral judgment of your response and write down the reasons for that assessment.

Step: _____

Reasons: _____

_____

_____

_____

_____

_____

_____

2. Reread the definition and examples of the stage at which you evaluated your response. Do you think that this level of moral judgment is typical of

you at this point in your life? In the space provided, write a brief paragraph explaining your answer to this question. One way of getting at the answer to this question is to consider a moral judgment that you've recently made, focusing on your reasons for having made it. Does the example seem to fall at the same stage as your reply to the R.A.'s dilemma? Here is how two students responded to this task:

△ I think my response to the R.A. story was a 4—she'd have to decide who her first obligation was to. As far as my typical moral judgment, I'd say it's often one step down (3), because I have real doubts sometimes about whether any standards make much sense. In some ways, no institution lives up to its values, and that makes me wonder how individuals can.

△ My response about what the R.A. should do was a 2. I thought she should consider school policies and the law first in deciding what to do. I guess that's usually how I make up my mind about stuff. Family and church standards play an awfully big role, even if they don't always seem right to me.

Now write your response to the question of how your answer to the R.A.'s dilemma fits or doesn't fit with your current moral judgments in real life.

_____

_____

_____

_____

_____

_____

_____

_____

Systematic Self-Assessment: Real Values Versus Notional Values

Select a value that you claim as your own. Here are some examples:

△ It is wrong to take something that belongs to someone else.
△ A promise is sacred.
△ Loyalty to friends above all else.

What Do I Believe in? Values and Development

133

△ Treat others as you'd like to be treated.
△ Do your fair share.

In Part 1 of the space provided, write at least two examples of actual behavior that reflects this value in your life. Here is one example of a response to this task:

Part 1—Consistency between Value and Behavior

Value: Friends deserve loyalty even when they do things that hurt.

Deborah has been in a terrible mood for several weeks. I think there's real trouble at home. She doesn't do stuff with us like she used to. So far, at least, I haven't gotten mad at her. I just wish she'd let me know what's going on.

In Part 2 of the space provided, write at least two examples of behavior that you feel are at odds with a value you've chosen. Here is one example of a response to this task:

Part 2—Inconsistency between Value and Behavior.

Value: We should be grateful to parents for their sacrifices on our behalf.

Pretty often I think I get so wrapped up in what I want to do that I don't think about my folks' needs. The other day, they loaned me the car for the day with the understanding that I'd be home by supper time. The group I was with wanted to stay later (and so did I), so I didn't get back until 8:30. As a result, my parents missed a play they had tickets for; one they'd been looking forward to.

List the value(s) that are important to you, and give examples of behaviors that are consistent and inconsistent with them. You may use the same or different values in Parts 1 and 2.

Part 1—Consistency between Value and Behavior.

Value: _____

a. *Behavior:* _____

_____

_____

_____

_____

b. *Behavior:* _____

_____

_____

_____

_____

_____

Part 2—Inconsistency between Value and Behavior.

Value: _____

a. *Behavior:* _____

_____

_____

_____

_____

b. *Behavior:* _____

_____

_____

_____

_____

Key Settings and the Development of Values

The key settings in your life contribute to your development in the area of values. In the following exercise, we invite you to reflect on whether these settings are providing the challenge and support necessary for your development.

Instructions: Using the form provided, list at least one key setting that is enhancing your moral development and one that seems not to be doing so. Then, write a brief description of the reasons for your responses. Here is an example of how one student responded to this task:

Positive influence.

Setting: Living situation

Reasons: For some reason, my roommates and I developed enough trust among ourselves so that we are pretty straight in discussing

What Do I Believe in? Values and Development

135

things that are on our minds. My views about drugs and sex have changed for the better because of knowing and talking to these guys.

Negative influence.

Setting: Church

Reasons: It seems funny to list my church here, but what I mean is that I always feel that someone who's morally superior is telling me what to do and judging me. I've never really felt that they understand what my concerns are. A lot of what's said there seems to have very little to do with what's going on in my life right now.

Now complete your own assessment of the impact of key settings on your values.

Positive influence.

Setting: _____

Reasons: _____

_____

_____

_____

_____

Negative influence.

Setting: _____

Reasons: _____

_____

_____

_____

_____

Structured Group Interaction: Values

1. Instruct one member of the group to read the R.A.'s dilemma aloud. Each member of the group should then read his or her response to the first exercise:

a. What would you do if you were the R.A.?

b. Why would you do that?

The group should then spend 10–15 minutes in a discussion of their responses to the dilemma. After participating in the discussion, decide whether or not you want to change your own response in any way. If you do, explain how and why.

2. Each member of the group should reread (aloud) his or her response to the R.A.'s dilemma, indicate at what level of moral judgment he or she evaluated it, and give reasons for the evaluation. Other members of the group will then be free to comment on the evaluation, raising any questions they may have or indicating their agreement. Continue until everyone has had an opportunity to share his or her evaluation and receive feedback.

3. Each member of the group should share one example of a key setting in his or her life that seems to have a positive impact on moral development. Be specific about *how* the setting has an effect.

4. Finally, if you wish, tell the group how you assess your current level of moral reasoning. At which level do you seem to be, and why? Then ask the members of your group for feedback.

Action Plan: Values

Instructions: Based on your reading and thinking regarding moral development and the behavioral expression of values, take the following steps:

1. Write a brief response to the following question: In what area of values in your own life (either level of moral judgment or real/ideal value discrepancies) would you like to see change? Why?

Target Area: _____

Reasons: _____

_____

_____

_____

_____

_____

2. Compile a list of possible resources that can help you to bring about change. One student responded to this task in the following way:

Target Area: Moving to Step III

Reasons: I'd like to be less dependent on what others think I should do and more certain of my own value positions. Here are some resources that occur to me:

△ reading material on values and how they change during these years,
△ friends who seem to have a fairly independent way of making decisions,
△ classes where independent reasoning is required,
△ values-clarification groups at the career center,
△ my older brother, who seems to be pretty independent. He's not tied up by the family rules, and
△ a minister who's down-to-earth and understands people my age.

Now compile your own list of potential resources.

Resources: _____

_____

_____

_____

_____

3. Select several of the resources you've listed and use them to formulate a list of action steps that you can take to move in the direction of the change you specified in Step 1 of this exercise.

Action Steps:

1. _____

_____

_____

_____

2. _____

_____

_____

_____

3. _____

_____

_____

_____

4. _____

_____

_____

_____

Summary

In this chapter, we've focused on the development of moral judgment, the behavioral expression of values, and concerns about religion. We invited you to reflect in various ways on your own level of moral judgment, on real/ideal value discrepancies that you observe in your behavior, and on the ways in which the key settings in your life foster or hinder your ethical development. Finally, you were asked to select and focus on one aspect of values in your life and to formulate action steps that will help you to move in the direction you desire.

In the following chapter, we turn our attention to a cornerstone of human development through life—psychosocial identity.

CHAPTER

Identity: The Bridge between Self and Society

In Chapter 6, we examine the development of identity as a key process during the years of moving into adulthood. We begin with an exercise that is designed to help you explore your thoughts about your own identity. Then we turn our attention to basic concepts of identity derived from theory and research. Using the material we present, you will reflect on yourself in a systematic way and take part in a structured group interaction focusing on identity. Finally, you will be assisted in planning an action process regarding identity.

Personal-Reflection Exercise: Who Am I?

Instructions: Using the space provided, answer the question "Who am I?" 20 times. Allow yourself only 15 minutes to complete this task. Since you have only a short period in which to respond, it's important that you write brief statements. If, after several statements, you "run dry," allow a few seconds to pass. New ideas are likely to strike you.

1. I am _____
2. I am _____
3. I am _____
4. I am _____
5. I am _____
6. I am _____
7. I am _____
8. I am _____
9. I am _____
10. I am _____
11. I am _____
12. I am _____
13. I am _____
14. I am _____
15. I am _____
16. I am _____
17. I am _____
18. I am _____
19. I am _____
20. I am _____

Identity: A Psychosocial Definition

As we indicated in our overview of the developmental tasks of moving into adulthood, identity can be defined as a fairly stable sense of who you are that seems to be shared by the people in your life who are significant to you. If you examine this definition, you will see that it has both an internal, or *psychological*, aspect ("a fairly stable sense of who you are"), and an external, or *social*, aspect ("that seems to be shared by the people in your life who are significant to you"). This dual nature led Erik Erikson (1968), the investigator who is credited with discovering the importance of identity development, to refer to identity as a *psychosocial concept*. Some definitions of identity place relative emphasis on the social dimension, such as Cooley's "looking glass self," Mead's "reflected appraisals as the basis of self," and Sullivan's "habitual interpersonal expression of self." As we will see, commitment plays an important role in fashioning identity. This is reflected in Newman and Newman's (1975) definition of identity as "the eventual commitment to a personal integration of values, goals, and abilities" (p. 219). Note that this definition involves competence, autonomy, and ethical development—issues that we treated in preceding chapters.

We stress the psychosocial conception of identity, because it is one of the most useful ways of calling your attention to an important fact about your development as a person: you become who you are as a result of the interactions (both verbal and nonverbal) that take place between yourself and the important people and key settings of your life. Although your identity is in a very real sense personal, it is not self-created.

Rather, it is the result of literally thousands of exchanges between yourself and the people you encounter during your lifetime. These exchanges with your parents, brothers and sisters, teachers, coaches, classmates, and so on occur as you work through the developmental tasks of early life as sketched by Erikson (1963): trust, autonomy, initiative, and competence. The way in which you've coped with these developmental tasks becomes part and parcel of your identity. A task (such as the development of competence) doesn't become unimportant after you've come to grips with it; it moves to the side of the stage while the next task (such as identity formation) moves to the center of the stage.

During this moving-into-adulthood period of your life, the sense of who you are is going through changes of real significance. What makes the years of moving into adulthood so critical to the development of identity? White (1976) has this to say:

> It is at this time when identity as a child no longer fits and when all the choices, problems, and unknowns of being an adult loom directly ahead, that the question "Who am I?" may be asked with special urgency [p. 433].*

From all the possibilities, fantasies, and hopes of childhood emerges a pattern of commitments to a life—*your* life. "Who will I be?" is no longer the question of your

*From *The Enterprise of Living* (2nd Ed.), by R. W. White. Copyright 1976 by Holt, Rinehart & Winston.

childhood but rather one that you face in very concrete ways in the form of major choices, career decisions, and relationship commitments. Your developing *Dream*, to use Levinson's term, is a way in which you begin to define yourself as a unique person in relationship to the world.

As you make crucial decisions, a sense of who you are—an identity—will develop that will (if all goes well) be much more stable and deep than the identities of your early life. This is not to say that, beyond this point, your identity is fixed in granite. On the contrary, major life changes during adulthood (such as marriage, career change, and parenthood) can be powerful stimuli for identity development. However, evidence suggests that these changes usually involve building on, refining, and deepening the identity achieved during the years of moving into adulthood.

Identity: Statuses and Stages

An extremely insightful analysis of the development of identity comes from a program of research conducted by James Marcia (1966). Marcia's work in attempting to understand identity development in college students led him to the conclusion that there are two critical signs that shed light on the status or condition of a person's identity: crisis and commitment. *Crisis* refers to the experience of confusion and anxiety regarding important life choices that you face (for example, career, values, and religious beliefs). *Commitment* refers to making stable choices in these areas of life—choices that establish the pattern of your life. Four combinations of crisis and commitment represent the four statuses, or conditions of identity, that Marcia found in his research: identity achieved, moratorium, identity foreclosure, and identity diffusion. Figure 6-1 illustrates these identity statuses.

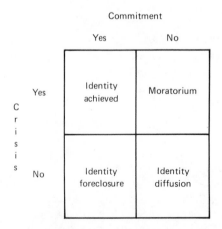

FIGURE 6-1. Identity statuses.

Let us take a brief look at each of these conditions.

Identity achieved. The individual who has experienced a personal crisis, questioned values and decisions, and resolved those questions by beginning to make personal choices is said to be in the *identity achieved* status. His or her behavior is no longer dictated by rules and paths laid down by others. This person's actions are a result of authentic personal choice. This doesn't mean that the values and influences of family, schools, church and so on are disregarded, but it does mean that the individual has decided what role, if any, these values will have in his or her life choices.

Moratorium. The individual who is experiencing the personal crisis of belief and decision but who has not yet resolved it is said to be in a status of *moratorium.* He or she is in the process of struggling with decisions and coming to personal choices in critical areas but hasn't resolved them as of yet. The college years can offer a kind of free period (moratorium), during which decisions can be pondered. It should be stressed that the moratorium period involves a healthy process of struggle—a testing period for behaviors and values, some of which will become stable aspects of your identity. Individuals with a mature sense of identity do not simply carry out the directions they received as children; they have either internalized or rejected those directions. The moratorium is an important step toward adulthood.

Identity foreclosure. A situation in which a person seems to have experienced no crisis and has made stable decisions regarding values and career is referred to by Marcia as *identity foreclosure.* By this, he means that the person has simply accepted the values and decisions of others without struggling through personal choices as to whether or not they "fit." The danger here is that, since the values and decisions do not really belong to the individual, he or she might not have the depth of personal commitment required to live by them. The commitments of others, when taken on secondhand, can lead to real difficulties in adult life. Values not personally chosen may grow hollow over the years and a person may have vague or strong feelings that he or she is living a lie. For instance, without apparent warning, Sally leaves her husband and two teenage children and moves in with another man. Those who know Sally (or think they know her) are startled, because she has been a "solid citizen" ever since she was a young girl. Sally had gone through adolescence and into marriage without struggling at all with traditional values concerning marriage, family, and the roles of wife and mother. Her supposedly solid values were hollow, and her rejection of them was not the drastic step her friends and acquaintances thought it to be. Foreclosed identity can be thought of as living out someone else's dream. Many young people today appear to be foreclosing their identities by accepting the prepackaged identities issued by religious cults.

Identity diffusion. This status is occupied by people in the moving-into-adulthood years who don't experience crises regarding life commitments and, therefore, haven't made stable choices. On the other hand, they have neither accepted nor rejected the beliefs and values of others. We speak here not of individuals who haven't yet undergone the belief-choice crisis, but of those who apparently will not experience it and are not particularly concerned about it or about the life choices to which the crisis is related. This identity status is often associated with the aimlessness of individuals who drift through life by responding to the demands of particular situations and by pleasing others rather than setting their own course. For instance, Anatoly is seen as a nice person by some, as an inoffensive person by others, and as a rather colorless and bland person by still others. Although he shows signs of being intelligent and talented, he never seems to make any demands on himself. No cause, personal or social, has ever galvanized him into action. He seems to be a victim, in almost dramatic ways—though *dramatic* seems to be an inappropriate term to use in describing his life—of the psychopathology of the average. To casual observers, his life seems to be comfortable enough, but he is living a life of "quiet desperation." He is often depressed, and he seems at times to be suffering from what some people have called "learned helplessness." When asked to do the simple "I am" task featured at the beginning of this chapter, he gave up.

Marcia's model of identity illustrates a progression—a sequence of steps—on the bridge from the world of childhood to the world of adulthood. Figure 6-2 illustrates these steps in the development of identity during the college years.

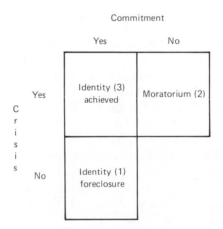

FIGURE 6-2. Steps in the development of identity.

Step 1 (identity foreclosure). If you reread the definition of identity foreclosure, you will see that, in the sense that everyone begins life by taking on the values, beliefs, and behaviors of others, we all take on identities given by others. All individuals live the early part of their lives in a state of identity foreclosure—they haven't yet become their own persons. Therefore, identity foreclosure is Step 1 (the beginning phase) in the process of identity development.

Step 2 (moratorium). Once you've begun to ask questions regarding the values that were given to you in childhood, the process of becoming your own person has begun. Some people never experience this crisis, and they continue to live out the beliefs of others (identity foreclosure) or drift with no central identity (identity diffusion). Step 2—the moratorium—is the period during which you struggle through a maze of alternative thoughts, behaviors, and values in an effort to define who you are in an autonomous sense. It can be an exciting time, though typically it has its fair share of unpleasant moments. The image of a hot-air balloon comes to mind—drifting nicely above familiar landscape, and yet subject, sometimes continuously, to battering gusts of wind that can range from uncomfortable to terrifying. Riding under such a balloon can be exhilarating, but eventually there is a pressing desire to anchor oneself to something that will add direction and stability to life.

Step 3 (identity achieved). This is the process of anchoring. The anchor involves a set of choices regarding values and life direction. These choices will, in all likelihood, reflect your childhood (or foreclosed) identity but will not be defined by it. Some of the beliefs and values of your earlier life will be strengthened and internalized, others will take different forms, and others will be discarded. In the third phase of the process of identity development, you begin to experience yourself as a person with a fairly stable sense of who you are, and this sense of self is consistent with the messages that you receive from others concerning yourself.

Identity is not something that you can simply demand of yourself; its development depends on your movement through phases in settings where adequate levels of challenge and support are available. If you are in a state of moratorium, torn and undecided, you are on the road to maturity. If you are overly comfortable and perhaps even smug in your life commitments and plans, this could be a sign that you haven't yet faced the crisis of personal commitment.

Identity and Personal Commitments

As we have seen, Newman and Newman's (1975) definition of identity as "the eventual commitment to a personal integration of values, goals, and abilities" emphasizes choices insofar as they reflect a sense of identity. In Marcia's words:

> If one has achieved a sense of ego identity in late adolescence, then he may be expected to express commitments (regarding occupation and values) both verbally and behaviorally. . . . One does not achieve an identity *because* he has made these commitments; nor does he make these commitments because he has achieved an identity. Simply, commitments in occupation and ideology are the observable signs of identity achievement [p. 553].

In other words, although identity is not directly observable, certain events that accompany it (for instance, values and career choices) are observable. In fact, you can assess your identity status by examining your values and initial career-related decisions.

The development of a stable personal identity provides the foundation on which career and value commitments are built. Much of our early thinking regarding careers and values tends to reflect either fantasy or the automatic playing out of the expectations that important people in our lives hold for us.

The concept of identity is like a summary, a hinge, or an arrow. As you might have noticed, it repeats and summarizes a great deal that has been said about competence, autonomy, and the development of values. Your identity is like a hinge in the sense that, if you have a stable sense of who you are, and, if this is reflected in the way in which others see you and act toward you, then it serves as a solid hinge on which you can hang the behavioral ways in which you relate to yourself, to others, and to the world. Identity is an arrow that points toward the future. It not only summarizes what you are achieving in terms of competence, autonomy, and commitment but it also points toward achievements to come in the areas of friendship and intimacy, love and commitment, career, involvement with community, country, and the world, leisure and recreation, and the development of a life-style that is the concrete expression of significant elements of your Dream.

Chickering (1969) has suggested that the development of identity is the keystone of the entire process of human development through life. Everything that happened previously in your life can be viewed as building *toward* identity; everything that happens beyond the development of identity can be viewed as building *on* identity. The time of transition in which you find yourself is often referred to as *a time of passage*. The struggles you experience in making decisions and commitments are referred to as *rites of passage*. Once you have weathered this passage, you will find that you possess something of great value—a self that is neither dominated by the world nor insensitive to it. You will be able to relate deeply and effectively to the world without being possessed by it.

The development of your identity will never be final. It is quite likely that you will stabilize your identity during the years of late adolescence, deepen and extend that identity during your 20s, and perhaps undergo a fundamental reevaluation of identity during mid-life. Moreover, the development of identity often remains unfinished in the sense that your identity might be initially achieved in one area (such as career), but still in flux in another (such as religious beliefs or marriage).

Systematic Self-Assessment: Identity

1. Refer to the "Who am I" exercise that you completed earlier in this chapter and review your responses. Write one paragraph summarizing the most important response. Here are the responses of two students.

I'm a thoughtful and somewhat shy person. Other people's opinions about things interest me, but quite often I end up keeping my opinions to myself. I change my mind a lot about where I'm going. It concerns me, but I just can't seem to settle on any one thing. I have good friends, a small number of them. I don't think I'll ever be a real social-set person.

I'm a hard worker—my whole family is. School has one purpose for me—a degree in accounting and the job that'll go with it. I tend not to have much time for other things—reading, music, and so on. Maybe I'll get back to all that later. For now, I want to join my Dad's C.P.A. firm just as Dad joined Grandpa's.

In the space provided, write your own paragraph summarizing your "Who am I?" exercise.

_____

_____

_____

_____

2. Refer to the four identity statuses that were discussed earlier in this chapter. In the space provided, select the status that you think most accurately reflects your current phase in identity development. Give at least three examples of behaviors that illustrate the reasons for your self-assessment. Two students who worked on this task responded by writing the following:

Status: Moratorium

Behavioral examples:

—I keep changing my major.
—I can't decide whether to attend church or not.
—I find myself spending less time with my old group.

Status: Foreclosure

Behavioral examples:

—I accept what teachers say as gospel.
—I am pursuing a business major mostly to please my folks.
—I have never questioned anything from my religion.

Now make your self-assessment and illustrate it behaviorally. If you think that your present position on identity reflects more than one status, indicate each status and the behaviors that underlie them.

Identity Status: Self-Assessment

Status: _____

Behavioral examples: _____

_____

_____

_____

_____

_____

Key Settings and the Development of Identity

The key settings in your life can either enhance or inhibit your development in the area of identity. In the following exercise, you are invited to reflect on the ways in which certain key settings in your life affect the development of your identity.

Using the space provided, evaluate your family, friendship group, and classroom experience as sources of challenge and support regarding the development of your identity. In each case, you are asked to assess positive and negative aspects. Here is an example of how one student responded to this task:

Family

Positive: My parents really do seem to want me to be independent, to make up my own mind about things. They supported my decision to get an apartment, even though it was cheaper if I stayed at home. They don't generally quarrel with my decisions about things.

Negative: My Mom and Dad are so concerned about the job market for me that they tend to push me toward majors "with a future"—meaning a job. I see a career or profession as a lot more than just a job, but I'm not sure they think that way. It's kind of funny, because I think my Dad is caught in a job he's never liked. You'd think he'd understand where I'm coming from.

Friendship Group

Positive: My friends support one another as far as making choices that families don't like, and so on. We stick together, even if we don't always agree. Being able to talk with them openly helps me get clear on my own ideas and values about where I'm going.

Negative: Sometimes we start to sound a lot alike. Same beliefs, same prejudices, even the same language. I feel like we need a breath of fresh air—some other viewpoints to keep us from being too comfortable, a closed clique.

Classroom

Positive: My best profs always get me questioning, thinking about things. They don't accept all the stuff I take for granted. I feel like I'm doing my own thinking more after a course like that, instead of just relying on what someone told me to think or believe.

Negative: My only negative comment would be that some profs don't seem to realize how painful and disturbing it can be to have old assumptions taken away; for instance, about the American government. They're so used to thinking like that that they forget we've always believed that stuff. I think they lose some people that way.

Now do your own assessment of these key settings in your life. One blank is provided so that you can assess a setting of your choice.

Family

Positive: _____

_____

_____

_____

Negative: _____

_____

_____

_____

Friendship Group

Positive: _____

_____

_____

_____

_____

Negative: _____

_____

_____
_____
_____

Classroom

Positive: _____
_____
_____
_____
_____

Negative: _____
_____
_____
_____

Setting: _____

Positive: _____
_____
_____
_____

Negative: _____
_____
_____
_____

Structured Group Interaction: Identity

Step 1. First, each member of the group shares one insight into his or her personal identity that has been gained from the work in this chapter. Try to share something that was particularly significant to you.

Step 2. Next, each group member shares one example of a positive influence and one example of negative influence of a key setting on his or her identity development. Be specific in your description of these influences.

Step 3. Next, each member of the group shares his or her self-assessment of current identity status (achieved, foreclosed, diffused, moratorium, or any combination) and the reasons for that assessment.

Action Plan: Identity

Instructions: Review the Competence Checklist in Chapter 3 as a guide to help you complete this exercise.

1. In the space provided, write a brief response to the following question: What is your reaction to the level of identity development at which you have assessed yourself? Why?

_____

_____

_____

_____

_____

2. Write a brief personal-goal statement regarding your identity development—describe one concrete change that you would like to make in this area. One student, Norma, chose the following goal:

> I want to see in what areas of life I have done some premature "foreclosing" and work at doing some "unforeclosing." Concretely, I will look at the areas of career and religion. Over the next two months, I will see what decisions I have made or have failed to make in these areas. If I have done some foreclosing, I will make some concrete decisions in these areas.

Now write your own goal statement.

_____

_____

_____

_____

_____

_____

3. List some of the steps you might take to achieve your goal; that is, construct a program. Norma included the following steps in her program:

—move onto campus or into an apartment next semester.
—do some reading in the areas of career development and religion.
—do the life planning seminar at the counseling center.
—talk to someone about how what is happening in my life is affecting my religious beliefs.

Now list the steps in your program.

_____

_____

_____

_____

_____

_____

4. In the space provided, draw up a list of possible resources that will provide support and challenge as you carry out your program. Norma identified the following resources:

—Ray and Ellen seem to know who they are and are moving in directions they've chosen for themselves. Talk to them about issues that concern me.
—Our counseling center is actually called the Center for Student Development. Explore what they have to offer besides the life-planning seminar.
—Talk with the campus minister about suggestions in the area of religion. I've heard that she's understanding and honest.

Now list the resources available to you, and give a brief indication of how they might help you in your program.

_____

_____

_____

_____

_____

_____

_____

_____

5. *Implementation and evaluation:* (a) Explain how you are going to monitor your participation in your program.

_____

_____

_____

_____

_____

_____

_____

(b) What obstacles do you anticipate? How can you overcome them?

_____

_____

_____

_____

_____

Summary

In this chapter, we've focused on the development of identity. We invited you to reflect on the current status of your own identity and on the settings that affect its development. Finally, you were asked to focus on a goal regarding your own identity development and to think about programs and resources that could help you to achieve that goal.

In the next chapter, we turn our attention to sexuality and identity.

CHAPTER

7

Sexuality and Identity:
Who Am I as a Sexual Person?

154

Developmental theory and research, as well as common sense, suggest that the way in which you see yourself as a sexual person is an important aspect of your overall identity. Sexuality, together with its various forms of behavioral expression, can be seen as a bridge between identity and intimacy. It is in that light that we encourage you to examine sexuality.

Sex as Commodity: Double Messages

It is unfortunate but true that, for many reasons, the subject of sex tends to set off a complex set of conflicting reactions—curiosity and fear, excitement and guilt, longing and avoidance. As a result, many people find it difficult to assess and understand their sexual feelings, values, and behaviors. Hettlinger (1974) argues that contradictory feelings regarding sex have their roots in cultural "double messages" that affect the members of our society.

> While impressing on their children that sex is something sacred to be kept for marriage, the adult world has no hesitation in taking full advantage of erotic responses to sell everything from chutney (*Chut-Nut* is "the sexier chutney") to automobiles. We are invited to "Make Love Not Beds" on *Slumberdown*, to "Make out better at both ends" with *Big Tip Pall Mall Gold*, and to let *John Kloss* dress us for bed when we're not the least bit sleepy. The smart boats this year are said to be wearing "topless power," and *Capri* is "the first sexy European car under $2,300." We learn from ads "What to wear on Sunday when you won't be home till Monday," and "Where to shop for underthings if you're not thinking of wearing any." And so it goes [pp. 7–8].*

Your own exposure to television and magazines would enable you to update Hettlinger's list. (Most of us would find any European car under $2300 a good buy, "sexy" or not.)

The commercial use of sex angers some people, because it robs sex of its power.

> Sex, our birthright and one of our strongest sources of pleasure, has been taken away from us. It has become America's obsession; America's darling of the marketplace. It has been systematically channeled, diverted, turned against us, allotted the role of carrot or stick, reward or enforcer. Our erotic needs have been co-opted, defused. Sex has been reduced to the status of commodity: women's sexuality is dispensed as payment to men for successful performance [Votichenko & Winter, 1979, p. 63].

*From *Sex Isn't That Simple*, by Richard F. Hettlinger. Copyright © 1974 by Richard F. Hettlinger. This and all other quotations from this source are used by permission of the publisher, The Seabury Press, Inc.

This represents a social-systems view of sex—individuals become victims of de-humanizing cultural blueprints.

You face a constant bombardment of sexual stimuli, and yet you are warned, on social, religious, moral, and hygienic grounds, against translating sexual feelings into behavior. All of us live with this cultural contradiction.

Some people draw fairly sharp distinctions between the "old" sexuality (morality and practice) and the "new."

> I guess that I have been fortunate, for my parents are truly in love and share a deep respect for each other. The vows they made long ago have been kept, commitments have been honored, responsibilities fulfilled. My parents seem to feel as though their relationship has worked, and that love, monogamy, respect, and sexual privacy have protected and reinforced the invisible tapestry of their human bond. For me, the monogamous love/life relationship offers beauty and stability. This kind of relationship seems to help develop trust, clarity, sensitivity, and commitment, qualities that are said to encourage the exchange of love between two people.

> On the other hand, I have also grown up with a generation of men and women for whom sexuality is a changing, thrilling, playful thing. Sex is discussed openly, exchanged freely, experimented with, and often experienced casually. As more and more of us begin to travel, move to new regions, and enter into our own self-exploring adventures, we feel teasingly free to examine our minds, bodies, feelings, and, of course, the dynamics of sexuality that had previously lived only on the edges of our fantasies. Along with these attitudes and practices, a new morality has been struggling to emerge which places a great deal of emphasis on personal freedom, inner awareness, independence, equality of the sexes, and the open experience/expression of feelings in the "here and now."

> Surely there are many advantages as well as disadvantages to both these generational preferences. I will not attempt to present the "correct" approach to sexuality, for I simply feel that *there is none.* Rather, with the enormous amount of sexual and lifestyle experimentation going on, as well as the rapid decrease in the number of successful long-term marriages, it seems as though there are many like myself who are stuck between two worlds and who apparently share my yearning and confusion [Dychtwald, 1979, pp. 48–49].*

A statement such as this is based on assumptions that may or may not be true; not enough sociological data are presented to support them. These two different life-styles are identified with two different generations, the assumption being that older people identify with the former and younger people with the latter.

*From "Sexuality and the Whole Person," by K. Dychtwald, *Journal of Humanistic Psychology*, 1979, *19*(2), 47–61. Copyright 1979 by the Association for Humanistic Psychology. Sections of this passage initially appeared in *Bodymind* (Jove 1978), also by K. Dychtwald. This and all other quotations from this source are reprinted by permission of author and publisher.

However, it could be that some members of the older generation have adopted the "new" style and that many members of the younger generation maintain "old" sexual styles. There is no clear evidence to support the assumption that Dychtwald is speaking for a majority of persons. For instance, although evidence indicates that the number of men and women living together outside marriage has risen dramatically during the past ten years, it is also true that this life-style is still the life-style of relatively few people. It is a life-style that is more newsworthy than more traditional styles of living and, therefore, is discussed more frequently in the media. Media coverage can give the impression that the sexual revolution is more intensive and extensive than it is in reality. Dychtwald's personal statement *does* describe two anchor points. People range from one end of this continuum to the other, but precisely how many people in our society are at any given point is not clear. Moreover, it is probably true that any given individual's position on the continuum is not static—there is developmental movement. Also, participation in the sexual revolution can be partial rather than total. For instance, some people who once thought contraception was wrong now use it freely. But these same people might remain monogamous.

The following statements indicate some of the assumptions on which the discussions in this chapter are based:

△ Questions concerning a person's sexual behavior should be considered in light of the personal and social values of that person.

△ Decisions regarding sexual identity, preference, and expression should be the result of free personal choices made with the benefit of up-to-date information (physiological, psychological, sociological, theological, and ethical) and candid discussion of sexual matters in a supportive environment.

△ People should conduct their relationships, including sexual relationships, in ways that are not limited by rigid sex-role stereotypes.

△ Mutuality, in terms of a growing mutual sensitivity to the feelings, needs, wants, and values of other people, is the hallmark of mature sexual relationships.

△ People's individual sexual styles are profoundly influenced by factors in their individual developmental histories, including the patterns of reward and punishment that have been associated with both overt and covert sexual behavior, adult and peer role models, and cultural "blueprints" found in principal social settings—the family, peer groups, church, school, social class, neighborhood, and workplace. The decisions that people make are conditioned by their understanding of the ways in which their present style has been influenced by these factors.

According to this view, people who are maturing sexually make their own decisions in sexual matters with an understanding of cultural traditions and current social mores, but they don't totally accept the injunctions of parents, ministers, *or* peers. They make decisions that are consistent with the system of values they espouse. These decisions do not spring from rigid sex-role expectations. Finally, their sexual behavior is characterized by a growing sensitivity toward others.

We will begin by encouraging you to reflect on yourself as a sexual person. Then you will be asked to look more specifically at issues of sexual preference, sexual expression, and sex-role stereotypes. Then we will examine current theory and research in the area of sexuality and sexual relationships, emphasizing the most practical aspects of such research. You will then be asked to reflect on yourself in a systematic way, using the information presented here. Next, you will be asked to take part in a structured group interaction that focuses on sexuality. Finally, you will be encouraged to explore possibilities for concrete action in the area of your development as a mature sexual person.

Personal-Reflection Exercise: Sexual Identity, Sexual Preference, and Sexual Expression

Sexual Identity

1. Complete the following sentences:

When I think of myself as a sexual person, I _____

_____

_____

When wondering whether others are attracted to me sexually, I _____

_____

_____

What I like most about sex is _____

_____

_____

What bothers me most about sex is _____

_____

_____

When it comes to sex, my area of greatest confidence is _____

_____

_____

My greatest doubt about myself in the area of sex is _____

_____

When I think about the person who has been most significant in my life sexually, I _____

_____

_____

My greatest confusion about sex is _____

_____

_____

For me, the most difficult thing about relating sexually is _____

_____

_____

When I think about the ways in which sex relates to the rest of my life, I ____

_____

_____

For me, the most challenging thing about sex is _____

_____

_____

   2. List three values that are important to you and that you think relate significantly to your sexual life:

Value #1: _____

How this value relates to your sexual life: _____

_____

_____

Value #2: _____

How this value relates to your sexual life: _____

_____

_____

Value #3: _____

How this value relates to your sexual life: _____

_____

_____

3. Using what you have learned about yourself in the first two sections of this exercise, write a short paragraph describing your view of yourself as a sexual person.

_____

_____

_____

_____

_____

_____

Sexual Preferences

1. Read each of the following statements, mark the scale beneath in a way that reflects your personal position, and briefly explain your response.

a. Men who prefer other men as sexual partners should be able to do as they wish in private.

1	2	3	4	5
Strongly disagree		No preference		Strongly agree

One student marked *1* (strongly disagree). He thought that, on both religious and natural-morality grounds, sexual relations among men are immoral.

Another student marked *3* (no preference). She said that, although she obviously preferred heterosexual men, she had no reason to care about what men did sexually with other men.

Now mark the scale yourself and explain your response.

Reason: _____

_____

_____

b. Women who prefer other women as sexual partners should be allowed to do as they wish in private.

1	2	3	4	5
Strongly disagree		No preference		Strongly agree

Reason: _____

_____

_____

    c. For me, sexual relations with a partner of the same sex would be . . .

1	2	3	4	5
Completely acceptable		Neutral		Totally unacceptable

Reason: _____

_____

_____

    d. I find the idea of sexual experimentation with a person of the same sex . . .

1	2	3	4	5
Completely acceptable		Neutral		Totally unacceptable

Reason: _____

_____

_____

    2. Complete the following sentences.

When I think of having a homosexual experience, I _____

_____

When I hear that someone is bisexual, I _____

_____

When I think of closeness or intimacy with a person of the same sex, I _____

_____

When I see "masculine" traits in women, I _____

_____

_____

When I see "feminine" traits in men, I _____

_____

(Women) When I see the "tougher" or more "masculine" side of myself, I ____

_____

(Men) When I see the "softer" or more "feminine" side of myself, I _____

_____

Sexually, men should _____

_____

Sexually, women should _____

_____

_____

Forms of Sexual Expression and Underlying Values
   Complete the following sentences:

For me, masturbation _____

_____

In my opinion, premarital sexual intercourse _____

_____

_____

Living with someone without being married _____

_____

_____

I think that contraception _____

_____

For me, marriage _____

_____

For me, sexual thoughts and fantasies _____

_____

If I had to deal with an unwanted pregnancy, I'd _____

_____

_____

Sexual Stereotypes

Under each of the two headings below, list adjectives or phrases that indicate your personal beliefs.

Women Should Be	*Men Should Be*
_____	_____
_____	_____
_____	_____
_____	_____
_____	_____
_____	_____
_____	_____
_____	_____
_____	_____

Sexual Identity

As we noted in Chapter 6, personal identity is a stable sense of who you are as confirmed by others who are important to you. Your view of yourself and your feelings about yourself specifically *as a woman or as a man* are central to your overall identity. Impulses regarding sexual exploration and experimentation are similar in many ways to impulses regarding independence from home, relationships with new and different people, and the establishment of new areas of competence—these are all, in part, identity-testing experiments. In the process of carrying them out, you discover more and more about who you are and who you are not.

Two Principal Issues of Sexual Identity

Two major questions are associated with sexual identity: Who am I sexually? and How do I relate to others as a sexual person? The first question has much to do with your feelings toward your own body and its sexuality. Such feelings do not simply appear for the first time at the onset of puberty. As Hettlinger (1974) has pointed out, "Everyone has sex before marriage. We're born with it and express it in our relationships from infancy on" (p. 45). Sex is a dimension of your being rather than something you do every once in a while. People who try to solve the problems associated with being a sexual person by denying or repressing their sexuality can appear cold and incomplete. In their attempts to establish and maintain control of sexual impulses and to manage intimacy, they inhibit a dimension of themselves that provides warmth and contact. Only when you are reasonably certain of who you are and care about yourself in reasonable ways will you be able to become intimate with another person.

Preoccupation with the Body

As you strive to establish a stable sense of sexual identity, your body is likely to be on your mind in a special way. You might even wonder whether you are abnormally preoccupied with sex. Initial sexual expression can sometimes feel "mechanical and self-centered, in contrast to the mutuality and commitment associated with mature sexual involvement" (Eddy, 1965, p. 31). The person who is overly concerned with his or her body, making an artificial distinction between "me" and "my body,"

> seldom enjoys any real intimacy with his or her partner. Concerned more with his body, he becomes preoccupied with his performance and technique and less aware of himself and his partner as persons in relation. He doesn't make love *with* another person, but *to* another body [Nevins, 1979, p. 27].

Nevins cites the experience of one of his students:

> When I had sexual relations, I only thought about having a good time and getting all the pleasure I could out of the act. The thought about experiencing myself or my partner as a person never occurred to me. Having sex was like a game. I either succeeded in it or I didn't. But I never really enjoyed it. It seemed I always was watching my moves. How long should I use my hands? Where should I put them next? . . . My deepest satisfaction never

came during the act of sex, but only afterward, if I could look back on having done a good job [pp. 27–28].

This initial inability to integrate "body" with "self" is one of the hurdles on the road toward an integrated sexuality.

Toward an Integrated Sexuality

The achievement of integration in the area of sexuality is an important developmental task—one that can't be achieved overnight. During the moving-into-adulthood stage, you will take significant steps toward integration, but there is no rigid timetable that says you must achieve complete integration before the age of 22. On the other hand, if your sexuality at age 22 is much the same as it was when you were 19, this might call for some soul-searching. Whitehead and Whitehead (1979), drawing on the writings of Erik Erikson, relate developing sexuality to the process of identity formation:

> Shared sexual experience and genital expression are important contexts for the young adult's development of psychological intimacy. Sexual maturity is reached as one's capacity for mutually satisfying sexual expression with a loved partner is developed and stabilized. "Such experience makes sexuality less obsessive," Erikson (1968) remarks. "Before such genital maturity is reached, much of sexual life is the self-seeking, identity-hungry kind; each partner is trying to reach only himself. Or it remains a kind of genital combat in which each tries to defeat the other" [p. 137].

The Whiteheads suggest that sexual experience that moves toward mutuality fosters identity formation:

> The experience of sexual play and orgasm in young childhood can contribute to our willingness to risk self-disclosure, to let down our defenses in the presence of another. Sexual intimacy thus opens out into a larger psychological resource, the "flexible capacity for abandoning [oneself] to sexual and affectual sensations, in a fusion with another individual who is both partner to the sensation and guarantor of one's continuing identity" (Erikson, 1959, p. 124) [p. 77].

Sexuality that leads to true mutuality depends on and affirms the individual's sense of his or her own identity.

Developmental Timetables

There is no single style or rate of progress that characterizes the development of sexual identity.

Individuals vary in their progress toward establishing a sense of identity. An adolescent whose need for closeness has been frustrated or overindulged in childhood frequently grasps at sex now that it has become available, and premature commitments follow. Sex may also serve primarily to demonstrate dominance or to express hostility toward the opposite sex. Also at work among adolescents are cultural and psychological pressures to validate one's masculinity or femininity through sexual experiences. In the American culture, with its uneasy tolerance of closeness among men, the male student may seek out a girl to confide in and the relationship may become a sexual one [Eddy, 1965, p. 31].*

The rate at which you develop toward sexual maturity is influenced by the unfinished emotional business of childhood, by the fears and misgivings you experience in becoming your own person, and by cultural pressures to be a "real woman" or a "real man." The exact age at which individuals come to grips with the issues of sexual identity varies widely as a result of differences in the rate of physical development, family and religious background, early sexual experiences with peers, the degree of exposure to sexual stimuli, and so on. Therefore, when it comes to sexual identity:

△ you might be discovering some of the issues being discussed here,
△ you might have begun to sort through these issues and taken initial steps toward sexual self-definition, or
△ you might have arrived at a tentative (though relatively stable) sense of yourself as a sexual person.

There is no rigid time schedule that you must follow in order to be "normal." However, if you are in the early stages in this process, encounters with those who are further along can provoke anxiety ("This person is too far ahead of me!") or confidence ("It's good to meet someone who has some sense of stability in the area of sex!").

Sexuality and Values

You can't divorce your sexual behavior from the system of values within which you work. Two extreme positions can be identified that are, in some ways, caricatures of the two positions outlined by Dychtwald (1979) earlier in this chapter: repression and the funsex mentality.

Repression. At one extreme, we find the individual who, in order to remain faithful to the rules of family or church or society regarding sex, comes to repress his or her sexual feelings, avoiding people and situations in which such feelings might be stimulated. In Masters and Johnson's (1970) view, "channel-visioned

*From *Sex and the College Student*, by the Group for the Advancement of Psychiatry, Inc., H. P. Eddy (Ed.). Copyright © 1965 by The Group for the Advancement of Psychiatry, Inc. Used by permission of Atheneum Publishers.

religious orthodoxy" is a major source of sexual difficulties in marriage. Religious development that is needlessly rigid espouses approaches to sexual morality that emphasize taboos and dwell on the goodness and badness of isolated acts rather than a more comprehensive development toward sexual integrity that encourages reasonable experimentation and allows for mistakes. Such rigidity can be a factor in foreclosed identity formation, and it can be ultimately self-defeating. This is not to suggest that religion stands in the way of full sexual development. On the contrary, in our view, full religious development both affirms and challenges sexual development (see Whitehead & Whitehead, 1979, pp. 11–23 and 71–109).

Funsex mentality. At the other extreme, there are individuals whose values with respect to sex reflect a *funsex mentality:* "If it feels good, do it." Their response to what has been called the *sexual revolution* takes the form of greater or lesser degrees of promiscuity—they go out and "have sex." In reviewing the funsex, or recreational, approach to sexual behavior, Hettlinger (1974) raises four interrelated questions:

△ Is sex as simple as it is made out to be in the recreational approach?
△ Is such sex honest?
△ Are there dehumanizing aspects to recreational sex?
△ Is recreational sex healthy?

Hettlinger concludes that the advocates of a funsex mentality fail to appreciate the consequences of such a mentality, including possible damage to one's sense of self-worth and the worth of others. Does your own experience or that of your friends help you to answer the questions posed by Hettlinger?

As we have noted previously, the critical question is whether you are arriving at moral judgments in the area of sexual behavior in a way that reflects a personal commitment to your own values or simply responding by conformity *or* rebellion to the values of parents, teachers, ministers, peers, the general culture, or a prevailing subculture. If you feel trapped at either the funsex or the no-sex extreme, your challenge is to accept the responsibility of making free and informed choices with respect to your own sexuality.

Sexual Expression

In this section, we focus on masturbation, sexual relations and commitment, contraception and unplanned pregnancy, homosexuality, and "sexual silence." All of these topics involve values and can require major decisions on your part. It is not our intention to discuss these issues exhaustively in this section. We will simply outline some of the dilemmas involved and encourage you to reflect on your personal position regarding each issue. In the area of sexuality, where strong and spontaneous impulses arise, an unexamined life can be the source of unnecessary crisis and even tragedy.

Masturbation

In exploring the issue of masturbation, Hettlinger (1974) makes the following observation:

> The fact is that masturbation is a common phase of early human development, part of the natural infantile exploration of the body and better described as "self-discovery" than "self-abuse." . . . Masturbation is never a cause of emotional illness. Obsessive masturbation in adulthood which interferes with other responsibilities may be symptomatic of psychological problems. Some adolescents masturbate as an escape from social problems or personal relations; in such cases it is not the act of masturbation but the underlying problem that needs attention. . . . If the "awful habit" were as harmful as ignorant crusaders have maintained, the majority of the human race would be hospitalized [p. 14].

Hettlinger touches on some of the key aspects of masturbation as a form of sexual expression. The issues he brings up can be seen from a number of perspectives—(a) the recreational extreme, (b) the no-sex extreme, or (c) a viewpoint that falls somewhere between these two.

The basic (a) statement is "Masturbation is never a problem. If it feels good, do it."

The basic (b) statement is "Masturbation is always a problem, because it is evil and sinful." From this point of view, the no-sex extreme is not considered an extreme at all.

As Hettlinger implies, it is possible to list a number of more moderate (c) statements. Some of these might be:

△ Masturbation is one means of sexual self-discovery and occurs naturally and unselfconsciously in the developing person. Whatever its moral interpretation, it is normative, rather than exceptional, during adolescence.

△ Masturbation in itself does not cause emotional problems, though in certain cases it might indicate that something is wrong. The guilt and anxiety that can become associated with masturbation are due to the power of the sensations and emotions aroused and to the opinions of others. Such anxiety and guilt can lead to emotional difficulties.

△ Many people see masturbation as a legitimate means of releasing sexual tension and of developing sensitivity to one's own sexual feelings and needs. Others believe that masturbation can easily become a self-centered act that is symptomatic of the kind of self-preoccupation that impedes the development of mutuality.

△ From a physical and psychological perspective, masturbation needs to be labeled a "problem" only when it becomes a means of avoiding intimate relationships and of developing a full adult sexuality.

Individuals who are committed to the development of a personal set of values do not swallow any of these statements whole. Ideally, they listen to cultural and religious traditions, to the collective wisdom of people they trust, and to their own experience and that of others. Then they make the kind of free and informed decisions that lead to solid values. In other words, they no longer base their decisions on religiously or culturally motivated scare tactics that lead to anxiety, confusion, and self-doubt.

Solid information, frank discussion with nonjudgmental peers and adults, and honesty with yourself will help you to deal in a healthy way with issues of sexuality.

Write three statements regarding masturbation that reflect your own present views and values:

Statement #1: _____

_____

_____

Statement #2: _____

_____

_____

Statement #3: _____

_____

_____

Sexual Relations and Commitment

Decisions regarding sexual relations prior to marriage or other forms of commitment can present dilemmas to young people who are trying to come to terms with their sexuality. Sexual attraction is often an important part of growing personal attachments. How is such attraction to be handled? You might decide

△ to postpone sexual intercourse or serious foreplay until your commitment has been finalized,

△ to engage in sexual expression short of intercourse prior to commitment, or

△ to engage in complete sexual expression whenever it is mutually acceptable.

Each of these options presents dilemmas.

If you decide to postpone sexual intercourse and serious foreplay, there is the question of how to handle the sexual arousal and tension that accompany your growing relationship.

1. Sexual feelings can be ignored or repressed, but they have a way of asserting themselves in indirect ways. (For instance, some of your arguments that seem to focus on inconsequential issues could stem from the unresolved sexual tensions you feel.)

2. You might have strong religious or moral convictions, beliefs, and values that make the postponement of sexual expression much more positive than the repression mentioned here; however, lapses on your part could be devastating to your sense of self-worth and could cause you to feel that your relationship is "tainted."

3. You could relieve the sexual tension by masturbating, but your reasons for limiting sexual expression in your relationship could render masturbation unacceptable to you. Or, as your relationship deepens, masturbation might seem too self-centered or too hollow a substitute for sexual relations with your partner.

4. You could change your wedding date in order to make sexual expression legitimate for you sooner, but this might interfere with other commitments, such as completing school, establishing yourself in a career, giving yourself time for a moratorium, and so on.

If you choose to engage in sexual activity short of intercourse, you will be giving expression to feelings that can help to deepen a relationship, but these same feelings can make complete sexual expression seem even more attractive. Moreover, you and your partner need to ask yourselves whether petting to orgasm and mutual masturbation are personally, culturally, and morally acceptable to both of you. If not, these activities can provoke feelings of guilt and loss of self-esteem. If they are acceptable to you and do not lead to even further frustration, these activities might provide a way of releasing sexual tension and expressing mutual affection without the risk of pregnancy.

If you choose to engage in complete sexual expression prior to commitment, you need to be aware of and willing to accept the consequences, whether they be positive, negative, or, as is often the case, mixed. The giving of oneself sexually to another person is not, for most persons in our culture, an act that is taken lightly.

The issues discussed in this chapter are addressed to you as an individual, since you must make decisions based on your own beliefs, values, and needs. But it is clear that decisions in the area of sexual relations are mutual; you and your partner must decide on a course of action that you can both accept physically, psychologically, and morally. Relationships in which one person directly or indirectly imposes his or her values on the other, especially when this is done by using termination of the relationship as a threat—"If you won't wait (or go ahead), I won't see you anymore"—are a major source of tragedy. Coercion, whether direct and physical or subtle and psychological, has no place in a loving relationship. Decisions concerning sex should be made by individuals who have reflected mutually and honestly on their needs and values. Once made, these decisions should be respected and honored. (If a decision proves to be a mistake, it can be renegotiated bilaterally.)

Understanding and expressing your needs and values while taking into account those of the people to whom you relate intimately is valuable in all relationships—not just those in which there is sexual expression. Self-awareness, honesty in self-expression, sensitivity to others, and mutuality in decision making are the cornerstones upon which deep and effective commitments are built. At this stage of your life, you are beginning to establish patterns in the way in which you build relationships. What you do now can influence all the intimate relationships of your life.

In the space provided, write three statements that express your feelings or values with respect to sexual relations prior to marriage (or any other form of extended commitment).

Statement #1: _____

_____

_____

Statement #2: _____

_____

_____

Statement #3: _____

_____

_____

Contraception and Unplanned Pregnancy

If you and your partner have decided that sexual intercourse is acceptable to you, you also need to decide whether a pregnancy is acceptable. If it is not, you must arrive at a decision regarding its prevention. Nondecisions—"We'll take our chances," "It's not likely if we're careful about times," "We'll stop before ejaculation," and similar statements—amount to an agreement to run the risk of bringing a child into the world or opting for an abortion—alternatives that involve very serious personal, social, and ethical implications. To shrug these off or to ignore them is not only foolish but also mutually harmful. Since sexual relationships are mutual by their very nature, decisions regarding contraception also should be mutual. Obviously, the most direct and immediate consequences of pregnancy affect women. It should be equally obvious that the personal, legal, moral, and financial ramifications of pregnancy are just as real to men. Unless you and your partner decide that you want children, to engage in intercourse without contraception is to court potential tragedy. This dilemma can be particularly painful for those for whom contraception is forbidden on ethical or religious grounds.

In the event that an unwanted pregnancy does occur, very difficult choices must be made. Should you marry? Are you and your partner prepared for marriage? In what ways would marriage affect your educational and career plans? Should you keep the baby even if you decide not to get married? Should the baby be given up for adoption? How do you and your partner feel about abortion as a possibility? What about the financial implications of any of these decisions? With regard to the illusion that either adoption or abortion are simple solutions, Eddy (1965) notes that:

> Once an unmarried student becomes pregnant, emotional difficulties cannot be avoided. The student herself [and her partner], sometimes the parents, and even some college officials may have the illusion that if abortion or adoption can be arranged, the whole experience will be erased. Nothing could be further from the truth. The consequences in either case will be less disastrous if the girl is aware of her contradictory inner feelings and is allowed to reach her own decision, with all possible help offered [pp. 66–67].

This issue is complicated further by the fact that we live in a society that is polarized by the issue of abortion. Many people see abortion as a nonviable solution personally as well as socially. As Eddy notes, abortion is never easy. (It seems most sensible to avoid abortion through effective contraception, but the ways in which people pursue sexual relationships are not always sensible.) Individuals need to deal with the question of what to do about an unwanted pregnancy in a way that reflects their own values and beliefs. If they have no particular beliefs and their values are fuzzy, the decisions will be difficult and painful. People need understanding, support, and respect as they struggle with such agonizing decisions.

Homosexuality

The issue of homosexuality (sexual preference for individuals of one's own sex) is a controversial one both socially and religiously. The social and political rights of gay people are matters of controversy in many areas of our country. Hettlinger (1974) has identified five major changes that appear to be taking place on the part of many people in our culture in their attitude toward homosexuality as both a personal and a social phenomenon:

△   Homosexuality is not equated with homosexual acts. Experimentation with a member of the same sex is no longer regarded as proof of a fundamental homosexual orientation.
△   "Straight" people are less likely to see homosexuality as a basic challenge to their way of life.
△   Homosexual acts are not viewed as necessarily degrading. Hettlinger suggests that any sexual act can be either degrading or loving. The sex of one's partner doesn't determine the quality of the sexual act.
△   Religious condemnation of homosexuality has been modified to some degree.
△   Gay people are not considered emotionally sick, even though their sexual orientation differs from the norm. The myth that homosexual

behavior is indicative of personality problems or psychopathology has been exploded. Gay *and* straight people vary widely in stability and social adjustment.

Although there may be some disagreement regarding the degree of attitudinal change that has taken place, there seems to be little reason for arguing that it is not substantial; it seems to be as substantial as the "sexual revolution" itself.

Sexual preference is not an arbitrary choice. To quote Hettlinger (1974):

> The roots of true homosexuality lie far below the level of simple choice: nobody makes up his or her mind to *be* a homosexual, though someone may choose whether or not to engage in homosexual acts or to accept the fact of being homosexual [p. 142].

Evidence suggests that homosexuality, like heterosexuality, is a result of a complicated interaction between personal characteristics and events in the family; this includes subtle patterns of reinforcement and punishment in sexual matters. Individuals are not responsible for their sexual preference, but they *are* responsible for their response to that preference.

Questions regarding sexual preference are common among people your age. Such questions do not call for either repression or dramatic public declarations. Honest exploration of the issues with people you trust (because they listen and respond empathically) can help you to sort out whatever concerns you might have in this area. Perhaps a word of caution is in order. Be wary of anyone whose support or advice seems to carry with it a push in either direction—straight or gay. Someone who really wants to help you will not push you but will encourage you to discover your own identity. Admittedly, it will be difficult for someone who is close to you and who has strong personal or religious convictions regarding homosexuality not to push his or her values in such an important area of life.

Sexual Silence

Sexual silence—the absence of sexual behavior—among young people isn't necessarily a positive sign. As Eddy (1965) has noted:

> It is important to examine the meaning of sexual "silence" among college students who apparently are not engaged in overt sexual behavior. The manifest presence or absence of sexual behavior alone provides no indication of the meaning of sexuality in relation to the total personality.... Silent patterns may range from students who have severely restricted personalities and for whom close contact with others is painful and frightening, to those students with more open personalities who are comfortable enough with their own sexuality to be able to delay sexual activity in a manner consistent with other important personality needs [pp. 81–82].

In other words, it isn't *whether* you engage in overt sexual behavior or not, but *why*. The individual who copes with the challenges of maturing biological sexuality by retreating into isolation could encounter as much difficulty as the individual who responds to the same challenges by becoming sexually promiscuous.

Sex-Role Stereotypes

Every culture has expectations regarding male and female behavior. In recent years, the traditional rules of male/female interaction in our culture have been questioned, and alternatives have been proposed. We raise the issue here in order to encourage you to see where you stand with respect to male/female interaction. Women's movements have challenged not only the usefulness of some of the traditional rules but also the very assumptions on which they are based. When cultural "blueprints" regulating the interaction between women and men outlive their usefulness, it could mean that they are based on assumptions that aren't valid.

Consider your reactions to the following statements:

△ She never calls him. He calls her.
△ He makes all the plans and invites her. She accepts.
△ He pays. When he can't pay, she doesn't go.
△ He always calls for her at home and takes her back to her home.
△ He does not involve her sexually unless they are engaged to be married.
△ She does not plan any career which may not fit in with his future.
△ She does not commit her time to other people or activities. Rather she remains "on call" for him.
△ You call each other when you have something to say or share.
△ You both make plans together, or go places separately.
△ You both pay, or either one, or decide on things that don't take money.
△ You meet wherever is convenient for both of you.
△ You decide together on your sexual relationship.
△ You each plan for the future individually.
△ You each do things and see people you like. You feel you are more interested and interesting this way.*

Sexual relationships are, first of all, relationships between people.

The right combination of a man and a woman is you the way you want to be, no lies and no performance, and [your partner] the way he or she wants to be, no mask and no pretenses. You will be happy with him or her and apart. . . . It will not depend on the size of her breasts or the size of your penis, upon her eyelashes or your reputation as a mighty hunter. It will

---

* From *You've Changed the Combination*, Rocky Mountain Planned Parenthood. © 1974. This and all other quotations from this source are reprinted by permission of Rocky Mountain Planned Parenthood, 1525 Josephine, Denver, CO 80206.

depend upon the persons who are involved who are friends with each other. *The right combination always starts with friendship.* It can't be more than that until it has been at least that [Rocky Mountain Planned Parenthood, 1974, p. 19].

If your attitudes and your behavior typically reflect sensitivity for the dignity and worth of your partner, no techniques of relating or making love will add much to what you already do.

Systematic Self-Assessment: Sexuality and Sexual Identity

1. *How I see myself sexually.* Refer to the first exercise in this chapter and review what you wrote regarding your view of yourself as a sexual person. In the light of your reading and reflection on the material in this chapter, what comments or questions occur to you as you look back at your initial statement? Is there anything in the statement that you would like to modify? Is there anything you would like to add? Would you like to explore any issues more fully? Use the space provided to answer these questions.

_____

_____

_____

_____

_____

_____

_____

_____

2. *Sexual preference.* Review what you have written in response to the second exercise in this chapter. Is there anything you would like to change or add to your initial response? If so, use the space below.

_____

_____

_____

_____

_____

3. *Sexual expression.* Review what you have written in the section entitled *Forms of Sexual Expression and Underlying Values.* Using the scales on the following pages, rate the extent to which you feel settled or "up in the air" on each of the issues discussed in this chapter. Then, in the space provided beneath each scale, indicate the source of any dilemma or concern you might have. Here are the sources of dilemmas experienced by a variety of students.

△ lack of factual information
△ conflict with religious values
△ conflict with family
△ conflict with partner
△ no one to talk with openly
△ conflict with community or cultural values
△ inability to express what I think and feel in this area
△ peer group pressure
△ ambiguous messages from the society in which I live
△ lack of clear values
△ my own stereotypes or prejudices
△ the stereotypes or prejudices of others
△ lack of experience
△ lack of opportunity

Sexual Expression and Underlying Values

Masturbation

1	2	3	4	5
Quite settled	Fairly settled	Settled/ unsettled	Fairly unsettled	Very unsettled

Source(s) of dilemma: _____

Premarital Sexual Relations

1	2	3	4	5
Quite settled	Fairly settled	Settled/ unsettled	Fairly unsettled	Very unsettled

Source(s) of dilemma: _____

_____

_____

Contraception

1	2	3	4	5
Quite settled	Fairly settled	Settled/ unsettled	Fairly unsettled	Very unsettled

Source(s) of dilemma: _____

_____

_____

Living Together before Marriage

1	2	3	4	5
Quite settled	Fairly settled	Settled/ unsettled	Fairly unsettled	Very unsettled

Source(s) of dilemma: _____

_____

_____

Handling Unwanted Pregnancy

1	2	3	4	5
Quite settled	Fairly settled	Settled/ unsettled	Fairly unsettled	Very unsettled

Source(s) of dilemma: _____

_____

_____

Now review the sources of the dilemmas that face you. Do any patterns emerge? Are any sources listed more than once? If so, indicate the source or sources in the space provided and explain how you feel about them.

Principal Source(s) of Dilemmas

_____

_____

_____

_____

_____

_____

_____

_____

_____

4. *Sexual stereotypes.* Review your response to "Women Should Be" and "Men Should Be." Do any of these expectations limit you in your relationships to either men or women? For instance, one male student indicated that he expected men, including himself, to be "tough." On reflection, he realized that that expectation made it difficult for him to give or receive support to other male peers. He wrote the following: "I don't want to be 'soft' nor do I like 'soft' males. But to be honest I include things like being sympathetic in the category of 'soft' behavior. I can be sympathetic to my kid brother, but it's harder with my dad, and it would take a catastrophe for me to be sympathetic with a male friend."

Indicate three sex-role expectations you think you have and the ways in which you believe each expectation limits you in your relationships.

Expectation #1: _____

_____

How it affects your behavior: _____

_____

_____

Expectation #2: _____

_____

How it affects your behavior: _____

_____

_____

Expectation #3: _____

_____

How it affects your behavior: _____

_____

Key Settings and Sexuality: An Assessment

A great deal of the support and challenge you receive with respect to your sexual identity and behavior comes from the key social settings of your life. Consider each of the social settings listed here and indicate what you experience in those settings that helps you (+) or hinders you (−) in the development of a mature and healthy sexuality.

Family

(+)

_____

_____

_____

_____

(−)

_____

_____

_____

_____

Peer Group

(+)

_____

_____

_____

_____

(−)

_____

_____

_____

_____

Church or Religious Group

(+)

_____

_____

_____

_____

_____

(−)

_____

_____

_____

_____

_____

School

(+)

_____

_____

_____

_____

_____

(−)

_____

_____

_____

_____

_____

Your Society or Culture

(+)

_____

_____

_____

_____

_____

$(-)$

_____

_____

_____

_____

_____

Your Closest Relationship(s)

$(+)$

_____

_____

_____

_____

_____

$(-)$

_____

_____

_____

_____

_____

Other: _____

$(+)$

_____

_____

_____

_____

_____

(−)

_____

_____

_____

_____

_____

Structured Group Interaction: Sexuality

1. After reviewing what you have written in response to the systematic self-assessment exercises in this chapter, list the four most significant personal statements or concerns about your own sexuality on 3 × 5 index cards. List only one statement, concern, or problem on each card. Write as personally and concretely as you can, but remember to remain anonymous.

2. The cards will be collected and read aloud. Note any issues, problems, or concerns that occur repeatedly.

3. Using the information you gathered in the second step, rate the issues from most important to least important; this will give you an idea of how the group as a whole stands at this moment. (Remember, even if one of your personal concerns is not ranked high, it is still a legitimate concern.)

4. Group members should have an opportunity to elaborate on any question or concern and to receive feedback from other group members. Everyone should have an opportunity to speak.

Action Plan: Sexuality and Sexual Behavior

1. The exercises you have done up to this point have given you an opportunity to review what you like and what you don't like about the ways in which you are developing sexually. At this point, list three goals, or valued accomplishments, you would like to achieve in the near future in the area of sexual development. Be as concrete as possible. The following are examples of goals set by students.

(A male sophomore) I feel very close to a girl at school. I trust her, and I think she trusts me. There's been no explicit sex in our relationship. By the end of the month, I'd like to have a few conversations with her. I'd like to discuss some of my own thoughts and feelings about my own sexuality with her. What I'd like to do is to go through this chapter with her and share how we responded to the various exercises and how we feel about what we have learned. I've never talked to anyone that explicitly and personally about sex.

(A female student at the beginning of her junior year) Justin and I have sexual relations every once in a while. We've never talked about it. We just more or less fell into it and take it for granted. I've talked to a girl friend a bit about it and thought about it fairly much myself. Justin and I have never really talked about what we're doing and what it means. I have some suspicions that I'm not the only person he has sex with. I'd like to do two things. First, join a women's consciousness-raising group sponsored by the counseling center. I feel I'm loaded with too many woman stereotypes. Second, I'd like to put off having sex with Justin until we talk about what we're doing. I'd like to talk with him as soon as possible.

(A male student in his freshman year) I'm convinced that I'm gay, even though I have not had direct sexual experience with another male. I'm too chicken to go to the Gay Student Alliance meetings, but there's a branch of Dignity that has special meetings for gay males under thirty downtown. I'd like to attend a couple of meetings to see what they're like. But I'd also like to meet some guy with whom I could experiment with sexually—someone like myself, I suppose. I want to do this before the end of this school year.

Your Goals

Goal #1: _____

_____

_____

_____

_____

Goal #2: _____

_____

_____

_____

_____

Goal #3: _____

_____

_____

_____

_____

_____

   2. Review the planning and problem-solving methodology presented in Chapter 3. Choose the goal that is most important to you and apply this methodology to it. In the area of sexuality, as in other areas of development, you can "let things happen," or, without losing your spontaneity, you can take charge of your own development. Setting concrete, realistic goals and developing programs to accomplish them is one way of taking charge.

CHAPTER

Friendship and Intimacy:
The Challenge of Deepening Interpersonal Relationships

In this chapter, we examine the first of several major life challenges that face you now and in the years to come: the challenge of deepening the interpersonal bonds in your life—the challenge of developing friendship and intimacy. We begin with an exercise that is designed to assist you in considering the current state of your personal relationships. Then we present several concepts from theory and research in this area that will shed light on relationships; you will be asked to use this information in reflecting on your relationships. You will take part in a structured group interaction that focuses on friendship and intimacy, and you will be encouraged to complete a self-directed action plan.

Personal-Reflection Exercise: Friendship and Intimacy

1. Complete each of the following sentences.

For me, an acquaintance is _____

_____

_____

_____

For me, a friend is _____

_____

_____

_____

For me, an intimate is _____

_____

_____

_____

2. Using the form provided, write the first names of several people to whom you relate at each of the levels shown (as you understand them).

Depth of Relationships: An Overview

Acquaintances	Friends	Intimates
_____	_____	_____
_____	_____	_____
_____	_____	_____

_____   _____   _____
_____   _____   _____

3. How would you describe the depth of relationships in your life? In the space provided, write a brief paragraph in response in this question.

_____
_____
_____
_____
_____
_____
_____
_____

The Impact of Identity on Relationships

In Chapter 6, we examined the meaning of the term *identity* and the process whereby identity is initially achieved. We noted that many developmentalists have suggested that your ability to cope with the challenges of adulthood depends on the achievement of a stable sense of who you are—an identity that is confirmed by others' response to you. One of the most noticeable and important results of the attainment of a stabilized personal identity is what White (1958) has called "the freeing of personal relationships." According to White, the individual who has a healthy sense of who he or she is will begin to create:

> . . . human relationships that are less anxious, less defensive, less burdened by inappropriate past reactions, more friendly, more spontaneous, more warm, and more respectful. Social interaction becomes more free . . . from the impulsive inconsiderateness and egocentricity of youth. The person learns not to be so immersed in his own behavior . . . that he fails to perceive the people around him. .·. . He notices more things in the people with whom he interacts and becomes more ready to make a place for their characteristics in his own behavior (p. 343).

White presents an image of a person who, having initially resolved the "Who am I?" questions we discussed in Chapter 6, can now become genuinely interested in and available to others. This is a person who is capable, perhaps for the first time, of asking "Who are you?"

Chickering (1969) suggests that tolerance characterizes relationships in the life of individuals who have a stable sense of personal identity. They no longer need people to behave in particular ways for their benefit, and, therefore, they are willing to allow people to be who they are—to accept and value differences between themselves and others. Individuals who have a stable sense of who they are find differences in others less threatening; this enables them to approach people more openly. On the other hand, individuals who have foreclosed identities are often defensive when they meet people who do not accept and follow their standards. Individuals who have diffused identities are indifferent to or fearful of intimate relationships; because they have no firm sense of their own boundaries, they fear that they will be swallowed by other people. They avoid this perceived threat by keeping their relationships shallow.

Although White has correctly described the process of stabilizing identity as one of freeing interpersonal relationships, in this chapter we have chosen to emphasize the *deepening* of relationships—a process that describes an important aspect of the development of friendships and intimate relationships.

Deepening Your Relationships with Others: Stages in the Process

Psychologist David Hunt (1971) has outlined a series of developmental stages related to the ways in which individuals orient themselves to the people they meet. A modified form of Hunt's model is found in Figure 8-1.

Stage I: Culture Bound

Stage I is characteristic of the "pre-identity" years—the years that precede your development of a stable sense of who you are. During this stage, relationships tend to be dictated by the values, rules, and norms of your family, school, peer group, church, and other personal settings. It is extremely difficult for the person in this stage to make a distinction between "what I think, feel, and believe" and "what I ought to think, feel, and believe." Hunt refers to this phase as *Culture Bound*—a time during which we tend to see the world through the "lenses" provided by our culture. As Figure 8-1 indicates, we operate within the boundaries laid down by our culture. The figure also indicates that the boundaries of the self (dotted lines) are open during this phase. Note the relationship of this stage to the idea of identity foreclosure described in the previous chapter. Hunt's culture-bound stage describes the interpersonal behavior of individuals who haven't separated themselves from the identities given to them by their parents, teachers, religious leaders, and friends.

Stage II: Unique Selfhood

The next phase in Hunt's model, unique selfhood, refers to the establishment of interpersonal relationships during adolescence. According to Hunt, "self-delineation" occurs as one breaks away from the cultural rules of Stage I.

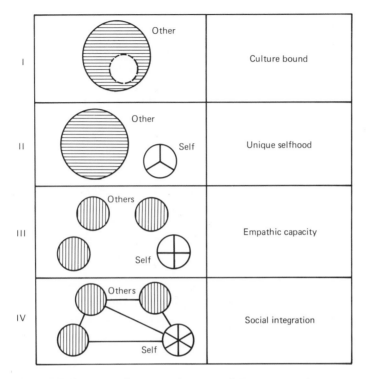

FIGURE 8-1. Developmental stages of interpersonal orientations.

The learning about how one is distinctively oneself provides the basis for beginning to accept individual responsibility for outcomes. The initial expression of independence may appear in exaggerated form. Nonetheless this stage marks a person's first awareness of his own feelings as cues for . . . action [p. 19].

The exaggerated form of independence is similar in nature to the rebellion that is so characteristic of adolescence. The moratorium period of identity development, which we discussed in Chapter 6, is one in which interpersonal relationships characteristic of Stage II of Hunt's model would be likely to occur; there is often an oppositional quality in relationships during this period. Individuals seem to say, either verbally or behaviorally, "leave me alone." Behavior such as this has prompted some people to refer to adolescence as a time of "natural neurosis."

Stage III: Empathic Capacity

As you enter the third stage in Hunt's model, you develop the capacity to put yourself in the shoes of other people—to see things from their perspective. It is as if the ability to understand yourself as a unique person provides a foundation for an appreciation of the uniqueness of other people. You begin to view others in their uniqueness ("Joan is a strong and caring person") rather than in terms of stereotypes ("Women are emotional"). As your capacity for empathy becomes stronger, you become more capable of relating to people as they are rather than on the basis of stereotypes regarding the groups to which they belong. Empathy has accurately been called the cornerstone of all effective human relationships. Without it, friendship and intimacy—the deepening of interpersonal relationships—cannot occur. In Hunt's words: "The first awareness of others in terms of their own personal feelings and values occurs at Stage III."

Stage IV: Social Integration

In Stage IV—social integration—you not only appreciate yourself and others as unique individuals but you also see that you are connected to them by a network of social bonds. Figure 8-1 illustrates the fact that individuals in Stage IV are linked to others but not enveloped by them. In Stage IV, a personal awareness of the relatedness of self to others—a sense of *interdependence*—becomes an important part of your way of looking at the world.

The four stages of interpersonal relationships presented here offer a picture of the way in which relationships tend to change as they move toward friendship and intimacy. Hunt's model provides guideposts to be used in assessing the depth of your current relationships.

Acquaintanceship—Friendship—Intimacy: A Continuum

We can think about the degree of intimacy in human relationships as lying along a continuum. At one end of the continuum, we have acquaintances—people we know casually. At the other end of the continuum, we have intimates—people who know us at the deepest levels. It is possible for two individuals to start at the acquaintanceship end of the continuum, move into friendship, and, over a period of time, become intimate. On the other hand, individuals can remain acquaintances or friends, never reaching the intimate end of the continuum. *Not all relationships should have intimacy as their goal.* The values of the other forms of relationships are real in their own right.

In distinguishing friendship from intimacy, White has written:

It is not uncommon for a pair ... to do everything and go everywhere together, to be inseparable, but never to exchange a word about their inmost secrets. One might say figuratively that they stand side by side looking out at the world but never look at or into each other. Friendship in such instances does not involve intimacy, but it may be characterized by firm loyalty, strong mutual support, and a certain shared validation of external experience [p. 340].

White offers us a working definition of friendship that has three elements:

△ firm loyalty,
△ strong mutual support, and
△ a shared view of the world.

How does intimacy differ from friendship? Intimacy is characteristic of a relationship in which the individuals involved share their thoughts, feelings, values, and experiences with each other directly and at the deepest levels of which they are capable. The type of sharing characteristic of an intimate relationship comes, in White's words, "from one's inmost being." An intimate relationship is one in which you allow yourself to be known as fully as possible by another person, and he or she reciprocates. Being intimate means, among other things, being vulnerable. When you allow another person to know you, you open yourself to the possibility of being hurt. Intimacy is not possible without risking this kind of vulnerability.

The elements of the working definition of intimacy that we are presenting are:

△ firm loyalty,
△ strong mutual support,
△ a shared view of the world,
△ deep, mutual self-disclosure, and
△ shared vulnerability.

Intimacy includes the elements of friendship, but it goes beyond friendship, deepening the relationship between yourself and another person.

The Areas of Intimacy

Some important forms of intimacy cannot be seen as a stage beyond friendship; that is, they do not fit easily into the continuum we've described. In these forms, intimacy is not an all-embracing, friendship-plus relationship. Two people might share themselves intimately in one area of life but not in others. For instance, Schmidt and Carver work together in the city desk of a newspaper. They share their feelings, their values, their hopes, and their expectations as they relate to their work. They enjoy working together, meeting challenges, and providing strong mutual support. They reveal their misgivings about the newspaper and its policies, and about themselves as professionals. All the elements of the working definition of intimacy are present—loyalty, strong mutual support, shared views, deep mutual self-disclosure in work-related areas, and, because they share their values and misgivings about work and themselves as workers, shared vulnerability. However, their relationship doesn't extend beyond the office. They don't see each other socially or share any of the other important areas of their lives. "Work intimacy" is extremely important to both of them.

Mason and Montoya attend the same church. They also belong to one of the small prayer groups sponsored by the church. In their meetings, they explore religion and the ways in which it relates to the rest of their lives. They also explore and engage in different forms of prayer. The time they spend in this group each week is very important to them. They find the meetings enriching, because they provide a forum in which people can speak freely, personally, and deeply about an area of life that has great meaning for them. They always leave these meetings feeling recharged and ready to face the tasks, joys, sorrows, and uncertainties of life more peacefully and more resolutely. However, Mason and Montoya do not see each other outside these meetings. Again, all the elements of the working defini- tion of intimacy apply to the area of life they share, but they don't share a day-to- day intimacy in other important areas. Theirs is a faith-sharing, or religion-based, intimacy.

Barnes and Silverman are in their early 30s. They play basketball together with a group of eight others once or twice a week. They like the game and play it intensely. For them, it provides a serious "play time" in which they forget their cares. They enjoy playing together, whether on the same team or on opposing sides; that is, they enjoy working together and competing. They enjoy the game so much that it is rarely dropped from their weekly schedule. During warm-ups and breaks, their conversation focuses on sports, physical fitness, and their basketball game. They talk about their interest in the world of sports, their goals in terms of physical fitness, the loss of the physical elasticity and resiliency of their youth, and similar topics. They know a few things about each other's personal life—things that they joke about when they warm up or meet over an occasional beer and pizza after the game—but these are not central to their sharing. Whenever one of them fails to show up for a game, the other feels a sense of loss. They see each other only on "basketball" nights. Is theirs an intimate relationship? Do they share a recrea- tional, or play, intimacy? Take the elements of the working definition of intimacy and see if they apply to this relationship.

Perhaps it is better to discuss "the intimacies" of relationships, or different areas of intimacy, rather than *intimacy* in the singular. In this case, any given intimate relationship can be described in terms of the areas of intimacy involved and the depth or intensity of the relationship.

Intimacy and Sexuality

Intimate relationships are not synonymous with sexual relationships. Although a relationship can be both intimate and sexual, intimate relationships aren't necessarily sexual. The identification of intimacy with sexuality by televi- sion, movies, and popular music constitutes a great disservice to us all. Sexual intimacy is portrayed as primary, whereas all other forms of intimacy are seen as second-class.

Janet had reached the point at which she wanted to experience sex in all her close relationships. As far as Janet was concerned, if a relationship wasn't sexual, she and the other person were not really intimate. The effects of this type of misunderstanding are hard to calculate, but they certainly include:

△ a tendency to equate physical intimacy with relationship intimacy,
△ the distortion of our image of the relative importance of sexuality compared to other forms of intimacy in marriage and other forms of commitment, and
△ the establishment of cultural "rules" that make it difficult for members of the same sex to develop relationships that are characterized by intimate communication.

Interpersonal Style

Your interpersonal style refers to the usual, ordinary, day-to-day ways in which you behave when you're with other people. Your style includes the ways in which you act toward everyone. ("I am self-effacing with everyone—members of my family, people in authority, peers, and strangers.") Your interpersonal style includes the ways in which you tend to treat particular sets of people. ("I am quiet and well-behaved at home and in front of authority figures such as teachers, but I act like a buffoon when I'm with my peers.") Your style includes the skills you possess and use, the skills you lack, and your characteristic successes and failures in relating to other people.

We'll make this description of interpersonal style as concrete as possible. If someone were to ask you "What are you like when you are with people; how do you act?" you might answer "Well, it depends on the people I'm with. I'm comfortable with friends—I talk easily, but I don't like to argue. I'm very uncomfortable with strangers—I feel very shy and quiet." By answering the question this way, you would give a brief description of your interpersonal style—how you act, what you do, how you think and feel when you are with people. Moreover, note that the answer indicates that your interpersonal style isn't a simple thing: it's complex, because you behave differently with various kinds of people. And perhaps you behave one way when you're in a bad mood and another way when you're in a good mood.

You can make the term *interpersonal style* come alive by asking yourself the questions listed here. As you begin to ask yourself these questions, you'll notice two things: (1) the questions will force you to think about yourself in relationship to other people and to think about yourself in clear, concrete, and specific ways, and (2) you'll notice how complicated and enriching relationships can be. By answering at least some of the questions in each of the ten sections that follow, you can begin to form a description of your own individual interpersonal style. You needn't answer all the questions right now.

How big a part of my life is my interpersonal life?
△ How much of my day is spent relating to people?

△ Do I want to spend a lot of time with people, or do I prefer being by myself?
△ Do I have many friends?
△ Do I spend a lot of time with my friends?
△ Is my life too crowded with people?
△ Are there too few people in my life? Do I feel lonely much of the time?
△ Do I prefer smaller gatherings or larger groups? Or do I prefer to be with just one person most of the time?
△ Do I plan to get together with others, or do I leave getting together to chance—if it happens, it happens?

What do I want, and what do I need when I spend time with others?
△ What do I like in other people; that is, what makes me choose them as friends? Is it intelligence or physical attractiveness? Is it the fact that they're good-natured and pleasant or that we share the same values?
△ Do I choose to be with people because they're important or are in positions of authority?
△ Do I choose to be with people who will do what I want to do?
△ Do I choose to be with people who will take over and make decisions for the two of us?
△ Do I just spend time with whoever happens to come along?
△ Are the people I spend time with like me or unlike me? Or are they like me in some ways and unlike me in others?
△ Do I feel that I need my friends more than they need me?
△ Do I let other people know what I want from them? Do I let them know directly, or do they find out what I want in indirect ways?

Do I care about the people in my life?
△ If I care about other people, how do I show it?
△ Do other people know I care about them?
△ Do I take people for granted?
△ Do I wonder at times whether I care at all?
△ Do I see myself as selfish or generous?
△ Do others see me as self-centered? If so, in what way?
△ Do people care about me? How do they show it?

What are my interpersonal skills?
△ Do I understand people and let them know that I understand?
△ Do I respect other people? How well do I communicate that respect?
△ Am I my real self when I'm with others, or do I play games?
△ Am I open—that is, willing to talk about myself—when I'm with people who want to be intimate with me?
△ Can I confront people without trying to punish them or play the game of "I'm right and you're wrong"?
△ Do I ever talk to another person about the strengths and weaknesses of our relationship?

△ Do I make attempts to meet new people? Does the way in which I meet new people encourage them to make further contact with me?

△ Am I an active listener; that is, do I listen carefully and then respond to what I've heard?

△ Do my friends come to me when they're in trouble? If they do, do they leave me feeling understood or helped?

△ Am I outgoing, or do I sit back and wait for others to make the first move?

Do I want to be very close to people?

△ What does closeness or intimacy mean to me? Does it mean deep conversations? Does it mean touching?

△ Do I enjoy it when people share their secrets and their deepest feelings with me?

△ Do I like to share my secrets and my deepest feelings?

△ Who am I close to now?

△ Do I encourage certain people to get close to me? How do I do this?

△ Does closeness frighten me? If so, what is it about it that frightens me?

△ Are there many different ways of being close to others? What are they? Which ways do I prefer?

How do I handle my feelings and emotions when I'm with others?

△ Do people see me as a very feeling person, or do they think I'm cold and controlled?

△ Which emotions do I express easily to others? Which emotions do I tend to hide?

△ Is it easy for people to know what I'm feeling?

△ Do I let my emotions take over when I'm with others?

△ Do I try to control people with my emotions—for instance, by being moody? Do I manipulate others?

△ Do I think that it's all right to be emotional?

△ How do I react when others are emotional?

△ Which emotions do I enjoy in others? Which emotions do I fear?

△ What do I do when people keep their emotions locked up inside themselves?

How do I act when I feel that I'm being rejected?

△ Does loneliness play a part in my life?

△ If I feel rejected, how do I handle my feelings?

△ Do I sometimes avoid a person or a group of people because I'm afraid that I will be rejected?

△ Can other people scare me easily?

△ Have I ever been rejected?

△ Am I hurt easily? What do I do when I'm hurt?

△ Do I ignore or reject people who might want to get close to me?

△ What do I do when a person wants to get close to me and be my friend?

Do I want a lot of give-and-take in my relationships?

△ Do I play games with people, or do I prefer to be straightforward and direct with them? Do people play games with me?

△ Do I like to control others—to get them to do things my way? Do I allow people to control me? Do I give in to others most of the time?

△ What do I ask of my friends? What do my friends ask of me?

△ Are there ways in which my friendships or my other relationships are one-sided?

△ Am I willing to compromise—that is, to decide with another person what would be best for both of us?

△ Do I think that it's all right for others to influence me and for me to influence others, within reasonable limits?

△ Do I expect to be treated as an equal when I'm with others? Do I want to treat people, especially my friends, as equals?

△ Do I feel responsible for what happens in my relationships, or do I just let things "take their course"?

How do I get along in my work and school relationships?

△ How do I relate to people in authority?

△ At school and at work, do I treat people as people, or do I see them as other workers or other students?

△ Am I too friendly at school and at work? Do I get my work done?

What are my interpersonal values?

△ Do I want to grow in my interpersonal life and relate to others?

△ Am I willing to work, to risk myself, and to put myself on the line with others in order to be involved in a richer interpersonal life?

△ Am I willing to allow others to be themselves?

△ Is it important for me to be myself when I'm with others?

△ In what ways am I too cautious or too careful in relating to others? What are my fears?

△ Do I get along with people who have opinions and views and ways of acting that differ from my own?

△ Do I have any prejudices regarding other people?

△ Am I rigid or unbending in my relationships?

△ Do I share my values with others?

△ Do I put so much emphasis on my interpersonal relationships (for instance, my friendships) that they interfere with my work or with my other involvements in life?

This Is Me: An Exercise in Awareness of Interpersonal Style

1. From the list of questions regarding your interpersonal style, choose the issues that seem important to you. Which questions capture your interest?

2. Which questions do you find difficult to answer? Which questions would you like to avoid in your group discussions?

3. Using the questions as a guide, write a brief description of your interpersonal style. Write only what you would be willing to read or show to members of your group. At the same time, try to show them a side of you that usually remains hidden.

Loneliness

Since loneliness is such a common experience in our culture, we think it will be useful for you to develop a basic working knowledge that will help you to deal with loneliness. First, describe your most recent experience of loneliness. Describe briefly what led up to it or caused it, how you felt and what you did, and how you worked through it (if you have).

_____

_____

_____

_____

_____

_____

_____

_____

_____

_____

The Experience of Loneliness

Being alone and being lonely aren't necessarily identical experiences. In a book called *The Broken Heart: The Medical Consequences of Loneliness*, James Lynch maintains that people who live alone are more susceptible than others to serious illness. However, he assumes that people who live alone are lonely, and that isn't always the case. As Rubinstein, Shaver, and Peplau (1979) point out, *alone* is an objective term that indicates whether a person lives with someone else, how many friends he or she has, and so on. On the other hand, *lonely* is a subjective term that describes a state of mind. "Feelings of loneliness do not inevitably follow from solitude or circumstance; they depend on how people view their experiences and whether they decide to call themselves lonely" (pp. 58, 60).

Here are some of the facts regarding loneliness that have been gleaned from the research of people such as Rubinstein, Shaver, and Peplau.

△   The highest degree of loneliness is found among members of your age group (18–25). Some people estimate that 70% of the members of this age group experience loneliness as a problem at one time or another. If loneliness is a problem for you, it has much to do with the transitional developmental stage you find yourself in.

△   Loneliness seems to present a problem to the poor, the uneducated, members of minority groups, and the unemployed.

△   Perception of reality is one of the most important factors of loneliness. If you believe there is a mismatch between your actual social life and the kind of social life you want, then you are likely to feel lonely. Dissatisfaction with relationships can lead to loneliness.

△   Feelings of loneliness tend to affect a person's entire social life: "Lonely people are dissatisfied with everything about their lives: their living arrangements (whether solo or with others), the number of friends they have, the quality of those friendships, their marriages and love affairs, the number of conversations they have each day, and their sex lives" (Rubinstein, Shaver, & Peplau, 1979, p. 61).

△   Lonely people tend to become trapped in a vicious circle: it's difficult to approach guarded, defensive people; therefore, they tend to remain isolated. Lonely people tend to lack social skills. They are poor at conversation and empathy. Their lack of skills keeps them locked in their loneliness. They are sometimes hostile, especially if they attribute their loneliness to external factors that are beyond their control ("This university is so big and so impersonal that it's impossible to develop a decent social life!"). Often, lonely people see themselves or their situations as hopeless and do little to remedy their condition. Self-pity often keeps them locked in a passive role.

△   Researchers have discovered four sets of feelings that characterize different subjective experiences of loneliness:

△   some people feel desperate and abandoned—they feel helpless and afraid;
△   some people feel bored and impatient;
△   others feel unattractive, ashamed, and deserving of their fate; and
△   still others feel sorry for themselves (these people often long to be with one special person).

△   Loneliness can be situational and temporary, or it can be chronic and generalized.

△   It seems unrealistic to suppose that one special relationship will satisfy all your social, emotional, and intimacy needs.

In view of these findings, review the experience of loneliness you described and answer the following questions.

1. How do I contribute to my loneliness (for instance, through my lack of social skills, my shyness, my feelings of unattractiveness, and so on)?

_____
_____
_____
_____
_____

2. How does my situation contribute to my loneliness (for instance, the size of my school, its impersonal atmosphere, the cliques here, and so forth)?

_____
_____
_____
_____
_____
_____

3. Do I see my loneliness as transitory or permanent?

_____
_____
_____

4. What can I do about my loneliness (for instance, my lack of social skills)?

_____
_____
_____
_____
_____

5. What can I do with respect to my environment (for instance, join clubs, ask for dates, and so forth)?

_____
_____

_____
_____
_____
_____

Forms of Intimacy: An Exercise

List as many forms of intimacy as you can and explain how the elements of the definition of intimacy apply to each form.

_____
_____
_____
_____
_____
_____
_____
_____
_____
_____
_____
_____

Systematic Self-Assessment: Friendship and Intimacy

1. Using the checklist provided, assess the depth of three of your current relationships. Whenever you answer yes, give one or two concrete examples of the kind of experience on which you base your answer.

Relationship Checklist

1. This relationship is characterized by firm loyalty.
2. This relationship is characterized by mutual support.
3. We often see things the same way.
4. This relationship is characterized by self-disclosure on both sides. (This

could refer to sharing either one important area of life or all areas of life.)

5. We are willing to be vulnerable, to risk being hurt or disappointed.

One student analyzed a relationship this way:

Person: Agatha

1. Yes.
—We always check with each other to see what's happening on weekends and during vacations.
—I spent a great deal of time with her last year when she was out of circulation with a broken leg.

2. Yes.
—We've worked out a note-taking and study system that's been mutually beneficial.

3. Yes.
—We're both from small towns and have discussed our mutual —and sometimes limited—views on a lot of things: sex, religion, career. Both of us see ourselves as having done some "foreclosing," and we discuss this.
—Even though we belong to different church denominations, we share a lot of the same values regarding family life, feelings about American materialism, urban versus semirural living, and the like.

4. Yes.
—We talk a great deal about our other friendships, especially our relationships with males.
—We have visited each other's homes, and we have shared the ups and downs of family life.

5. Yes.
—I was rather hurt when she made arrangements for the big school dance without letting me in on it or doing any planning with me.
—Agatha was disappointed when I switched majors last month. Up to then, we were both majoring in history.

Now fill out the following forms.

Form 8-1

Relationship Checklist

Relationship #1

Person: _____

1. Yes _____   No _____

If you answered *yes*, list one or two examples.

_____

_____

_____

2. Yes _____   No _____

If you answered *yes*, list one or two examples.

_____

_____

_____

3. Yes _____   No _____

If you answered *yes*, list one or two examples.

_____

_____

_____

4. Yes _____   No _____

If you answered *yes*, list one or two examples.

_____

_____

_____

5. Yes _____   No _____

If you answered *yes*, list one or two examples.

_____

_____

_____

Relationship #2

Person: _____

1. Yes _____ No _____

If you answered *yes*, list one or two examples.

_____

_____

_____

2. Yes _____ No _____

If you answered *yes*, list one or two examples.

_____

_____

_____

3. Yes _____ No _____

If you answered *yes*, list one or two examples.

_____

_____

_____

4. Yes _____ No _____

If you answered *yes*, list one or two examples.

_____

_____

_____

5. Yes _____ No _____

If you answered *yes*, list one or two examples.

_____

_____

_____

Relationship #3

Person: _____

1. Yes _____   No _____

If you answered *yes*, list one or two examples.

_____

_____

_____

2. Yes _____   No _____

If you answered *yes*, list one or two examples.

_____

_____

_____

3. Yes _____   No _____

If you answered *yes*, list one or two examples.

_____

_____

_____

4. Yes _____   No _____

If you answered *yes*, list one or two examples.

_____

_____

_____

5. Yes _____   No _____

If you answered *yes*, list one or two examples.

_____

_____

_____

2. Refer to the descriptions of acquaintanceship, friendship, and intimacy and to your responses in the Relationship Checklist. Use the definitions and your responses to assess the level of the three relationships you choose. Then write a brief explanation of your assessment. Here is a sample response to this task:

> *Relationship #1:* David
> *Level:* friendship
> *Reasons:* I could answer *yes* to 1, 2, and 3, but not to 4 and 5. We don't share very much personal stuff with each other, even though we're good friends.
>
> *Relationship #2:* Sara
> *Level:* acquaintanceship
> *Reasons:* I couldn't answer *yes* to any of the questions on the list. We're in the same lab group for chemistry, and we've ended up at the same party a few times, but that's it.
>
> *Relationship #3:* Paul
> *Level:* intimacy
> *Reasons:* I said *yes* to every question. We've been close for two years now. I'm not sure that anybody knows me better. We know each other intimately in a number of areas of life. However, I haven't shared the crisis back home and the pain I experience in family life.

Now do the same for the relationships you chose to assess.

Relationship #1: _____

Level: _____

Reasons: _____

_____

_____

_____

_____

_____

Relationship #2: _____

Level: _____

Reasons: _____

_____

_____

_____
_____
_____

Relationship #3: _____

Level: _____

Reasons: _____

_____
_____
_____
_____
_____

3. Refer to Figure 8-1 and the descriptions of relationships at various levels. Which level describes the way in which you relate to others? Why? Here is one student's response to this exercise.

> *Level:* II
> *Reasons:* I picked level II, because that's the one pertaining to people who are rebelling—trying out new things, not just buying into all the old rules. I'd say that's my style right now, especially with my profs and my parents.

Now write your own response. (If you think that a mixture of levels represents your style, indicate the levels and your reasons for including each one.)

Level: _____

Reasons: _____

_____
_____
_____
_____
_____
_____
_____
_____

Level: _____
Reasons: _____

_____

_____

_____

_____

_____

_____

_____

Key Settings and the Deepening of Interpersonal Relationships

Your ability to form relationships of real depth is created in the key settings of your life, especially your family and friendship groups. In the exercise that follows, we ask you to reflect on the effects that those settings have had and are presently having on the deepening of your relationships.

Using the form provided, list at least one key setting that is having a positive effect and one that seems to be having a negative effect on friendship and intimacy in your life. Then write a brief explanation of your answer. Here is one student's response to this task:

Positive Influence

Setting: family
Reasons: My parents always talked openly with one another and with us. I guess they always stressed saying what was on our minds and listening to one another. They had to pay a certain price. We four kids did speak our minds, and sometimes we weren't very good at it. I mean, we did a fair amount of arguing and yelling. But our parents listened and, by their example both with us and with each other, taught us how to speak out in close relationships in reasonable ways.

Negative Influence

Setting: commuter college
Reasons: I go to class, leave for work, and go home. The college is almost like a factory. We click around to different classes, then it's over. No one, myself certainly included, makes much of an effort to talk to anyone else. Maybe that happens during extracurricular

activities. But I'm at work then. It doesn't happen before or during class. I mean, the profs tend to lecture, and we don't talk to one another.

Now write your response in the space provided.

Positive Influence

Setting: _____

Reasons: _____

_____

_____

_____

_____

_____

_____

_____

Negative Influence

Setting: _____

Reasons: _____

_____

_____

_____

_____

_____

_____

Structured Group Interaction: Friendship and Intimacy

Step 1. Share the definition of *intimacy* that you wrote earlier in this chapter. Discuss the definitions written by the other members of your group. (Are there any common themes?)

Step 2. Share one important thing that you've learned regarding the depth of interpersonal relationships in your life.

Step 3. Share one example of the positive effects of a key setting on friendship or intimacy in your life.

Action Plan: Deepening Interpersonal Relationships

1. *Goals.* Now that you've read about, thought about, and discussed friendship and intimacy, what changes, if any, would you like to initiate with regard to these areas? List several concrete goals that you might pursue and describe the need or want or problem to which each goal is related. For instance, one student, Denise, wrote the following:

> Right now, I discuss the serious issues in my life only with adults —parents, advisers, my pastor. I'd like to develop a couple of peer relationships in which I can do the same thing. This does not mean finding new relationships. I have a lot of friends, but really no intimates. My need or want is this: I think some life issues need to be discussed with peers who are presently experiencing the same things. The adult perspective is important, but so is the peer viewpoint, and I miss it.

Now describe several goals that you might pursue and the need or want or problem to which each goal is related.

_____

_____

_____

_____

_____

_____

_____

_____

_____

_____

Return to your description of your goals within 48 hours and add any goals you might have thought of in that period. Then choose one or two goals that seem especially important to you and list them in the space provided.

_____

_____
_____
_____
_____
_____

2. *Resources.* In the space provided, indicate the people, books, or settings that might help you to achieve the goals that are important to you. For instance, Denise came up with the following:

—A book on intimacy and identity.
—An interpersonal-skills training course from the psychology department.
—Ray and Susan, who can talk seriously about themselves and who still know how to have fun.
—Bart, who tries to talk seriously about himself but who receives little cooperation from me.

_____
_____
_____
_____
_____
_____
_____

3. *Programs.* Indicate the steps of a program that will lead to the achievement of your goals. You might have to consider several programs before you adopt the one or the combination that suits you. Denise came up with the following program:

—Review the current status of my relationships from the viewpoint of the acquaintance-friend-intimate model.
—Sign up for the course in interpersonal-skills training.
—Review my own interpersonal style either by myself or in the context of that course.
—Pick out one or two peers who are friends and who I believe I can trust.
—Use this course on developmental tasks to review the areas of life I would like to explore with a peer.

—Slowly begin to share myself more fully and set up an atmosphere in which others will feel free to do the same.

—See if I can find someone to talk with in the interpersonal-skills course.

Now set up a program for each goal you've set.

Goals/Programs

_____

_____

_____

_____

_____

_____

_____

_____

_____

_____

_____

4. *Implementation/Evaluation.* (a) Outline the obstacles you might meet in trying to carry out your program and the ways in which you might handle those obstacles.

_____

_____

_____

_____

_____

_____

_____

_____

(b) How do you want to monitor your participation in your program; that is, how are you going to demand accountability of yourself?

_____

_____

_____

_____

_____

_____

_____

_____

Summary

In this chapter, we focused on friendship, intimacy, and the process of deepening interpersonal relationships. We invited you to reflect on the depth of your current relationships, on some current theories regarding friendship and intimacy, and on the impact of key settings in your life. Finally, you were asked to take part in a structured group interaction and create an action plan regarding the deepening of interpersonal relationships in your life.

In the next chapter, we turn our attention to love and commitment.

Love, Marriage, and Family: Commitments in Interpersonal Living

In this chapter, we examine the challenge of developing relationships that are characterized by commitment. We begin with an exercise that is designed to assist you in considering the current level of commitment in your personal relationships. Then we present several concepts from recent theory and research concerning the nature of committed relationships and ask that you use these concepts as a basis for self-reflection. We ask you to take part in a structured group interaction focusing on commitments in interpersonal living and complete a self-directed action plan.

Personal-Reflection Exercise: My Commitments to Others

1. Write a brief paragraph (4–5 sentences) beginning with the following sentence stem:

When I say that I am committed to another person, _____

_____

_____

_____

_____

_____

_____

2. Select one person with whom you've had what you consider to be a committed relationship, or something close to it. In the space provided, list the characteristics that made this relationship special. Here is one student's response to this task:

Relationship with David

Special Characteristics

—I especially look forward to our time together.
—He understands me at a deeper level than almost anyone.
—I would make a special effort to help him if he needed it.
—I have a feeling that the relationship will last, while many others are likely to fade away.
—We have a special type of mutual loyalty.

Now complete the task for yourself.

Relationship with _____

Special Characteristics

_____

_____

_____

_____

_____

_____

_____

3. In order to help you think deeply about committed relationships in your life, we would like you to respond to the following question: Why do you think that some relationships in your life move toward commitment, whereas others do not? Here is one student's response to this question:

> I guess I don't have a general answer to this question. Right now, I can only answer it for myself. When commitment happens between me and another person, I think it's because there's a special kind of attraction there somehow. I don't necessarily mean sexual-type attraction, but that can be part of it. I feel accepted and understood in a special way, and I naturally want to be with somebody who gives me that feeling. But it's not enough for just me to feel that way—it's got to go both ways. When it doesn't, commitment doesn't seem to happen. The other thing is that things sometimes click well at the beginning but never go anywhere. Unless the relationship gets deeper somehow—it has to have some of the intimacy we just studied—commitment won't be there. That initial attraction can wear off without leaving anything lasting.

Respond to this question in the space provided.

_____

_____

_____

_____

_____

_____

_____

How Social Competence, Relationships, and Commitment Are Related

In Chapter 3, we examined social competence, which was defined as the ability to relate decently and effectively to other people. You will recall that we divided the skills of social competence into several categories of basic skills. Three of these categories are:

△   the skills of self-presentation,
△   the skills of responding to others, and
△   the skills of challenging others responsibly.

We indicated that these skills are necessary in building decent working and living relationships; these skills are the *foundation* of effective interpersonal living.

In Chapter 8, we examined the challenge of deepening interpersonal relationships. Friendship and intimacy come about as people use basic interpersonal skills to create relationships that go beyond decency and effectiveness to become characterized by:

△   firm loyalty,
△   mutual support,
△   a shared view of the world,
△   mutual self-disclosure, and
△   a mutual willingness to be vulnerable.

Friendship and intimacy are built on the foundation of the basic interpersonal skills.

In this chapter, we examine commitment, which may be viewed as another level of depth in interpersonal living. There is a degree of commitment in our relationships with friends and intimates; however, some of these relationships become the special commitments around which our lives revolve. This chapter focuses on love, marriage, and family life.

Figure 9-1 is an illustration of the relationships among basic interpersonal competence, deepened interpersonal relationships, and commitments in interpersonal living.

Figure 9-1 illustrates two important facts regarding interpersonal life: (1) at each level, interpersonal living is based on the fundamental skills of self-presentation, the ability to respond to others, and responsible challenge, and (2) as we move up the triangle, the areas become smaller. Likewise, as we move toward

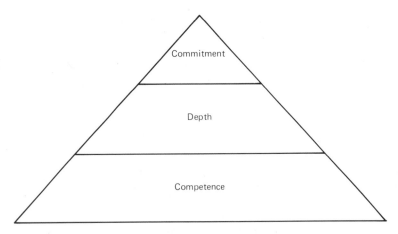

FIGURE 9-1. The levels of interpersonal living.

commitment in interpersonal living, the number of relationships at each level becomes smaller. Commitment is a rare and special thing.

Commitment: A Working Definition

The American Heritage Dictionary of the English Language offers several definitions of the word *commitment.* Two definitions are of particular importance for our purposes: "a pledge to do something," and "the state of being bound intellectually or emotionally to some course of action." When these definitions are combined, the following definition of *commitment* is created: "an intellectual or emotional pledge to do something."

We define commitment as an intellectual and emotional choice to pledge yourself in a special way to another person in an ongoing relationship characterized by depth and mutual vulnerability. The most common institutional form of such relationships in our culture is marriage; however, recently a number of alternative forms have emerged. Although we focus our attention here on the love/marriage/family triad, we don't imply a lack of respect for other forms of committed personal relationships.

Love: Responsiveness and Commitment

Many people think of love, marriage, and family life as phases in a deepening and widening process of commitment. *Love* is a much-used and much-abused term. Millions of words have been written about it—some sublime, many ridiculous. In this chapter, we consider love as it relates to marriage and family life. In this context, love is characterized by:

△ a degree of exclusivity,
△ romantic and sexual feelings,
△ an active and special concern for the other's well-being, and
△ a sense of a "future," however indefinite.

Generally speaking, the process of commitment to another begins in a relationship that has these characteristics. As Masters and Johnson (1970) have written: "This combination of emotions, this interaction in which each caring impulse reinforces the other . . . creates an overpowering sense of involvement and identification, of oneness. Some people call it love, and it is the original source of commitment."

Although the deeper commitments of marriage and family life have their roots in the experience of being in love, the intense emotions and sexual feelings that are a part of being in love often obscure this connection. Romantic love is characterized by both magic and turbulence; it tends to carry people on a tide of sexual and emotional attraction toward a commitment for which they are not prepared. One of our hopes in writing this chapter is that it will assist people who are beginning to experience romantic love or who are deeply in love to reflect on the demands of marriage and family life and talk openly and seriously with one another about mutual hopes, fears, and expectations regarding the succeeding phases of commitment in interpersonal living.

Marriage: A Public Commitment to Responsibility

Although marriage, like love, is an extraordinarily difficult concept to capture in a single definition, we are suggesting a fairly straightforward definition for our purposes: marriage is that phase of commitment in interpersonal living that involves a public commitment to extend a love relationship for an indefinite period of time. It typically includes the expectation of exclusivity in emotional and sexual involvement, a joint household, and reciprocal roles.

We have stressed the public nature of this commitment, because, although the experience of being in love is extremely private, marriage brings a love relationship into public view. Marriage involves a decision to stay together not only because you feel that you *want* to but also because you are publicly *obligated* to do so. Masters and Johnson capture the distinction between these two types of involvement in the following passage:

Caring—which is defined as paying attention, being concerned, solicitous and protective—flows from two related but different kinds of feelings. One is a feeling of being *responsive* to someone, of *caring* for that person; the other is a feeling of being *responsible* for someone, of wanting to *take care* of him or her. These feelings are generated in entirely different ways. Responsiveness occurs spontaneously, before the mind is consciously aware of what is happening—a sudden surge of interest and attraction, triggered by another person's physical presence. Responsibility is consciously, though often unwillingly, invoked by the mind—an acknowledgment of obligation [p. 252].

The important point here is that although being in love is primarily an emotional commitment, being publicly committed involves a choice to obligate oneself to continue caring for another person. In effect, marriage partners say to one another "I will care for you even when I don't feel like it." A bond that began as an emotional one goes beyond its beginning and becomes a bond of mutual responsibility.

Obviously, many relationships cannot tolerate the demands involved in the transformation from love to commitment. This is illustrated by the fact that, in the U.S., one-third of all marriages end in divorce. The outlook for successful marriages among teenagers is extremely bleak. The "honeymoon's over" phenomenon has become an accepted part of our folklore regarding marriage. The transition from love (responsiveness) to commitment (responsiveness plus responsibility) is not dependent on fate or statistical probabilities but rather on the working knowledge, skills, values, challenge, and support available to those who are making the effort to move their relationships to this deeper level. The stress and difficulty often experienced during the deepening of love and marriage shouldn't be interpreted as a sign that the relationship is in trouble. In fact, such difficulties could represent the growing pains of a maturing commitment.

The Competencies Needed for Commitment

In order to develop the kind of commitment that is demanded in marriage, you will need to develop the following competencies:

△ interpersonal skills,
△ the ability to delay gratification in view of a higher goal,
△ the ability to engage in collaborative decision making, problem solving, and life planning,
△ the ability to develop and pursue mutual interests,
△ the ability to coordinate multiple commitments,
△ the ability to appreciate a relationship,
△ the ability to be committed to another person without being possessive,
△ the ability to develop self-knowledge,
△ the ability to understand and appreciate conflicting cultural backgrounds, and
△ the ability to expect and deal with conflicts and disagreements.

We will now discuss each of these competencies in some detail.

Interpersonal Skills

We've reviewed the skills of self-presentation, responding, and challenging. One skill that is especially needed for deep commitment is immediacy. Immediacy refers to the ability of two or more people to talk to each other about their relationship. It is a complex skill that requires self-disclosure, empathy, self-confrontation, and the ability to challenge another person caringly.

Tina and George haven't developed the ability to discuss their relationship directly and nondefensively. They tend to "save up" little hurts and misunderstandings until they explode in a game of "uproar." This does little to strengthen or deepen their commitment to each other.

Clark and Mia take a different approach. When either of them notices little behavioral cues that indicate something is going wrong in their relationship (for instance, when one partner seems overly quiet or a bit sullen) the one who notices the cues examines his or her own behavior and invites the other to do the same. They have disagreements, but they make demands on themselves and on each other to work them out quickly. Every two weeks, they sit down and discuss what has been happening in their relationship.

What are your strengths and weaknesses in terms of the skill of immediacy?

The Ability to Delay Gratification in View of a Higher Goal

The ability to delay gratification is an important sign of maturity. Impulsive, self-centered people always experience difficulty with their commitments to other people. Marriage demands a great deal of self-control for the sake of the marital relationship.

Pia and Dominick married without having developed self-management skills. They wanted satisfaction immediately, without reflecting on each other's needs. Their fights were spectacular, and their relationship was short-lived. Eventually, they went their separate ways, only to start the same process all over again, each with a new partner.

1. Give an example from your own experience of how the ability to delay gratification has helped strengthen or affirm a relationship.

_____

_____

_____

_____

_____

_____

2. Indicate several ways in which you are successful in delaying gratification and several ways in which you are less than successful. In what ways does your degree of success in this regard affect your relationships?

_____

_____

_____

_____

_____

_____

_____

_____

_____

_____

_____

_____

_____

The Ability to Engage in Collaborative Decision Making, Problem Solving, and Life Planning

Right now, you feel fairly competent with respect to planning and decision making; however, as you look toward a deep commitment to another person, you need to review your ability to plan and make decisions collaboratively. Collaborative decision making involves the ability to negotiate fairly and engage in reasonable compromises. Many people enter into marriage with little or no experience in give-and-take decision making.

Before meeting Marilu, Henry had no trouble making plans and executing them. In groups, he spoke assertively and frequently, and many of the decisions made by those groups had his imprint on them. In his marriage, this trait proved disastrous. Although Marilu wasn't an assertive as Henry, she expected their relationship to be egalitarian. Henry's reaction was to tell her that he had not realized before they got married how stubborn she was. They terminated their relationship, and Henry found a more compliant partner.

1. How do you act toward aggressive people who want to make decisions that affect you? Give examples if possible.

_____

_____

_____

_____

_____

_____

_____

_____

_____

_____

_____

2. How do you act toward compliant people who allow you to make decisions that affect them? Give examples if possible.

_____

_____

_____

_____

_____

_____

_____

_____

_____

_____

3. Give an example of a way in which you engaged in collaborative decision making with a significant person in your life.

_____

_____

_____

_____

_____

_____

_____

_____

_____

The Ability to Develop and Pursue Mutual Interests

Your commitment to another person can be enriched and deepened by your ability to develop and pursue interests with that person. Although different styles can complement each other, extreme differences can affect relationships negatively.

Ethel is very gregarious and active. Somehow, she is able to fit a dozen things into a crowded schedule and still find time for volunteer work at Children's Hospital and dancing. She married Ed, who is stable, quiet, and unassuming. He enjoys solitude, classical music, and literature. During the first two years of their marriage, their vastly different styles didn't seem to matter. Ethel was out of the house a great deal, still the doer. Ed didn't mind, since he enjoys solitude. Eventually, they both realized that although their arrangement worked in the short run, they didn't have the marriage they both wanted.

1. List your main interests.

_____

_____

_____

_____

_____

2. Which of these interests do you pursue with other people?

_____

_____

_____

_____

3. Which interests do you pursue with your closest friends?

_____

_____

_____

_____

The Ability to Coordinate Multiple Commitments

Your ability to coordinate multiple commitments involves your ability to manage your time. We can look at this issue from the perspective of the roles you assume—wife, husband, father, mother, son, daughter, sister, brother, friend, church member, worker, community member, citizen, and so on. People who do not manage their time feel pulled apart by their roles: "I'm sorry we didn't have time to. . . ."

1. List the roles you presently assume.

_____

_____

_____

_____

_____

_____

_____

_____

2. Which roles demand most of your time?

_____

_____

_____

_____

3. Which roles do you find hardest to handle? Explain.

_____

_____

_____

_____

_____

_____

4. Indicate the ways in which your coordination of these roles affects your closest relationship.

_____

_____

_____

_____

_____

_____

_____

The Ability to Appreciate a Relationship

The ability to appreciate a relationship includes thoughtfulness. Perhaps one of the most rewarding experiences in life is to be contacted by someone you like—a thoughtful phone call from a friend during a time of crisis. Very often, little things say a great deal about the quality of one's commitment. The excitement that characterizes the beginning of relationships can be mistaken for this kind of thoughtfulness. Major commitments, whether they are in the form of intimate friendship or marriage, need to be worked at consistently. We talk of "cultivating" a relationship. Perhaps the agricultural image is appropriate: one need only observe the difference between the fruit of an apple tree that has been tended to and the fruit of one that has been neglected.

Gerda and Tim finally woke up to the realization that, in many ways, they had drifted apart. They found that their taken-for-granted marriage needed "reinvention," and they found this task to be a great deal of work. They envied the Slominskis, who continued to work at their relationship. For instance, the Slominskis would, on occasion, take a weekend off and go away together—away from friends, away from distractions—just to enjoy each other's company, work out their problems, and make plans together. The Slominskis' behavior had seemed overly romantic to Gerda and Tim, but now that they were in crisis, they had second thoughts about that "romanticism."

Complete the following sentences.

1. Here are the ways in which I am thoughtful in my closest relationship:

_____

_____

_____

2. Here are the ways in which I am thoughtless in my closest relationship:

_____

_____

_____

_____

3. I work hardest on my relationship with _____ . Here are some of the ways in which I work at this relationship:

_____

_____

_____

_____

The Ability to Be Committed to Another Person without Being Possessive

Interdependence allows both parties in a relationship to grow and develop in individual ways. Some people feel threatened when their partners develop new friendships, especially with members of the opposite sex. Some people become jealous of their partners' careers or their involvement in voluntary associations. "We love each other" doesn't mean "We own each other." It's much better to foresee problems in this area rather than handle problems that have been developing over a period of time.

Ingrid and Sal knew that the intensity of their courtship was probably covering up some issues that would eventually affect their relationship. When they discussed the ways in which intimacy and commitment can be contaminated by possessiveness, they found that they were much more prone to jealousy than they had imagined. They decided that they needed to "clear the air" every so often with respect to the issues of possessiveness and jealousy. This included making some initial decisions with respect to the amount of time they spent together, their relationships with each other's friends, their investment in school and work, and so forth.

1. Pick one or two of your relationships and describe the ways in which you concretely contribute to the other person's freedom to be different and to develop.

_____

_____

_____

_____

_____

_____

_____

_____

2. Describe the ways in which you can become possessive if you fail to check yourself.

_____

_____

_____

_____

_____

_____

The Ability to Develop Self-knowledge

It's very difficult to deal with people who lack self-knowledge: "We all told him more or less the same thing, but he kept saying 'I don't know what you're talking about.'" The ability to listen to reasonable confrontation and criticism from others can be the beginning of self-knowledge, and, as the philosophers say, self-knowledge is the beginning of wisdom.

Even in his relationships with his closest friends, Casper was sarcastic and cynical. He saw himself as a very witty person. He discounted negative feedback, because he thought it was offered out of envy; however, it was difficult for him to ignore the fact that people began to avoid him.

Check with two or three of your closest friends or intimates (including members of your family, if you wish) to find out whether they think you have any "blind spots." Remember, you might be unaware of your good points as well as your bad points.

1. Here's what I learned about my good points:

_____

_____

_____

_____

_____

2. Here's what I learned about areas of my behavior that need improvement:

_____

_____

_____

_____

_____

_____

The Ability to Understand and Appreciate Conflicting Cultural Backgrounds

The cultural factors to which we refer include family, style, ethnic background, religious upbringing, locale, social status or class, and so forth. Many of us are almost completely unaware of the cultural and subcultural "blueprints" that abound in life, and, as a result, we trip over them in our relationships.

Katie projected her own cultural stereotypes onto Bud. He seemed warm and friendly, but when she got closer to him, she perceived what she considered to be "rigidities" in his personality. Finally, she realized that she was relating to a young man who had a great deal of highly religious and close-knit family-oriented rural Midwest in his background. Her ignorance of his cultural roots had prevented her from really knowing him. She had projected her own cultural background onto him.

1. List some of the cultural blueprints that affect the attitudes and behavior of two of your closest friends.

Friend #1: _____

_____

_____

_____

Friend #2: _____

_____

_____

_____

2. Check out your perceptions with these friends and ask them to discuss the cultural blueprints that are most influential in their lives.

The Ability to Expect and Deal with Conflicts and Disagreements

Most people in committed relationships have an occasional fight. Since some degree of fighting is universal, many psychologists believe that couples should learn how to "fight fairly." In some individuals, anger is an emotion that is in overabundant supply, always lurking below the surface. Some people express their anger in a variety of unsubtle and unproductive ways. Still others see anger as a normal emotion of human life; they don't revel in it, nor do they apologize when it surfaces.

Write a short paragraph describing your style in handling conflicts and disagreements with people who are closest to you.

_____

_____

_____

_____

_____

_____

_____

_____

We ask you to examine the ways in which you relate in these areas of competence, because one of the best predictors of your future performance is your present performance. Before you commit yourself to a relationship, you should ask yourself the following questions:

△ Have I developed the competencies discussed in this chapter?
△ Has my partner developed these competencies?
△ Do we bring these competencies to bear in our relationship?

Family: Broadening Your Commitment to Responsiveness and Responsibility

The family can be thought of as an important type of *human system*. A human system is a group to which individuals belong, by which their lives are affected, and in the context of which they move through stages and cope with crises. Ernest Andrews (1974) offers the following illustration of the family as a human system:

One might construct a physical model of [the family] by using paper clips to represent each family member and connecting rubber bands to represent the relationships [between them]. . . . Plucking any of the rubber bands will reverberate the entire model. Similarly, any action or reaction pattern between any two family members will resonate throughout the entire family [p. 8].

The decision to create a family—to extend your mutual commitment to include children—is a decision to transform a two-person system into a larger system. The children who become a part of your family system will affect you and your spouse; the quality of the relationship between you and your spouse will affect the development of those children. You aren't free to choose whether your children will affect your marital relationship—they will. Your children aren't free to choose whether your marital relationship will affect them—it will. In fact, many experts on child development and family life argue that the most important factor in the healthy development of a child is a positive relationship between his or her parents. This position was expressed by a clergyman who said "The most important thing that a father can do for his children is to love their mother."

The commitment to family life involves a decision to extend your responsiveness and responsibility to other people. It also can be thought of as a commitment to create a more complex human system. We have stressed the demands and great complexity of family life; these are real indeed, but so are the deep rewards of caring and being cared for in a loving family. Such a family often becomes the social and emotional axis around which its members' lives revolve.

Perhaps you've read articles suggesting that the family is in trouble, that it is disappearing, that other arrangements are rapidly taking its place, and so forth. In *Here To Stay*, Bane (1976) examines the evidence related to the family. Although the family is undergoing significant transformations because of a host of rapid changes in our society, the evidence points to the fact that it is here to stay. Before you and your partner establish a family, however, you should examine the significant ways in which your family would differ from the kinds of families from which both of you have come.

Systematic Self-Assessment: Love, Marriage, and Family

1. Refer to Figure 9-1 (The Levels of Interpersonal Living). Reflect for a moment on your own interpersonal life. Using the form provided here, write a brief description of the current level of the relationships in your life. Here are two students' responses to this task:

The Levels of Interpersonal Living

Lack of Competence	Competence	Depth	Commitment

(Student #1) I put my check just past competence, because I feel that I'm just beginning to have the ability to relate in a basically decent way to other people. I hope to move toward deeper relationships, but I'm not there yet.

The Levels of Interpersonal Living

```
|_____|_____|_____✓_____|
Lack of              Competence          Depth        Commitment
Competence
```

(Student #2) I'd put myself out toward the commitment end. I feel like I'm on the verge of commitment in a particular relationship. It has been a deep one, but now it seems to be getting even deeper. It's scarey but very good as well.

Now do your own assessment and description.

The Levels of Interpersonal Living

```
|_____|_____|_____|
Lack of              Competence          Depth        Commitment
Competence
```

(Reasons) _____

_____

_____

_____

_____

2. Write a brief paragraph in response to each of the following phrases.

a. For me, a love relationship _____

_____

_____

_____

_____

b. For me, a good marriage_____

_____

_____

_____

_____

_____

c. For me, a good family life _____

_____

_____

_____

_____

3. Ask someone who is close to you to respond to the same phrases. Compare your responses, discussing similarities and differences. If you are in love, contemplating marriage, or married, we suggest that you do the exercise with your partner.

Key Settings and Love, Marriage, and Family

What settings in your life affect your capacity to form the types of committed relationships discussed in this chapter? Using the form provided, name two such settings and briefly describe the effects they seem to be having.

One student wrote the following paragraph in response to this task:

> I don't think my own family life is the best preparation for marriage, except maybe as a warning. My parents don't seem to relate much to each other at all. My father travels a lot, and both of them seem happiest when they are apart. My mother brightens up when he goes. When he comes home, there are no real greetings, no sign of any kind of joy in reunion. It's all so bland that it makes me hesitate to get too close to any of the guys I go out with. Home isn't a turbulent place; it's just a dead place. I heard someone describe marriage as one year of flames and forty years of ashes. I don't want that!

She also wrote of a setting that provided more hope for her:

> Following a psychology course in interpersonal relations last year, six of us decided to keep meeting. The prof called these kinds

of groups "life-style" groups. We try to continue to use the skills we learned to provide some challenge and support for one another. We talk about a lot of the issues in this book—friendship and intimacy, how we feel about ourselves, our values and what we're doing about them, religion, dating, our dreams, possible careers, all sorts of things. I think we're good friends and intimates. We care quite a bit about one another. It's a mixed group. Peg and Jerry have become more deeply involved. If I fall in love and get married, I want it to grow out of the kind of deep relationship we experience with one another in the group. The difference between this group and what I experience in my family is like night and day.

Key-Settings Assessment

Setting: _____

Effects: _____

_____

_____

_____

_____

_____

_____

_____

_____

_____

Setting: _____

Effects: _____

_____

_____

_____

_____

_____

_____

_____

_____

_____

_____

_____

Structured Group Interaction: Love, Marriage, and Family

Step 1. Share one thing in this chapter that had particular meaning for you. Why did this item strike you?

Step 2. Share your assessment of the level of interpersonal living which you feel you have reached. Describe the behavior, the successes, and the failures in relating on which you base your estimate.

Step 3. Share one example of positive or negative effects of a key setting on your capacity to form love, marriage, or family commitments.

Action Plan: Creating Committed Relationships

1. On the basis of your reading and thinking in this chapter, answer the following questions:

How does the way in which you relate to other people facilitate your development of committed relationships?

_____

_____

_____

_____

_____

_____

How does the way in which you relate to other people hinder your development of committed relationships?

_____

_____

_____

_____

_____

_____

2. Write down a list of potential resources for you in developing your capacity to form committed relationships:

_____

3. Using your list of resources, develop a set of action steps to help you move toward your goal.

Summary

In this chapter, we focused on commitments in interpersonal living, especially love, marriage, and family life. We invited you to reflect on the committed relationships in your life at the moment, presented concepts regarding the levels of commitment in interpersonal living, and asked you to engage in a structured self-assessment. Finally, we asked you to take part in a structured group interaction and complete an action plan related to these themes.

In the next chapter, we turn our attention to another major life challenge—the choice of a career.

10

Work/Career Choice
as a Process

The purpose of this chapter is to sensitize you to a number of work/career decision-making issues. The material in this chapter shouldn't be seen as a substitute for more formal career-counseling processes. In this chapter, we examine the challenge of making decisions regarding your work/career. We begin with an exercise designed to help you think specifically about the issue of career choice. Then we present a basic model that sheds light on the initial phases of career development and ask that you reflect on it with respect to your own career development. Finally, we ask you to take part in a structured group interaction that focuses on career development and to complete a self-directed action plan.

Personal-Reflection Exercise: Career Development—Where Do I Stand?

1. Complete the following sentence by writing a brief paragraph.

This is what I mean by choosing a career: _____

_____

_____

_____

_____

2. Complete the following sentence by drawing up a list.

I've considered the following occupations: _____

_____

_____

_____

_____

3. Complete the following sentence by writing a brief paragraph.

My ideal career _____

_____

_____

_____

_____

_____

Work/Career Choice: Phases in a Process

The following is part of a conversation overheard on a train somewhere in the Midwest. Two strangers were talking. One man described himself this way:

> I never did develop any special abilities. So now I'm a salesman. I almost said "just a salesman." It's really all I know how to do. I guess I don't really like it—all the travel and that—but I make a buck at it. It's all that I have now.

This man expressed some degree of career dissatisfaction. He also felt locked in, as though there was nothing he could do about his situation. How can you avoid making a similar statement twenty years from now?

Many people think that an initial work/career choice is made at one moment in time—that at some point you simply "make up your mind." Such thinking has two major negative effects: (1) it tends to make an initial career choice more anxiety provoking than it should be, and (2) it ignores a process (or series of steps) that leads to initial career decisions. We now invite you to reflect on this process.

Another important issue concerns the distinction between "work" and "career." Many people view their occupations as jobs, as means of financing things of more importance to them. Other people are inclined to think of their occupations in terms of professional career development. Whether you tend to think in terms of work or career, you will spend a significant portion of your adult life "on the job." The information and exercises contained in this chapter are intended to enhance your freedom to make your work or career a constructive experience as well as a means of survival.

Career development can involve an initial census of career possibilities, followed by a four-phase process. First, a word about the initial census. Many people fail to seek out certain kinds of jobs because they don't even know that they exist. One function of school-based career-development programs is to give students a view of the occupational possibilities available to them. For instance, when they think of the field of medicine, most people immediately think of doctors and nurses but are unaware of the literally dozens of different kinds of jobs available in that field. Most people know relatively little about such jobs, since they don't learn about them in the ordinary course of studies offered in high schools and colleges. We believe that students should be made aware of a very wide spectrum of occupations, especially those that are relatively new, _before they graduate from high school._ This will help them to decide whether they should go to college or attend a technical or occupation-specific school or program. If you weren't made aware of career possibilities during your high school years, then we believe that you should become aware of them early in your college career—that is, if you don't want to be locked into the traditional career choices suggested by ordinary school curricula.

The four-phase career-development process involves two basic types of "movement"—expanding and narrowing. Through the expanding movement, you broaden your horizons by considering a wide variety of options and alternatives. In the narrowing movement, you contract your focus and eliminate some alternatives in favor of more promising ones.

Figure 10-1 represents Phase 1 in the initial career-choice process.

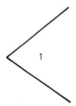

FIGURE 10-1. Phase 1 in the initial career-choice process.

In Phase 1, you consider various fields of study as possibilities. This phase usually occurs at the end of high school and the beginning of college. This is a time during which you experience and consider the "fit" between various courses of study and your interests, aptitudes, and values. Concretely, this phase usually involves taking introductory courses in a variety of areas in the physical and social sciences and the humanities. One student described her experience of this phase in these words:

> I found myself shifting between really different ways of looking at the world during this time. What went on in biology lab was worlds apart from my English Lit. survey, and psychology and economics also seemed removed—on a different plane. It felt like there was no pattern to what I was getting, just a variety of interesting looks at things. I couldn't begin to pick one at that point. It would have been a real stab in the dark.

Figure 10-2 includes the second phase of the initial career-choice process.

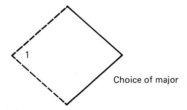

FIGURE 10-2. Phase 2 in the initial career-choice process.

This phase involves a process of narrowing, of selecting an area of study based on the exploration you carried out in Phase 1. Your task during Phase 2 is to select a major field of study.

Having examined the fit or lack of fit between your interests, aptitudes, and values and various courses of study, you are now forced (in a very real sense) to choose one course of study. This is one of the key choice points in the history of your career. Having gone through a particular door, you will find that, as time goes on, it will become both more difficult and more expensive to reverse this choice and to set out in an entirely new direction. No doubt, this is why the choice of a major has a certain aura of urgency about it.

Having said this, we must add that the choice of a major doesn't necessarily dictate the choice of a career. In many fields, there are a variety of functions that are performed by people who have pursued similar courses of study. The choice of a major tends to move a career in one direction rather than another. In fields that require a high degree of specialization (such as nursing), the choice of a major can effectively eliminate other possibilities, since there is little room in the curriculum for other kinds of course work. To summarize, the choice of a major—the end point of Phase 2 in our model—represents an *important* choice, but not a *final* one. It is one more phase in an ongoing process. One of our students described his experience of this phase in the following words:

> Toward the middle of sophomore year, the pressure was on. According to college policy, I had to declare a major during second semester. A lot of things came up that I guess I'd been avoiding. Part of me has always loved literature, and teaching has been somewhere in the back of my mind. On the other hand, I've done well in business courses and the job market looks better for business majors. I had pretty well decided against the sciences or math as a major. Just the two were left. A double major was possible, but I was afraid that might lead to a sloppy job with both. Anyway, the choice couldn't be put off any longer.

Figure 10-3 includes the third phase of the initial career-choice process.

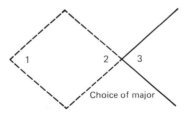

FIGURE 10-3. Phase 3 in the initial career-choice process.

This phase involves another process of expanding. Having selected a major field of study, you need to explore the various career possibilities that exist for someone with a background in that area. Once again, you need to test the fit between various career possibilities within a particular field and your interests, aptitudes, and values. As you pursue advanced course work in a major area, you will be exposed to theory, research, and (in many cases) applications of knowledge to actual situations. Your reactions to this exposure can tell you a good deal about your aptitudes and preferences. Moreover, you can test the fit between yourself and various career possibilities by taking part in an internship or work experience in the field you are considering. The difference between learning in the classroom and applying knowledge to life situations can be staggering. Many colleges and universities have recognized this fact and are designing internships and field placements for their major curricula. In some cases, however, you may need to seek out career-related experiences on your own initiative. One student described his experience of this third phase in these words:

> I was extremely interested in psychology. It was my major, and the course work had been really involving. I began to realize that, while studying the stuff was interesting, that didn't mean that I'd like a career in it. Also, psychologists do a lot of different things—research, therapy, consulting, teaching. Psych majors seem to have a lot of opportunities other than psychology. So I got a part-time job on the psychiatric unit of a hospital and learned an awful lot about the difference between theories of personality and actually helping somebody.

Figure 10-4 includes the fourth and final phase of the initial career-choice process.

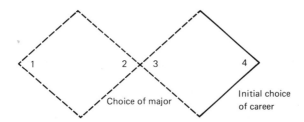

FIGURE 10-4. Phase 4 in the initial career-choice process.

This phase involves another narrowing process, in which you select an initial area of work specialization based on the exploration you completed in Phase 3. Your task in this phase is to make an initial career choice. This choice might lead you to seek an occupation immediately or to make arrangements for advanced education in a particular field.

Having experienced the fit or lack of fit between your interests, aptitudes, and values and various concrete occupational possibilities, you will need to choose a direction that you will pursue. This is another key choice point in the history of your career: it is often expensive in terms of energy, time, and money to change major career decisions. As we've noted, the choice of a major area of study often has a certain aura of urgency about it; the initial choice of a career often seems earthshaking.

We would like to make two comments regarding the relative importance of the initial career choice. On the one hand, it is a decision of real importance that is worthy of active and serious consideration on your part. A good deal of your adult life will be affected by the satisfaction and accomplishments (or lack of them) that result from the development of your occupation. This choice, and the process that it culminates, should not be taken lightly. On the other hand, as we have stressed throughout this chapter, we are speaking here of an initial work/career choice. It is important that you put this first set of career choices in a long-term perspective. You aren't deciding once and for all what you will be doing with your life 30, 15, or even 5 years from now. Rather, you are setting out in a particular direction, and you will continue, through a process of expanding and narrowing, to create a career path for yourself over the years. The initial career-development process that faces you during these years of moving into adulthood doesn't lead to a final decision regarding your career, but it does lead to the first in a series of decisions.

The Four-Phase Model of the Initial Work/Career Choice: Process or Tool?

In one sense, the four phases in the initial career-choice process that we have described can be thought of as parts of a natural process that we all go through as a result of the structure of our society's educational and economic institutions. In other words, as a student and a member of our society, you need to:

1. take courses in a variety of fields,
2. choose an area of major study,
3. consider career alternatives, and
4. make an initial career choice.

We present this model of career choice with the hope that you will use it as a tool in directing yourself more effectively with respect to your initial career choice. We don't mean to imply that all college students follow this model carefully, or that it is absolutely necessary to follow it in order to get a good job. Some people go through junior college or college because they feel that they should or because their parents feel they should. They choose majors haphazardly without trying to relate their choices to future career decisions. Furthermore, some people give relatively little thought to the kind of job they would like, and, as a result, they fail to make an initial career choice. They get involved in college life and don't give too much thought to what lies beyond it. We know people like that who have found good jobs in fields that are unrelated to their college majors.

It is also true that many companies provide on-the-job training. They hire people who have certain basic competencies and motivation, and provide job-specific education and training for them. To be absolutely truthful, although the companies might hire college graduates, many of these jobs don't require a college education. Some career counselors suggest that, if a high school graduate wants to go to college only to become eligible for a good job, he or she should rethink such a decision, take a careful look at job statistics, and determine whether a college education will significantly increase the chances of getting a good job. Obviously, there are other reasons for going to college—reasons that relate to the other developmental challenges we are considering.

We feel that students who take a systematic approach to career orientation and development increase the probability of finding career satisfaction. The decision-making process doesn't work magic, but it does help people to develop a sense of self-direction.

Initial Career Choice: Two Possible Pitfalls

The logic of the four-phase (expanding-narrowing-expanding-narrowing) model of initial career choice points to two major pitfalls to be avoided as you move through this process. The first pitfall involves a failure to expand adequately. If you attempt to narrow too rapidly, without actively considering a variety of possibilities, your choice of a major or initial career direction could prove unsatisfactory. In order to narrow effectively, you must have a sufficient number of options from which to choose; otherwise, you might neglect possibilities that could be very fruitful.

The second possible pitfall involves the failure to narrow. In the model we presented, there are two points at which you must stop developing alternative possibilities and make a choice. Individuals who find themselves "circling," continually seeing new prospects from new perspectives, tend to make impulsive and unsatisfactory choices.

An adequate balance between exploring alternatives (expanding) and choosing from among them (narrowing) leaves you open to new information and alternatives, but it doesn't paralyze your ability to act. As we noted earlier, the process of expanding and narrowing is one in which you will engage throughout your life. You can make the process work for you by using it to help yourself fashion the career you desire.

A Systems Perspective of Career Choice

The initial choices you make with respect to either a course of study or an occupation are influenced by the systems we discussed in Chapter 1. We will review some of these systems with respect to their impact on the process of choosing a career. These systems can influence your choices subtly or blatantly. They can provide opportunities for or set limits on what you would like to do. Try to discover both positive and negative influences in the settings you examine.

Level I: Personal Systems

As we've pointed out, personal systems are the immediate settings of your life, such as your family, peer group, church groups, and the like.

Family. One or perhaps both of your parents work. Maybe you have older siblings who have jobs. Naturally, you get some feeling for the occupations in which your family members are involved. Your father or mother might have some expectations regarding your future. These expectations might be subtle and unstated, or they might be clearly enunciated. Conversely, you might see your father or mother as a model. The workers in your family might like their jobs, be indifferent to them, or hate them. In one way or another, their attitudes toward work and toward their particular occupations are communicated to you.

Conrad's father is a doctor; he is away from home most of the time. He sees his job as a vocation, not merely an occupation or a profession. When he talks to Conrad, he tells him to forget medicine unless he's willing to dedicate his life to it. He expresses contempt for doctors who see their profession as a lucrative occupation. He pushes himself and those who work with him. Conrad feels very ambivalent toward his pre-med studies.

Lorrie's mother likes to describe herself as a housewife. She prides herself on her traditionalism and wants nothing to do with the women's movement. She never did think that college was necessary for Lorrie. She hopes that her daughter won't become involved in a career. Lorrie feels that she can't talk about her career expectations at home.

Jobs. Perhaps you have had a number of part-time jobs. These provide your first experiences in the world of work. Whether the jobs were uplifting or depressing, they have probably influenced your attitudes toward work.

Sheila has a part-time job as a salesperson in the household-wares section of a large department store. Her supervisor is a personable middle-aged woman who provides a great deal of direction and support. Sheila's coworkers are industrious and friendly. She enjoys going to work. She's interested in a career in social work, but she has learned that working as a salesperson need not be the depressing experience that some of her friends said it would be. She believes that she is learning about human nature through her relationships with her supervisor, her coworkers, and the steady stream of customers. She has learned to deal with various kinds of people.

Review the personal settings in your life—your family, friendship groups, jobs, peer groups, classrooms, extracurricular groups, clubs, and so on—and write a paragraph explaining the ways in which you think you have been influenced by one or more of these settings in terms of your career choice. How have these settings influenced your attitudes toward work and your feelings about certain occupations?

_____
_____
_____
_____
_____
_____
_____
_____
_____
_____
_____
_____

Level II: The Network of Personal Settings

Since you belong to a variety of personal settings, you serve as a linking pin. The effects of these settings with regard to the process of choosing a career can be positive, negative, or neutral.

Positive effects: Family/school interaction. Theus' father is a manager in a large business firm. He likes his work and is interested in the new approaches to management coming from the behavioral sciences. Theus' major is business; his minor is psychology. When his management prof discussed approaches to management, Theus saw how the principles of behavior he is learning in his psychology courses relate to these new methodologies. Now he and his father have exciting discussions about careers in management and management consultation. In this case, two settings—family and school—cooperate in reinforcing Theus' initial career choices. He is very stimulated in his work, and he feels quite fortunate.

Negative effects: Job/school interaction. Lisa, a psychology major, has a part-time job as a ward attendant in a nearby hospital. Due to her practical and experience-based courses in counseling and the applications of the principles of learning, she is excited about a career in psychology. In the literature and in the classroom, the field appears to be exciting. At the hospital, however, she encounters people who see what they are doing as just a job. She is disturbed by the fact that the professional staff—especially the doctors and psychologists—do not seem to be excited about what they are doing. They don't seem to know about or use the approaches to helping that she is being exposed to at school. A disturbing number of the professional staff seem to be "burned out." She is torn and confused by the excitement of one setting and the depressing character of the other.

Neutral effects: Peer/church interaction. Jeff's family participates in modest ways in their local church. Jeff has belonged to the church youth group for a few years now, and he is being influenced a great deal by the church's youth minister. At school, Jeff has a group of peers with whom he associates. He decides that he might be interested in a career in professional ministry. When his peers at school learn of his plans, they neither encourage nor discourage him. They do not influence his decision one way or the other.

Write a paragraph explaining the ways in which your career-related attitudes and decisions have been or are presently being influenced by the settings in your life.

_____

_____

_____

_____

_____

_____

_____

_____

_____

_____

Level III: The Larger Organizations and Institutions of Society

Large organizations and institutions can either facilitate or stand in the way of your pursuit of a career. You might find that a particular field is overcrowded and that many people are looking for jobs or have already settled for jobs in some other field. Perhaps your ability in this field is outstanding and will move you toward the head of the employment line. The point is, however, that the environment sets limitations on the development of careers, and you should be aware of these limitations. Economic systems, professional organizations, governmental agencies, the changing policies of educational institutions, popular fads, and a host of other realities will affect the choice and development of your career.

Louise decides that she wants to pursue a career in hospital administration. Right now, she is finishing her third year in nursing school. There is concern nationwide regarding the cost of health care. Many people want to impose a moratorium on the construction and expansion of hospitals. Louise learns about this and begins to gather information concerning job prospects for hospital administrators. She works through the college career counseling center and gathers information from organizations such as the American Medical Association. She interviews one of the administrators at the hospital where she is receiving training. When she puts the whole picture together with the help of one of the counselors in the career center, she decides to finish her nursing degree and get a job as a nurse for a few years. She knows that jobs for nurses are plentiful. Eventually, she decides that she won't enter a graduate program in hospital administration. She plans to reassess her decisions after working a few years as a nurse.

Write several paragraphs explaining the ways in which larger organizations and institutions might influence your decision-making process in choosing a career. Try to answer questions such as:

△ What are the employment predictions for your chosen occupation?

△ What larger organizations or institutions might possibly affect your decision-making process?

△ How much money do you expect to make?

△ How do the media—newspapers, TV, magazines, movies—affect your decision-making process?

△ What large organization or institution might be most influential in helping you to achieve your career goals?

△ What large organization or institution might put obstacles in the way of your career goals?

△ If you have no answers for these kinds of questions, where might you find the answers?

Level IV: Culture

The various cultures and subcultures to which we belong provide unwritten "blueprints" that affect the way in which we carry out certain tasks in life. When a working-class couple declares that "no child of ours is going to grub for a living the way we have," they are talking of breaking out of cultural restrictions. When a young woman says "I have just never thought of being a doctor. I have never met a woman who is a doctor," she, too, is talking about cultural limitations, or her perception of cultural limitations. If a person says "I come from good

German peasant stock; we work well with our hands," he or she is voicing cultural expectations that are both promising and limiting. Cultural expectations and "blueprints" change over the years, but they constantly influence our decisions.

By developing a working knowledge of the cultural influences in your life, you can make informed decisions. You will never be free of your culture, but you can use working knowledge to help free yourself of oppressive cultural expectations. Cultural blueprints are found in the country in which you live, your ethnic and social background, your religious affiliations, and your family. All the systems of which you are a member contain cultures and subcultures that influence you. More to the point here, they influence your approach to the decision-making process. One student, Raul, felt that the following cultural influences affected his approach to his career.

North American culture. Everywhere I turn, I think I hear such things as "Be your own person," "Watch out for number one," "Make as much money as you can," and "Don't be a sucker for others." I'm thinking of a career in nursing, and, in many ways, it seems countercultural.

Sexual stereotypes. Although I know that the cultural stereotype of the male nurse is changing, a lot of eyebrows are still raised when I say I'm in nursing school. Sometimes I laugh it off and realize it's their problem, not mine, but sometimes I'm defensive and wonder whether I'm doing the right thing.

Family culture. My family has a tradition of being very enterprising business people. This actually has not been the case for the last generation. I think my family came to the States to try to reestablish this tradition. They don't say anything to me, but I think they're both proud of me because I'm making my own money and am in college. At the same time, they seem disappointed that I'm in nursing school.

In a similar way, review three systems of which you are a member and review the ways in which unwritten cultural blueprints or expectations might be influencing your decision-making process with regard to your career.

System #1. _____

_____

_____

_____

_____

_____

_____

System #2. _____

_____

System #3. _____

_____

Systematic Self-Assessment: Initial Career Choice

1. Write a brief paragraph in response to the following questions: Where would you locate yourself in the four-phase process outlined in this chapter? Why would you locate yourself there?

_____

2. List some activities you've engaged in that relate to each of the four phases of the career-choice model.

Phase 1. _____

_____
_____
_____
_____
_____

Phase 2. _____
_____
_____
_____
_____

Phase 3. _____
_____
_____
_____
_____

Phase 4. _____
_____
_____
_____
_____

3. List some activities that you *could* engage in at each of the four phases in the career-choice model.

Phase 1. _____
_____
_____
_____
_____

Phase 2. _____

_____

_____

_____

_____

_____

Phase 3. _____

_____

_____

_____

_____

_____

Phase 4. _____

_____

_____

_____

_____

_____

Structured Group Interaction: Initial Career Choice

Step 1. Discuss the following questions with the members of your group: Where do you stand regarding your initial career choice? How far along are you? How are you feeling about it?

Step 2. Share one thing that you've learned regarding career development from your work in this chapter.

Step 3. Share a description of the type of career you desire.

Action Plan: Self-Directed Career Choice

1. *Goal.* Write a brief description of an immediate goal regarding your career development. Be as concrete as possible. One student, Penny, set the following goal:

I've taken a number of basic courses in the school of business. I want to come up with an integrated set of electives. I want to decide which area of business to specialize in, and then gear my electives in some systematic way to that area. I'd like to achieve this goal by the end of the semester, before registration for next semester.

Your Goal

_____

_____

_____

_____

_____

2. *Resources.* List the settings and people that can provide resources to help you achieve your goal. Indicate what concrete help each might be able to provide. Penny described the following resource:

I belong to the school Business Club. We've had the opportunity to talk in depth with people from various management and technical areas of business. It really helped bring some things in focus for me. I now realize that the technical end of things is really closer to what I'd like to do. I don't think management is for me. At least, that's how I see it right now.

Your Resources

_____

_____

_____

_____

_____

3. *Program.* Develop a concrete set of steps to help you move toward your goal. Penny outlined these steps:

—In the next two weeks, I will attend the last two Business Club meetings dealing with areas of specialization within business— for instance, accounting, finance, and others.

—With my adviser, I will review the basic business courses I have already taken and discuss with him my interests and aptitudes.

—I will briefly interview three of my father's friends who are in different areas of the business world.

—I will take Part II of the career-counseling seminar offered by the Center for Student Development—that is three weeks from now.

—I'll do some final discussing with my dad and with people who have actually taken the courses that are on the elective list.

—The week before registration I will make my final selection of courses.

The Steps in Your Program

_____

_____

_____

_____

_____

_____

_____

_____

_____

SUMMARY

In this chapter, we focused on the challenges of an initial career choice. We invited you to reflect on your current thoughts and goals regarding your career, on a four-phase model of the process of coming to an initial career choice, and on the implications of that model for you. You were asked to assess the impact of key settings on your career development and to take part in a structured group interaction. Finally, you were encouraged to develop appropriate self-directed action steps regarding your initial career choice.

In the next chapter, we turn our attention to involvement in the community and in the larger systems of life.

11

Involvement in the Community and Society

In this chapter, we turn our attention to the challenge of involvement in the community and in the larger social systems of your world. We begin by asking you to reflect on your current understanding of the role of the community and of the larger social systems in your life. Then we present some working knowledge of these systems and ask you to reflect on your participation in them. Finally, we invite you to take part in a structured group interaction and complete an action plan.

Personal-Reflection Exercise: Social Involvement

1. In the space provided, explain what comes to your mind in association with the term *community member*. Concentrate on your personal reflections and feelings.

_____

_____

_____

_____

_____

_____

_____

2. In the space provided, explain what comes to your mind in association with the term *citizen*. Concentrate on your personal reflections and feelings.

_____

_____

_____

_____

_____

_____

_____

3. List the social organizations and institutions that will probably have an important influence on you and your family (after you marry) in the years to come.

_____

_____

_____

_____

_____

_____

_____

4. Complete the following sentence:

When I think of my chances of having an influence on society by becoming involved with my neighborhood, community, local government, church, school, state or national government, and similar social systems,

_____

_____

_____

The World beyond Personal Settings

In this chapter, we would like to present some concepts that can help you to reflect on the ways in which you want to invest yourself in the human systems that lie beyond the immediate social settings of marriage, family, friends, intimates, and workplace. You are and will be both community member and citizen, even though you might reflect very little on those roles. You might even say "I've got enough on my hands trying to do something about developmental challenges without thinking about what kind of a community member or what kind of a citizen I am." On the other hand, you might be investing a great deal of yourself in your school and your community. Perhaps your overall goal is to live contentedly in the world. Or maybe you feel a sense of mission in having a positive impact on society. Consider these various positions and your reactions to them.

An Appreciation of Context

Earlier we mentioned that the word _developmental_ conveys the notion of increasing complexity. For instance, you now juggle more complicated developmental tasks than you did earlier in life. We believe that your complete development includes the ability to place yourself, both conceptually and behaviorally, in successively wider contexts in life. When you were a child, the world revolved around your family. As you grew up, you discovered the world of your neighborhood, your school, and your town. (Perhaps you've traveled to or lived in other parts of the country or in foreign countries and have found that, because of that experience, you have a less provincial view of the world.)

McLuhan (1964) claims that newspapers, magazines, radio, movies, and television have turned the world into a "global village." Because of the mass media, you have an opportunity to know more about the world than your forebears did. Moreover, when something of importance happens anywhere in the world, you can learn about it almost instantly. You have the somewhat questionable opportunity of watching wars on your television screen. The news media, as you know, can give you a distorted picture of the world, but they also can present its realities. Through the media, the world, with its wonders and horrors, is at our fingertips.

Since you are bombarded with images of the world, you have a task that earlier generations did not have to face, at least not with the same intensity. You need to ask yourself how the world relates to you and how you relate to it—your task is to "put yourself in context." For instance, the position of a middle-class North American college student is somewhat extraordinary when placed in context. If we were to arrange all the people in the world in a pyramid, with the "have-nots" at the bottom and the "haves" at the top, you would find yourself near the top of the pyramid. Your place in the economic world is not an ordinary one. The task of developing a world view and deciding how you want to respond to this view is a lifelong task. In this chapter, we begin by presenting some working knowledge of community and what it means to be a member of a community.

What Does *Community* Mean?

Sociologists have pointed out important differences in the types of human systems in which we spend our lives. One type of system, the *primary group*, is characterized by emotional bonds, unspoken expectations, broad involvement of members in one another's lives, and loyalty to members, even when their behavior is "out of line." The family is the classic example of a primary group. In our society, the nuclear family has primary responsibility for the social and emotional development and sustenance of its members. It is the key human system—the crucial locus of developmental challenge and support.

Perhaps the most tragic failure of our social systems can be seen in the lives of those whose experience in their primary group was a destructive one. In the words of Erikson (1958), "There is nothing so terrible as the mutilation of the spirit of a child" (p. 255). The spirit of a husband or wife can be similarly affected by membership in an ill-functioning primary group.

Your capacity to love is initially shaped in your primary group. This shaping can affect your ability to form meaningful and decent relationships throughout your life. Fortunately, the effects of shaping are subject to change through development, education, training, counseling, and psychotherapy.

The second major type of human system, the *associational group*, is characterized by nonemotional relationships, specific expectations regarding performance, narrow involvement of members in one another's lives, and loyalty based on continued performance of duties. The workplace is the classic example of an associational group. Other examples include neighborhood councils, parent/teacher associations, political parties, and classrooms. In our society, the associational group has primary responsibility for the socialization of adults. In the associational group, your capacity to work competently and with a sense of meaning is either nurtured or destroyed. Events that take place in associational groups have a profound effect on the entire fabric of your life.

It has been said that the productive human being is one who is capable of love and work. If the primary group nurtures your capacity to love and the associational group strengthens your ability to work, what is the role of the social form known as *community?* Whitehead (1978) describes the basic function of communities:

> Some communities will incorporate several elements and expectations of primary groups; other communities will manifest some of the concerns and more formal patterns of (associational) life. All, however, meet the requirement of community—that is, they are social settings beyond the family in which group members can experience themselves . . . more completely and authentically, apart from the sometimes restricting prescriptions of their social roles [p. 388].

In other words, community combines the characteristics of the primary group with those of the associational group. A social system that functions as a community is one that draws on and supports its members' capacities to love *and* to work; it helps them to return to the primary and associational groups of their lives with renewed energy.

Community that characterizes a functioning family or friendship group differs in many ways from community in a corporate system or in a classroom. A group of neighbors working together on an area-improvement project experience community in a way that differs from the experience of a cohesive self-help group for alcoholics. Moreover, the specific forms of community vary according to cultural and ethnic background. The important issue here is the presence of a sense of community in people's lives, not the particular forms of a community's interactions.

Some Reflections on Being a Citizen

Webster's Collegiate Dictionary defines the term *citizen* as "a native or naturalized person who owes allegiance to a government and is entitled to reciprocal protection from it." Being a citizen is a legal reality. *Citizenship* is defined as "the status of being a citizen," but the same dictionary suggests that it means "the quality of an individual's response to membership in a community." If "being a good citizen" involves contributing to the common good, then there are many different ways of manifesting "quality responses" to the challenge of being a citizen. For instance, a person who obeys the laws of a society could be considered a good citizen. A teacher contributes to the common good by educating students and instilling respect for their fellow citizens. Since there are many ways in which people can contribute to the common good, there are many ways in which they can express quality citizenship. We are going to consider citizenship from the viewpoint of direct or indirect participation in governmental or political processes.

The Degrees of Citizenship

Since we are going to restrict ourselves to a discussion of participation in governmental and political processes, we can refer to degrees of citizenship, or degrees of participation. We will use an adaptation of a schema first offered by Robert Carkhuff (1974) to assess degrees of participation.

Detractors. Detractors are people whose behavior tends to impede the work of a group. They keep the other members of the group from achieving their goals. People who disobey laws, disrupt public order, and attempt to subvert legitimately functioning governments are, in terms of citizenship, detractors. People who fight for their own and others' legitimate rights under an oppressive government are seen as detractors from the government's point of view, but others might see them as excellent citizens (perhaps even heroes). Notice that this category—detractor—admits of degrees (this also is true of the categories to follow). For instance, a person who is a scofflaw in terms of parking violations is a relatively mild, though annoying, detractor when compared to members of organized crime who run "juice" rackets, commit murder, and so on. Detractors tend to place heavy demands on a government's resources in terms of police, investigative units, regulatory agencies, and courts. Therefore, the fact that a detractor votes does not remove him or her from this category.

Mere members. This refers to citizens who pay little or no attention to what is happening in terms of the governance of their ward, town, county, state, or country. Such individuals might be good citizens in that they pay their taxes, generally obey laws, and even contribute in some ways to the common good, but they show little interest in governmental or political processes. They don't vote, nor are they informed of what is happening in the world of government or politics. From the mere members' perspective, government and politics take care of themselves. They may gripe at times about government service or policies, but they do not have well-formed political opinions.

Observers. Observers are aware of what is happening in the world of government and politics, but that is where their involvement ends. They watch the news on television, read newspapers and magazines, and discuss issues that relate to government and politics, but, for whatever reason, they do not vote, write letters to their congressmen or congresswomen, or belong to political parties or associations related to politics and better government. They have relatively well-formed political opinions, but they contribute nothing to the cause of good government.

Participants. Participants not only keep themselves informed of what is happening in government and politics but they also take some steps toward active participation. For instance, they vote, especially when encouraged to do so. Or they might send a small campaign contribution to a political candidate. They are more than mere members or observers. Many people think of participants as "ordinary citizens." They sign petitions if they agree with the issue, but they do not work to gather signatures. They register to vote, and they think that it's important to vote, but they don't help to register other people. Their active contributions to government and political processes are minimal.

Contributors. Contributors take *initiative.* They see to it that they are informed in the areas of government and politics, and they volunteer their services in these areas. They register and vote without being asked to do so, and they willingly work in projects such as voter-registration drives. They send donations to organizations such as Common Cause, and they're ready to work for those organizations. They write to members of Congress, and they encourage others to do so. Their citizenship includes direct involvement in civic processes. There are degrees among contributors. Government-related or politics-related activities are the major avocations of some contributors.

Leaders. Government and politics are the central life values of leaders; their careers focus on these activities. Many of these people enter government-related jobs. They might become civil servants and work in the diplomatic corps, or they might work for a political party or a government agency. For better or worse, leaders have an impact on government and its effectiveness. There are degrees of leadership. At one end of the continuum are those who form policies and make decisions. At the other end of the continuum are those who implement policies and carry out decisions.

Remember that we are talking about the degree of involvement in political and civic processes, not contributions to the common good. It goes without saying that political leaders can be self-serving. Lobbying is a major political activity on the part of special-interest groups, some of which contribute little or nothing to the common good; however, these special-interest groups are deeply involved in the political process. Politics involves both ideology and power. Some people espouse a certain political party because they are attracted by the values and ideology of that party. Some people enter politics because they are interested in power and social influence. Political activity can be self-serving and venal, because people can be self-serving and venal. People who avoid participation in political processes—whether as participants, contributors, or leaders—do not thereby solve the problem of political venality—perhaps they contribute to it.

These categories can help you to assess your participation in the communities of your life. When used this way, they refer to the degree as well as the quality of your participation. In the following exercise, you are asked to apply these categories to both community living and political involvement.

An Exercise in Self-Assessment: Participation in Community and Political Life

1. *Community*. Make a list of the communities to which you belong—family, church, neighborhood, dormitory, clubs, school-based communities, and so forth. Then, list the community-related behaviors that apply to each category of participation. One student came up with the following remarks:

Detractor	*Mere Member*	*Observer*
I spent a lot of school-election week making fun of people running for student-government offices.	I don't cause any kind of trouble in the dorm, but I don't participate in dorm life—no parties, meetings, nothing.	I actually read the school newspaper from cover to cover every week, but it doesn't move me to do much.

Participant	*Contributor*	*Leader*
No one knows, but when Pat asked me to vote in the school elections, I did.	I worked hard in the Hunger-Day Campaign. I thought it was worthwhile.	I'm one of the ones who got the Computer Club going. I'm its president, and I'm very active.

Now see if you can make some statements that convey the quality and degree of your participation in the various forms of community in your life.

Detractor	*Mere Member*	*Observer*
_____	_____	_____
_____	_____	_____

Detractor	Mere Member	Observer
_____	_____	_____
_____	_____	_____
_____	_____	_____
_____	_____	_____
_____	_____	_____
_____	_____	_____
_____	_____	_____

Participant	Contributor	Leader
_____	_____	_____
_____	_____	_____
_____	_____	_____
_____	_____	_____
_____	_____	_____
_____	_____	_____
_____	_____	_____
_____	_____	_____

2. _Political Processes._ Complete the same exercise with respect to degree of involvement in government/politics. One student's form looked like this:

Detractor	Mere Member	Observer
I smoke pot — does that fit here?	Nothing.	I read _Time_, including the stuff on politics and foreign affairs.

Participant	Contributors	Leader
I voted in the last national elections.	I joined the Young Democrats, but I haven't gone to meetings. I don't think it counts.	Nothing.

List the behaviors that reflect your degree of participation.

Detractor	Mere Member	Observer
_____	_____	_____
_____	_____	_____
_____	_____	_____
_____	_____	_____
_____	_____	_____
_____	_____	_____
_____	_____	_____

Participant	Contributor	Leader
_____	_____	_____
_____	_____	_____
_____	_____	_____
_____	_____	_____
_____	_____	_____
_____	_____	_____
_____	_____	_____

3. Write a paragraph explaining the ways in which you would like to participate in the political life of the country now and in the future. Be as realistic as possible.

_____

_____

_____

_____

_____

_____

Social Demoralization

Social experts tell us that people in our society are losing trust in large organizations and institutions, even in traditionally respected religious organizations. The reasons for this mistrust are evident—scandals and betrayal of the public trust at the highest levels of government; bribes, payoffs, and illegal political contributions on the part of our most prestigious multinational corporations; misuse on the part of union officials of union pension funds; conspiracies to defraud the public; the discovery that students graduate from our schools without the ability to read or write effectively—and the list goes on and on.

Many individuals feel that decisions made by people in high places behind closed doors often benefit the elite more than they contribute to the common good. As a result, although people might feel satisfied with their private lives, they feel demoralized with respect to the larger social scene.

The Naiveté/Cynicism Polarity

There are two extreme ways of reacting to social systems and of assessing one's own ability to affect them. On the one hand, we find naiveté ("Everything is fine or will be fine if we just work at it"). On the other hand, we have cynicism ("Everything is rotten or hopeless, and only fools get involved"). The following statements illustrate these two positions:

Naiveté. "Our society may be changing, but the family isn't. All we need to do is reassert traditional civic and religious values such as fostering the extended family and getting back to men at work and women in the home. Most people want the family to be as it used to be."

Cynicism. "Let's face it, the traditional family is dead. An entirely different style of life is taking over. This is the age of getting what you want for yourself. Everybody's living together outside marriage. The increasing divorce rate is another sign that the family has had it."

(One problem with both these statements is that they are sociologically inaccurate. In that sense, even the cynical statement is naive.)

Naiveté. "I can't understand why politicians today are having so much trouble doing their jobs. All it takes is a desire to serve and then some hard work. Our generation of politicians is going to be a lot different from what we see now."

Cynicism. "It is pretty obvious that the system has just gotten out of hand. Everybody is on the take. Politics today is just a bunch of people pursuing their own self-interest. The common good is a meaningless concept. I think a person's best bet is to pull back from it all and take care of himself."

Naiveté. "There is nothing hopeless about this neighborhood. All we have to do is get people working together. We can readily find the resources we need if we just look around for them."

Cynicism. "This neighborhood died a long time ago. Why can't people just face that fact? The city planners scratched it from the books and they're not going to give us anything. Anyone who thinks otherwise is a fool."

Naiveté

Some people see life as a process in which individuals move from naiveté to disillusionment, demoralization, and cynicism. We feel that there is a difference between young people who haven't yet learned about the world and those who protect themselves by avoiding the facts. When we, the authors, were in primary school, we learned a great deal about such things as "the principal products of Peru" without really learning anything about Peru as a social system. Therefore, we had the tendency to imagine foreign countries as idyllic places. (Recently, newspapers reported differences of opinion among the editorial staff of *National Geographic* magazine. One editorial camp claimed that the magazine had conveyed idealized views of foreign countries, often overlooking or minimizing bitter social problems. They wanted the magazine to provide balanced portrayals of the world without becoming political.) However, there seems to come a point in a person's life when he or she can no longer blame naiveté on poor education. If you want a balanced, realistic view of the society in which you live, you must reach out for it. Some people feel that it's important to be well-informed about the world; others do not. The choice is yours.

Cynicism

Those who are cynical see no hope. They often hold those who do have some hope for society in contempt. The naive have yet to face the limitations of self, others, and social systems; the cynical feel defeated by them and withdraw into smugness and arrogance. Like naiveté, cynicism is self-protective; it provides an excuse to avoid action. The cynic pretends to know what's going on, but often is as poorly informed as the naive person. The naive person avoids the possibility of demoralization; the cynic surrenders to it while pretending to transcend it. Both stances represent immature attempts to see the world "as I want to see it" instead of seeing it as it is.

An Informed, Realistic Optimism

People needn't respond to demoralization by enduring it stoically or by trying to take flight from it through naiveté or cynicism. Somewhere between the

extremes of naiveté and cynicism, we believe there is another stance toward society, its systems, and its problems. As we noted in Chapter 8, research has shown
that young people have a good chance of overcoming loneliness and the demoraliz-
ing feelings surrounding it, because they have not yet become locked into self-
defeating attitudes. Those who are willing to do something about their loneliness
have the best chance of dispelling it. In *The Social Psychology of Organizing*,
Weick (1969) suggests that chaotic activity is better than orderly inactivity.

We suggest that an informed, realistic optimism regarding one's ability to
influence society and its systems is possible. But we feel that this optimism must
be based on people's ability to organize voluntary associations. The Superman and
Wonder Woman fantasies—one person against the forces of evil—are pleasant
myths, and they find a ready soil in North American individualism; however, the
most realistic way in which people can affect an organization is through another
organization. Unions were the workers' response to the power of management.
Ralph Nader is successful because he knows how to organize people.

Self-Assessment: Naiveté, Cynicism, Realistic Optimism

As you were reading the sections on naiveté, cynicism, and realistic optimism, you probably began to think of instances in your life in which you
experienced each of these orientations. In this exercise, we ask you to take
a closer look at these orientations as they relate to the communities to
which you belong and examine your attitudes toward large organizations
and institutions. You should identify the community or organization and
describe the way in which the particular sentiment manifested itself. One
student wrote the following:

Naiveté—school/community: I really set myself up for a lot of
grief. I came to this school really green, expecting to be greeted,
taken into groups as a friend. I thought that, with all these kids,
there would be no problem with social life. Boy, did I overidealize
this campus. I never knew that I would feel so lonely.

Cynicism—church: I see people who get involved in religion as
simpletons. I don't even want to get to know them. My prejudices
about church are enormous.

Realistic optimism—politics: I'm working in a campaign for
someone running for congress. I know that I'm just one of hundreds
of workers. But I like him because he is a bit more independent of
the party than most candidates. I don't expect him to change the
world. He might even have a hard time getting elected. But I'm
learning a lot about political processes just by doing this. I meet all
sorts of people; it's a new world for me. I think it will help me
decide what kind of commitment I'd like to make to the political
world.

In the spaces that follow, try to come up with two systems for each category.

Naiveté

System #1: _____

_____

_____

_____

_____

_____

System #2: _____

_____

_____

_____

_____

_____

Cynicism

System #1: _____

_____

_____

_____

_____

_____

System #2: _____

_____

_____

_____

_____

_____

Realistic Optimism

System #1: _____

_____

_____

_____

_____

System #2: _____

_____

_____

_____

_____

Voluntary Associations as a Vehicle of Social Development

Berger and Neuhaus (1977) suggest that the immediate settings of life, including families, churches, neighborhoods, and voluntary associations, have both a private and a public face. They look inward toward their members' needs and wants, and they act as buffers between their members and the larger organizations and institutions of life. Individuals feel "at home" in their neighborhoods, which act as buffers between people and large impersonal cities. Berger and Neuhaus feel that it is in the public interest to support and promote the development of these settings, because they provide social stability and contribute to the common good.

Voluntary Associations as Exercises in Democracy and Community

We live in a society that prides itself on its democratic values. We hope (if we avoid cynicism) that our government works as well as any form of government. Even though we might be discouraged by excessively high or inequitable taxes, unwieldy bureaucracies, the proliferation of self-interest groups, and so on, we try to remain optimistic. Since government can seem so remote at times (except perhaps when its deficiencies are exposed in the mass media), one wonders how ordinary citizens can learn to become members of a democratic society. Berger and Neuhaus suggest that individuals can do this by participating in voluntary associations that are guided by democratic principles.

Berger and Neuhaus define a voluntary association as a "body of people who have voluntarily organized themselves in pursuit of particular goals" (p. 34). In their treatment, they exclude associations that are established for economic gain. There is a variety of clubs and voluntary associations in our society—block clubs, chess clubs, French clubs, debating societies, religious clubs, and so on. See how many voluntary associations you can list.

———————————————————————

———————————————————————

———————————————————————

———————————————————————

———————————————————————

———————————————————————

———————————————————————

———————————————————————

———————————————————————

Berger and Neuhaus see voluntary associations as important "exercises in democracy." They train people, often in quite haphazard ways, to invest themselves in organizations. Members choose leaders, discuss policy, set goals, vote, and elaborate and participate in programs. Millions of people belong to such associations and "exercise democracy" through them.

We suggest that participation in these voluntary associations is an exercise in community. In other words, voluntary associations can (and often do) have both task-oriented and relationship-oriented dimensions. Members of such associations have an opportunity to experience a sense of community, of belonging to a group where they are recognized, valued, and needed as individuals. At the same time, voluntary associations are formed as a means to an end—political, recreational, or social. In order to become effective participants in such associations, members need to combine the personal, social, and task dimensions that are characteristic of communities. If you are able to participate effectively in voluntary associations at this point in your life, you will probably be able to participate in community later in your life.

The Mutual-Help Movement

The self-help movement is one striking example of an active response to the threat of social demoralization. Since helping takes place in voluntary associations of one kind or another, it is probably more accurate to refer to *the mutual-help movement*—people banding together in order to satisfy personal and social needs. Some voluntary associations focus on a specific kind of personal problem, such as drinking (Alcoholics Anonymous), gambling (Gamblers Anonymous), or emotional breakdown (Recovery Incorporated). Other associations focus on social issues. For example, Bread for the World and similar organizations deal with hunger and starvation.

People who join a particular voluntary association have a common *cause* and a common *community*. People join Alcoholics Anonymous to obtain help (the initial cause); however, eventually many members try to help others. The cause is the need or group of needs that give rise to the goals and programs of the group. For example, a host of groups have been organized in recent years to defend the environment from the effects of our highly industrialized society.

The members of voluntary associations provide challenge and support for one another. For instance, the members of Alcoholics Anonymous challenge one another to change and help one another to cope with their problems.

The *Self-Help Reporter* has listed dozens of mutual-help groups, many of which have literally hundreds of chapters or local groups throughout the country. Through the mutual-help movement, people are able to reclaim some of the functions that they have surrendered to government agencies, school systems, institutional churches, social-service agencies, and a variety of professions. Although these large organizations and institutions play an important part in people's lives, when they perform many functions, people tend to feel impotent. Just as you are working on the task of individual autonomy during this transitional phase of your life, the people who commit themselves to these associations are working on the task of social autonomy, freeing themselves from excessive dependence on social institutions. The following examples illustrate the forms this "reclaiming" is taking.

In these days of astronomical medical costs, health cooperatives are being formed. Their members not only make sure that they have adequate health insurance but they also believe that they are the primary agents in the promotion of their own health. They eat a nutritionally sound diet, exercise, avoid unnecessary stress, develop solid social/emotional lives as a way of warding off psychosomatic complaints, avoid (as far as possible) the noxious agents of a highly industrialized society, carefully monitor their intake of drugs, and obtain physical checkups periodically.

In a number of churches, lay members are reclaiming their right to minister to others. In their view—one with a great deal of theological support—many forms of ministry are not restricted to ordained or otherwise officially designated ministers. Although they do not deny that ordained ministers have special functions in the life of the church, the lay members assert their prerogative to minister. They see the church as a ministering community. They teach, care for the sick and shut-ins, give support to those in crisis, counsel, and promote the community. We know of one group of lay people who specialize in visiting the convalescing, shut-ins, and those who have recently experienced a crisis, such as the death of a spouse. They receive training in basic helping and human-relations skills and develop a working knowledge of what it means to be in crisis. They meet regularly to encourage and support one another and to obtain in-service training. They have a *cause*, and they are a *community* within the community of the local church. Some churches are making the transition to community-based ministry smoothly, whereas others are experiencing tension as lay people, ministers, and church executives struggle to redefine their roles.

Many mutual-help groups are reclaiming functions they feel were too readily handed over to mental-health professionals. People who have been unsuccessful in managing their own lives (or one dimension of their lives) are rediscovering the ability to do so in the context of mutual-help groups. Distrust exists between some professionals and the promoters of mutual-help groups. The most distrusting professionals talk about the psychological harm that can take place in these groups, and they usually cite examples. The most distrusting representatives of the mutual-help groups talk about self-serving professionals who do more harm than good, and they, too, cite examples. We believe that the mutual-help movement is strong and healthy. We feel also that professional consultation would help some of these groups to be even more effective.

We stress the importance of mutual-help groups and voluntary associations, because they provide practical, and often exciting, ways of dealing with both personal and social-developmental issues. Most people don't learn about the wide range of such groups unless they get into trouble or find that the "help" they are receiving from a professional isn't really helping. Earlier we suggested that people who are bored are usually responsible for their own boredom. Within reason, it also can be said that people who are demoralized by the failures of the institutions of society to provide the services for which they were founded are responsible for their own continued frustration. They fail to act; they fail to form or join associations that can deal with these issues. We say "within reason," because we believe that some members of society have been victims of its organizations and institutions, including its educational institutions. They don't believe that anything can be done, and they live under social conditions that inhibit the development of the kinds of mutual-help groups described here. Even so, we suggest that, in the kinds of "communities" we have been describing here, there *is* hope.

Life-Style Groups

In a mutual-help group known as a *life-style group*, people who want to invest themselves both in their own development and in one another meet weekly or biweekly to discuss their lives, their feelings about themselves, intimacy, career, community and civic involvement, their relationships to the larger world, and the values that relate to these issues. For instance, one group is composed of three married couples—one middle-aged couple with three children (ages 7 to 13), and two young couples without children—a young woman who has just received a law degree, a middle-aged single man who teaches college, and a single man in his early 30s who is presently between jobs. These people constitute a community; that is, they provide support and challenge for one another. Their weekly meetings provide a forum. Moreover, they see one another individually, work together on various projects—for instance, the young woman and the older couple help direct volunteer services at a large local nursing home—and have parties from time to time. Ellen, the lawyer, has taken a temporary position in a large law firm. The life-style group provides a forum in which she can discuss such issues as her career, how her career relates to certain human-service values, the possibilities of marriage and family life, her feelings about herself, and her religious concerns. All the members of the group have misgivings about the culture in which they live, with its emphasis on materialism, competition, individualism, and self-centered life-styles. They challenge themselves and one another concerning the ways in which they tend to "buy" cultural values without critiquing them.

By participating in the group, members can pursue and act on values that move beyond self and the personal settings of life, such as marriage, family, and friends. They discuss political issues and political involvement. They've pooled their talents to help start a food cooperative in one of the poorer sections of the city. They are interested in their own growth in terms of the developmental challenges we've considered, but they also are interested in the relationship between these challenges and the wider social world.

In a recent human-relations training group with college students, we ran across an example of what we believe to be the overprofessionalization of life. One of the students asked to see us after class. He told us about an ongoing group to which he and some of his closest friends belonged. For all practical purposes, it fit the description of what we call *a life-style group*—they discussed life issues and provided support and challenge for one another. After he finished describing the group, he said "Do you think that it's all right for us to be doing that?" He was asking professional permission to grow and develop in the context of a community! His participation in the human-relations training course helped him to sharpen the skills he needed to participate effectively in a group, but he certainly didn't need our permission to relate intimately to his peers.

Systematic Self-Assessment: Involvement in Community and Society

1. Use the scale below to assess your current level of social involvement.

Current Social Involvement

High	*Medium*	*Low*
(Spend a good deal of my time in student and community organizations.)	(Spend some time in student and community organizations.)	(Spend almost no time in student and community organizations.)

2. Now list areas of potential social involvement that are available to you.

1. _____

2. _____

3. _____

4. _____

5. _____

3. Go back through the list of potential involvements and rank them in order of their relative attractiveness to you. Consider your interests, values, and competencies.

Most attractive   1. _____

                     2. _____

                     3. _____

                     4. _____

Least attractive   5. _____

Structured Group Interaction: Social Involvement

1. Share a significant learning from the degree-of-involvement exercise. Why is that learning important to you?
2. Share one learning from the naiveté-cynicism-realistic optimism exercise. Why is that learning important to you?
3. Discuss the following issues:

△   What hope do I see for the world of larger organizations and systems?
△   What can people like me do to contribute to that world?

Structured Action Program: Social Involvement

Now that you've assessed your stance toward community and large organizations, you can use what you have learned to involve yourself in one or two action programs.

1. *Goals.* Write two concrete goals—one related to community, and the other related to large organizations and institutions, such as politics

and government. If necessary, review the problem-solving process in Chapter 3.

Community-related goal: _____

_____

_____

_____

_____

Large-systems-related goal: _____

_____

_____

_____

2. List the resources that will help you to achieve each goal.

Resources for community-related goal: _____

_____

_____

_____

_____

_____

Resources for large-systems-related goal: _____

_____

_____

_____

_____

_____

3. *Programs.* Formulate a step-by-step program for each goal.

Step-by-step program for community-related goal: _____

_____

_____

_____

Step-by-step program for large-systems-related goal: _____

_____

_____

_____

_____

_____

4. Indicate the criteria that will tell you whether you have achieved your goals.

Community-related goal criteria: _____

_____

_____

Large-systems-related goal criteria: _____

_____

_____

5. *Implementation.* What obstacles do you anticipate with regard to the execution of your programs? How do you propose to overcome them?

_____

_____

_____

_____

_____

_____

_____

_____

CHAPTER

12

Leisure: What Do I Want to Do with My Free Time?

The Definition of Leisure

The ancient Greeks saw leisure as an opportunity for personal growth and development in body, mind, and soul. The Puritans, on the other hand, considered "idle hands" to be the "devil's workshop." According to them, idleness led to sin often enough to be considered sinful in itself. To factory workers who toiled during the early days of the Industrial Revolution—12 hours per day, 6 days per week— leisure meant an escape from the routine of work. Old people might see leisure as "empty time"—time on their hands, time that must be filled somehow.

When people are asked to define the term *leisure*, they usually refer to two things: (1) freedom from work, and (2) freedom from activities that are considered socially compulsory. Leisure, then, is "free time," though "freedom from what" might differ from person to person. Admittedly, this is a somewhat negative definition, but it is almost impossible to come up with a positive definition, because "freedom from" implies "freedom to." "Freedom to" can be defined in a number of ways.

Gilbert (1978) suggests that one of the most important reasons for increasing human competence is to give people more leisure time:

> There is a word that once described the most valuable aim of any attempt to improve human competence: that word is *leisure*. In a world that puts great store by the display of activity, especially in the form of hard work, this once delightful word has lost much of its earlier meaning. Gradually, it has taken on the disreputable connotations of laziness and frivolity [p. 11].

Gilbert points out that the *Oxford English Dictionary* defines *leisure* as "an opportunity afforded by freedom from occupations." The important word here is *opportunity*.

The same dictionary provides an even more delightful definition of *leisure:* "time allowed before it is too late." Moving into adulthood is a time during which you can develop an appreciation of leisure as "opportunity" and establish self-enriching patterns of leisure activities "before it is too late." Darwin saw himself as an example of a person trying to develop leisure pursuits too late. Toward the end of his life, he said he wished that he could find some pleasure and solace in literature; however, he had spent his life in scientific pursuits and had not taken time to learn to enjoy literature.

If you are a typical member of our culture, you can expect to have a fair amount of leisure time in your life. Whether or not you see leisure time as an "opportunity" depends on the behavior patterns you establish during the moving-into-adulthood years.

Since playing—playing games, playing sports, and so forth—is such a popular form of leisure (and since there is an element of play in many leisure pursuits) we will include a brief review of play in our examination of leisure.

The Use of Leisure Time

There is something paradoxical about leisure; although it's an important part of our lives, few of us reflect very much on it. Perhaps we feel that, because we are overly rational in many areas of life, we would rather forget about rational reflection when it comes to leisure. Leisure *should* be free and spontaneous; thinking too much about it robs it of its spontaneity.

For many of us, opportunities for leisure time (whether or not we take advantage of them) are increasing. We have moved from the 6-day to the 5-day work week, and some people predict that we will move on to the 4-day work week.

> One view is that over the next few decades the amount of time that human beings are required to spend at work will decline to such an extent that a new age of leisure will be ushered in with a transformed rhythm of life which will result in people developing novel methods of using their spare time [Roberts, 1970, p. 20].*

Many workers now have an opportunity to choose between more leisure time and longer working hours; a significant number of people choose the latter. Roberts' own view is that leisure time will continue to expand in our society, but more slowly and less dramatically than some people suggest. (It's difficult to make long-term predictions regarding a complex society that is beset by serious problems.)

We don't mean to suggest that ours is the only society in which people have had to deal with the problem of how to use leisure time:

> In medieval times, it does appear that people did less work than they do today. Over a hundred public holidays were recognized each year, and spells of work tended to be punctuated by regular occasions for amusement and recreation. Life was also based around leisure in this sort of way in the ancient civilizations of Greece and Rome. The development of industry, preceded in Britain by the influence of Puritanism, pushed hours of work up to exceptional levels and made an individual's employment the major determinant of the pattern of his life [Roberts, 1970, p. 20].

Our leisure differs from that of the Middle Ages in that it is based on technological efficiency. Whatever its source, however, some sociologists believe that the increase of leisure time has brought about more radical transformations in the life of people in our society than any other recent social change. More and more, we are facing the question of how to use our spare time.

*From *Leisure*, by K. Roberts. Copyright 1970 by Longman Group Ltd. This and all other quotations from this source are reprinted by permission.

Personal-Reflection Exercise: My Use of Leisure Time

For the purposes of this exercise, we will define *leisure time* as the time you have in any given day after you have taken care of study, work, and any other obligations you have. Leisure is "free time."

1. Using Form 12-1, record the ways in which you spend each free-time period that comes along in a 7-day period. Start as soon as possible; you can begin on any day of the week. One student, Di Ann, divided the school day into two parts. The first part began when she got out of bed and ended when she finished her last class in the afternoon. After class, she filled out the first half of the form. She filled out the second half just before going to bed.

Use the form to break the day into two parts.

2. Indicate what you do with each period of free time. Do not include periods of time during which you do anything you feel obligated to do, for whatever reason—study, work, family obligations, and so forth. For instance, Di Ann's Friday form looked like this:

8 A.M.–2:30 P.M.

—10:00–11:00—talking with
  friends
—1:30–2:30—reading a novel

2:30 P.M.–3 A.M.

—5:00–6:00—tennis
—8:30–9:30—on phone with
  friends
—9:30–3:00—evening with
  Mark, movie, disco

As in the example, indicate what you did and for how long.

Form 12-1

What I Do during My Free Time

Monday	*Tuesday*	*Wednesday*	*Thursday*

Period 1: from_____ to _____ .

Period 2: from_____ to _____ .

Form 12-1 *(continued)*

Friday   *Saturday*   *Sunday*

Period 1: from _____ to _____ .

Period 2: from _____ to _____ .

3. At the end of the 7-day period, use Form 12-2 to try to divide your use of your leisure time into categories—use as many categories as you need to make the distinctions you think are necessary. Indicate how much time you have spent in each category. For instance, Di Ann used the following categories:

—just talking or playing cards with friends and acquaintances
—serious talk with mainly same-sex friends, intimates
—reading newspapers, magazines
—reading books not required for class
—physical exercise, participating in sports
—watching TV
—spending time doing things with male friends
—being a spectator at sports events
—meditating, taking walks alone just to think
—movies, plays, rock concerts, and things like that
—writing for the school paper
—wasting time, seemingly doing nothing

These categories might not apply to your experience. Use categories that make sense to you.

Form 12-2

Category _____   Category _____   Category _____

Time spent _____   Time spent _____   Time spent _____

Category _____   Category _____   Category _____

Time spent _____   Time spent _____   Time spent _____

Category _____   Category _____   Category _____

Time spent _____   Time spent _____   Time spent _____

---

4. Once you've organized the ways in which you spend your free time, use Form 12-3 to write a brief paragraph describing how you feel about what you see. Indicate whether you think that the week you examined is fairly typical of how you spend your leisure time. If you don't think that it is typical, describe as concretely as possible a typical week and indicate how you feel about the ways in which you usually spend your leisure time.

Form 12-3

My Reactions to My Use of Leisure Time

Leisure: Working Knowledge

We thought it important to include a chapter on the use of leisure time in a book that deals with moving into adulthood. During these transitional years, you are terminating or modifying some of the ways in which you use your free time, experimenting with other ways, and moving toward time-use patterns that will characterize your adult years. At one extreme, you can let these patterns "just happen"; at the other extreme, you can try to systematically shape the exact configuration of the patterns. Perhaps the most realistic approach lies somewhere between these two extremes. Even now, you can begin to make decisions concerning the part you want leisure to play in your life. If you fail to plan or make decisions in this area, you might find a great deal of dissatisfaction and boredom in your life—an intensification of the psychopathology of the average. On the other hand, too much planning could certainly rob your leisure life of its spontaneity. Whatever option you choose, the fact remains that, during these years of your life, you are establishing patterns in your use of leisure time. As Roberts points out:

> Young people are keen to develop new tastes, and they are willing to experiment, with the result that leisure is extremely colorful and varied in contrast to the more stable and conventional pursuits of their elders. . . . Few new leisure interests are acquired after marriage. [Moving into adult-

hood] is the period during which interests are aroused and a liking for particular types of leisure activity is developed. As people mature into adulthood the tendency is for interests to be dropped [Roberts, 1970, pp. 46–47].

Although it is true that an individual's interests begin to narrow as work, marriage, and family obligations become more pressing, it is likely that they become more narrow than they need to be. One of the best predictors of future behavior is current behavior. If you develop a relatively wide variety of interests, leisure-related values, and satisfying patterns of leisure activities—that is, if you assume a sense of self-direction in your use of leisure time—it is much more likely that you will retain a degree of creativity in this area of life as you become older.

Play

If someone were to ask you whether or not you know what the term *play* refers to, you would probably answer "Of course, everyone does." The problem with such basic, simple concepts is that familiarity and simplicity are, in a way, deceptive. Philosophers and social scientists have been musing about the definition, nature, and function of play among human beings for a long time. In *Why People Play*, Ellis (1973) explores more than a dozen theories of play.

The Definition and Description of Play

Huizinga (1949) devotes an entire chapter of his book to a consideration of the various definitions of the term *play*. One definition is: "free activity standing quite consciously outside 'ordinary' life as being 'not serious,' but at the same time absorbing the player intensely and utterly" (p. 13). By implication, if an activity becomes too "serious," or if the players are no longer absorbed in an activity, it ceases to be play. Although Ellis admits that seeking a perfect definition of play is a somewhat fruitless task, he provides a definition of play that focuses on one of the central issues involved in play and other leisure pursuits: "Play is that behavior that is motivated by the need to elevate the level of arousal towards the optimal" (p. 110). In other words, in play we seek to be stimulated. The degree of stimulation sought differs from person to person, but stimulus is a part of all forms of play.

Play is a stimulating, pleasant "time out"—a manipulating of one's environment. Let's examine these characteristics in detail. (These are not necessarily all the characteristics of play, but they are characteristics that relate to all leisure pursuits, even the "serious" ones.)

Stimulating. Playing is a way of seeking out a natural "high." The stimulation involved can be either moderate or intense, depending on the kind of play and the preference of the player. We know a gambler who actually begins to shake when he nears the gaming tables. He comes dangerously close to moving beyond his "optimal" level of arousal, or stimulation. For him, and for most gamblers, the uncertainty of the outcome, the risks involved, and the constant expectation of winning are extremely stimulating.

People play basketball not only because it provides physical exercise but also because it is stimulating in other ways. It seems that we want to be aroused, stimulated, engrossed in some activity. From one point of view, play represents the pursuit of "highs"—moderate or intense, creative or destructive, legitimate or illegitimate. When activities are no longer absorbing or stimulating, they are either discarded or placed in the category of "obligation."

> Cassy enjoyed playing pool at the local parlor. She became very good at different games and even at trick shots. She enjoyed competing, though she refused to play for money. Eventually, she became so good that no one locally could beat her. Her interest in playing pool at this point began to diminish. Winning was so easy for her that it was no longer stimulating. Perhaps if she had played for money, her winnings would have stimulated her, even though competing no longer did.

The opposite of stimulation is boredom. Play and other leisure pursuits are ways of avoiding boredom (though they are certainly more than that). It has been said that boredom is a self-indictment—if I am bored, I probably deserve to be bored, even though, as with loneliness, I might blame it on my environment. Generally, people who reach toward some optimal degree of stimulation are able to avoid boredom.

Pleasant. Playing is an enjoyed activity. If, when you invite someone to play cards, he or she says "No, I don't feel like it," you might say "Come on anyway—we need a fourth." If the person agreed to join you, the game would not constitute play for him or her.

On the other hand, when the stimulation derived from an activity is too much for a person, that activity ceases to be a form of play for that person, because it goes beyond the optimal level of stimulation—it is no longer pleasant. A friend of yours might find skydiving extremely stimulating and very pleasurable, whereas you might find it terrifying.

"Time out." Play is time apart from "ordinary" time; it is "festive" time. Gerry described playing basketball in these terms:

> I'm no hotshot. I'm just a garden-variety player, but I love to play. During a basketball game, I forget about everything else—all my worries, all the things I ordinarily do. It's "time out" from the rest of my life. I don't necessarily mean "escape," but just time out. After I play a couple of hours, I go back to my regular life refreshed and with a better attitude. Of course, the physical exercise also is important to me.

Many people see the pursuit of "festive time" as important, and they realize that they can pursue play in either self-enhancing or self-destructive ways. Individuals who abuse alcohol and drugs pursue "time out" or "festive" time in self-defeating ways.

A manipulation of one's environment. Play can be seen as one way of exercising power or control over one's environment. Putting a ball in a basket or taking a trick in a card game can give a person a feeling of competence. If, when Gerry played basketball with people who play much better than he does, he never had a chance to handle the ball, much less make a basket, he would no longer be exercising control over his environment. The game would provide exercise for Gerry, but it wouldn't be pleasant—it would no longer be play. On the other hand, an occasional good pass, rebound, or basket might be enough to keep him coming back, especially if he really liked the exercise and saw the game as a social event.

Directed daydreaming can be a form of play, because it is not compulsory. It can be a stimulating, pleasant "time out," or "festive" time—a way of symbolically manipulating one's environment. Some psychologists see daydreaming as an important form of play that can provide a means of coping with the miseries of real life.

The Relationship between Leisure and Work

The effect of work on leisure. When people worked 12 hours per day, 6 days per week, work certainly affected leisure. People had little time or energy to engage in leisure pursuits as we think of them. Today, some people work long hours because they want to or *think* they should, not because they absolutely must; that is, an inner compulsion drives them to put in long hours.

Linda works 60 to 70 hours per week. She is making very good money. She sees money as the royal route to the kind of independence she wants. She spends the little time she has for herself outside work taking care of her apartment and occasionally visiting her family or perhaps a friend. Since some of these tasks are, in a sense, obligatory, she actually has very little leisure time.

What are your reflections on Linda's life-style? What is your present attitude toward work, including school work, and how does it affect your leisure?

Eric is a minister. He, too, works at least 65 to 70 hours per week. He would like to pursue all sorts of leisure activities, not least of which would be to spend more time with his wife and small son. However, he feels that his primary obligation is to his congregation. Even when he is not working, he is "on call." He likes the work of the ministry, and, when asked about leisure, he says that he can't have everything.

Now comment on Eric's life-style.

A number of people who dislike their work see leisure as a way of compensating for the frustration and monotony they find on the job. Some of these people pursue hobbies to use skills that they don't use at work. Other people drown themselves in various forms of amusement to repress the dissatisfactions they would otherwise feel. Still others do very little to counteract the adverse effects of work; instead, they develop stoical attitudes that make monotonous jobs tolerable. Their leisure lives are quite bland.

Compartmentalization of work and leisure. Current research seems to indicate that, for many people, work has very little impact on leisure. They put work in one compartment of their lives and leisure in another; ordinarily, the two do not meet. When these people leave their workplaces, they forget about work and involve themselves in a different life.

Enid is a secretary. She doesn't really mind her work. When asked about it, she says that it is a way of "paying my dues." It's something she must do in order to have her "other" life. She has many friends and does all sorts of things with them in the evening and on weekends. This, she feels, is her real life. At work, she is considered competent and unemotional. Her friends see her as creative, artistic, caring, and enjoyable.

Like many people, Enid works in order to be able to realize a life-style that she considers desirable. On the other hand, many people seem to enjoy their work. For them, work is part of the ritual of life.

The impact of leisure on work. It is evident that work can have an impact on leisure; it may not be as immediately evident that leisure can affect work.

Brenda works for a certified public accounting firm. She is bright, personable, hard working, and very competent. Her superiors feel that she could move toward a top managerial position quite easily. The only thing they don't understand is her reluctance to put in overtime. They know that people make it to the top of this firm through a combination of competence and dedication; and dedication can be translated into a fair amount of overtime. They wonder whether she is ambitious enough. When Brenda talks to her friends about this situation, she says "That company is not going to own me. Getting to the top is simply not worth it. They get about 45 good hours from me every week, and sometimes a few more. But that's enough. If it takes 60 hours to make manager, they can keep it. I like my work very much, but I'm not going to define my life by it."

Full human development requires a balance between work and leisure. This is indicated by the fact that unemployment tends to render people incapable of enjoying leisure. The unemployed drop out of the normal rhythm of life. For them, free time, and the loss of economic and social status that come with it, are disorienting.

Work as serious play. For some people, work is a form of serious play. They feel neither an inner nor an outer compulsion to put in long hours; they enjoy working and *want* to put in long hours. They do not tend to lie on white sand beaches doing nothing. They work, often long and hard, because for many of them work is stimulating, pleasant, and a way of making an impact on their environment; that is, their work, no matter how serious it is, has some of the characteristics of play.

Some of us see other people's work as a form of play—it looks like fun to us. Although the ideal seems to be to do the kind of work you enjoy, we cannot assume that any given person likes his or her work. At a recent oldtimers' reunion, a number of retired professional baseball players were asked how they had felt about being baseball players. A surprising number of them, even some of the "greats," said that it was just another job. What was immensely exciting for many fans was merely work for some of the players.

Leisure and Obligation: A Mixed Bag

It is probably unreasonable for you to think that all your leisure pursuits, present and future, will be *pure* forms of leisure. Leisure and obligation have a way of becoming intertwined. When you visit home, either briefly or for an extended period of time, you might enjoy yourself in many different ways; that is, much of what you do could be considered leisure activity. However, you might feel that you *should* visit home. Some of the activities in which you participate during your visit might be considered leisure from the perspective of your family, whereas you see the same activities as obligations.

Getting married and starting a family often have a feeling of leisure about them. Such activities, at least in the beginning, are stimulating and pleasant. However, as life goes on, what was once leisure becomes a mixture of leisure and obligation. One sign that a marriage is going sour is that almost everything seems to be obligatory. Although it is mature to talk about "working at a marriage," a marriage that is mostly work has in some sense died.

Self-Assessment: My Leisure Activities—Actual and Potential

1. List your leisure pursuits. Use the exercise regarding the use of free time, which you completed earlier in the chapter, to help you draw up this list.

2. Using Form 12-4, draw up a list of leisure activities in which you engage. Use the first self-assessment exercise in this chapter to help you

complete this step. Be as concrete and specific as possible; that is, do not indicate a category of activities such as "volunteer work" or "playing sports"; instead, indicate the specific activities within a category, such as "volunteer work as an aide in the hospital."

3. Using the spaces provided in Form 12-4, indicate how frequently you engage in each activity, and rate each activity according to how much you enjoy it.

Here is a portion of one student's response to this exercise:

Leisure Activity		Frequency					Satisfaction		
	Seldom	Moderate	Often		Low	Medium	High		
	1	2	3	4	5	1	2	3	4	5
drinking with guys	__	__	__	__	X	__	__	__	X	__
talking with Lois	X	__	__	__	__	__	__	__	__	X
reading science fiction	__	X	__	__	__	__	__	X	__	__
jogging, calisthenics	__	X	__	__	__	__	__	__	__	X
watching TV	__	__	__	__	X	__	X	__	__	__

As you read this sample, do you find discrepancies or contradictions in the way that this person has arranged his leisure life? If you were the kind of person who gives advice to others, what advice would you offer him?

4. Return to the "Frequency" portion of the form. Use an *O* to indicate the frequency you would *prefer*. If you decide to add items to your list, add the items and indicate the preferred frequency.

The student whose activities and ratings we considered earlier completed this step in the following way:

Leisure Activity		Frequency					Satisfaction		
	Seldom	Moderate	Often		Low	Medium	High		
	1	2	3	4	5	1	2	3	4	5
drinking with guys	__	__	O	__	X	__	__	__	X	__
talking with Lois	X	__	__	O	__	__	__	__	__	X
watching TV	__	O	__	__	X	__	X	__	__	__

5. Check the items in which you find a discrepancy or contradiction in the way in which you have arranged your leisure life (for example, items that are high in satisfaction but low in frequency). In our example, the student checked three items, indicating a desire to rearrange his priorities with respect to use of leisure time.

Form 12-4

Rating Leisure Activities

Leisure	Frequency					Satisfaction				
	Seldom	Moderate		Often		Low		Medium		High
	1	2	3	4	5	1	2	3	4	5
1. _____	—	—	—	—	—	—	—	—	—	—
2. _____	—	—	—	—	—	—	—	—	—	—
3. _____	—	—	—	—	—	—	—	—	—	—
4. _____	—	—	—	—	—	—	—	—	—	—
5. _____	—	—	—	—	—	—	—	—	—	—
6. _____	—	—	—	—	—	—	—	—	—	—
7. _____	—	—	—	—	—	—	—	—	—	—
8. _____	—	—	—	—	—	—	—	—	—	—
9. _____	—	—	—	—	—	—	—	—	—	—
10. _____	—	—	—	—	—	—	—	—	—	—
11. _____	—	—	—	—	—	—	—	—	—	—
12. _____	—	—	—	—	—	—	—	—	—	—
13. _____	—	—	—	—	—	—	—	—	—	—

In the group activity and planning exercises, you will be asked to use what you learn about yourself in these exercises.

The Systems That Influence Your Use of Leisure Time: An Exercise

Sociological research indicates that many people spend most of their leisure time with their families; however, during adolescence and the moving-into-adulthood years, the individual's attachment to family life is at its lowest ebb. As we have seen, in order to facilitate the development of autonomy and identity, people in your age group drift away from their families physically and emotionally. This is culturally normal. In deciding how to use their spare time, young people are influenced more by their peers than by their parents. Of course, this doesn't mean that they desert their families. During this transitional period, you are likely to modify your relationship with your family. For those who marry and establish a family, the odds are that home-centered leisure will become the norm.

The four levels of systems that we discussed earlier affect the ways in which you are presently developing patterns of use of leisure time. This exercise provides an opportunity to examine these sources of influence. Each level of systems is presented, along with an example of how a system at that level affects one individual's approach to leisure. Then, you are asked to assess the ways in which systems affect your approach to leisure.

Level I: Personal settings. As we've said, these include immediate settings, such as the family, classroom, peer group, workplace, and so forth. One student, Rose, wrote the following:

> One classroom or course has affected my use of leisure time tremendously—I mean my class in drama. The teacher was very good. We read and analyzed a number of plays, but we analyzed them in terms of our own lives. We went to the theater and saw a number of plays, both old and modern, and then we discussed what we saw. Each of us even wrote a brief one-act "play." It was all very involving and exciting. I now see theater as a serious and very fulfilling leisure activity.

Another student, Carl, shared a somewhat different experience:

> As long as I can remember, watching TV together has been our primary form of leisure time spent together. My two sisters, my parents, and I would watch all the popular programs. Being banned from watching a program was one of the worst kinds of punishment we would get. Now that I look back on it, we were not very selective in what we watched, We made no attempt to watch educational TV. So I feel saddled with lousy habits when it comes to the tube—both in terms of quantity and quality.

Now describe the ways in which one or two personal systems have affected or are now affecting the way in which you approach leisure. Choose examples that show the greatest impact. If possible, pick one positive and one negative example.

_____

_____

_____

_____

_____

_____

_____

_____

_____

_____

Level II: The network of personal settings. The personal systems of your life interact and, therefore, affect one another and you. You are a linking pin between systems. The following is an example of how an individual can feel pulled in different directions because of his or her membership in various systems. Al wrote:

> I belong to a young people's club at one of the local churches. The club promotes community-centered activities—dances, pot-luck suppers, group volunteer work, and things like that. A fair amount of my spare time is spent there. The guys I hang around with at school do a lot of drinking and are a bit into drugs. So I drink a bit and have smoked some pot. I can't say that I dislike doing those things. But sometimes I feel I'm living in two entirely different worlds, and something about both of them attracts me. I have two sets of feelings. Sometimes when I'm at a pot party with the guys I feel like a hypocrite, though I don't think what I'm doing is really wrong, even though it's illegal. And sometimes at church I feel that I'm not "with it." I feel that I'm involved because that's the way I've been ever since I was a kid, and yet I really like being there and doing these things.

Write a paragraph explaining the ways in which your position as a linking pin between two systems affects your approach to leisure. Try to choose an example that is important to you.

_____

_____

_____

_____

_____

_____

_____

_____

Level III: The larger organizations and institutions of society. People talk about the "leisure industry." The entertainment media, professional ball teams, discos, racquet clubs, and travel agents would be included.

1. List as many leisure industries as you can:

_____

_____

_____

_____

_____

_____

_____

_____

2. Ask all the members of your class or group to share their lists.

3. Write a paragraph indicating some important ways in which one or two of these leisure industries affect your use of your spare time. One student, Andrea, wrote the following summary:

> I'm a television addict. I mean almost literally an addict. Even when I'm not watching it, I have it on—you know, just as background. When I shut it off at bedtime, I actually feel alone. I know it sounds crazy. It's so easy to plop down in front of it, instead of planning something to do that has more substance. I let myself become so passive. I must admit that I'm writing this to show how one industry, the television industry, is affecting me and my use of time, but I have to admit that I'm the one that's letting this happen.

Choose one or two leisure industries and explain the ways in which they affect your use of leisure time in either positive or negative ways.

_____

_____

_____

_____

_____

_____

_____

_____

_____

Level IV: Culture. Your culture, and the subcultures within it, influence your pursuit of leisure. Consider the following examples:

> Toby feels caught up in rugged North American competition; he doesn't enjoy any sport or any kind of physical exercise that isn't based on competition. A competitive note filters into most of his leisure pursuits. For instance, at parties, he has to be more witty than his friends. He came to this college because of its history of winning teams.

> Wanda believes that a "culture" of helping and caring that characterizes her church group influences what she chooses to do with her free time and how she goes about her leisure pursuits. For instance, she likes volunteer work, such as tutoring disadvantaged kids. When it comes to parties, she's always ready to help in planning, getting everything ready, and then making sure that everyone has a good time at the party itself—especially people who seem isolated. She wants to take a closer look at all of this, because she does not want to swallow cultural values whole without reexamining them from time to time. It's not that she's dissatisfied with her style, but she wants to get a better grasp on why she does what she does.

> Vince is beginning to realize how the rhythms and lyrics of pop music affect the way in which he expresses himself emotionally. A class he has been taking in music appreciation has made him aware of the fact that, for the past 6 or 7 years, he has been immersed in pop music. He feels that he would like to see whether he is being affected by cultural blueprints of any kind that come from this kind of immersion. He is intrigued by the possibility that his "style" of intimacy with friends might owe something to the music he listens to.

Describe some of the effects of cultural blueprints on your approach to leisure time.

_____

_____

_____

_____

_____

_____

_____

_____

_____

Group Activity: My Learnings about My Leisure Style

1. Share your feelings concerning your present approach to leisure. Base your assessment on the theory you've read and the exercises you've done.

2. Share one effect of a social setting and one effect of culture on your approach to leisure.

3. Share your Dream in the area of leisure. What do you want your leisure life to look like 5 years from now? If necessary, reread the section on the Dream in Chapter 2.

Action Plan: Widening My Approach to Leisure

In order to make decisions regarding the ways in which you use your leisure time, it is important for you to determine your leisure values. The "mix" of leisure pursuits you adopt depends on what you prize or value. Early in this book, we discussed the values we promote; they include becoming an active, self-directed person in facing developmental challenges, and avoiding, as far as possible, the psychopathology of the average. However, if a person prefers to take a more passive approach to life, or if he or she is not particularly concerned about the psychopathology of the average (one of our students once said to us "I don't *want* to live with any more intensity!"), that is his or her business. We do not suggest that all individuals who develop an extensive working knowledge of the developmental tasks of life want to change their approach to life. We do, however, value free and informed choices; and working knowledge enables people to make informed choices. With respect to leisure, it's up to you to determine a "profitable" use of your time. If you are dissatisfied with your present approach to leisure, or if you would like to take a more challenging approach to your use of free time, the following steps can help. (For a complete review of all the steps of the planning/problem-solving process, see Chapter 3.)

1. *Setting goals.* First of all, review the exercises you've completed in this chapter. You've already implicitly or explicitly expressed dissatisfac-

tions and formulated goals in the area of leisure living. Think of one or two concrete ways in which you would like to improve your approach to the use of leisure time during the next 2 months. Be as concrete as possible. One student, Simon, made the following choice:

> I watch over 20 hours of TV a week. My goal is to cut down to a maximum of 10 hours. The second part of my goal is to replace the 10 hours I eliminate with some cultural pursuits—plays, concerts, lectures in areas not related to my studies, novels I want to read, and other things like that.

List one or two concrete goals of your own choice.

Goals

_____

_____

_____

_____

_____

_____

2. *Resources*. In the space provided, list the resources (people, places, institutions, and the like) that will help you to achieve your goal. Simon wrote:

> Arlette is in a theater group. She probably has all sorts of ideas as to what is happening with local theater. She probably knows about plays that won't cost me an arm and a leg. The fine arts department puts out a schedule of local events, such as exhibitions and concerts. I can get hold of that. I think Jimmy goes to a number of these. I'll check it out.

Resources

_____

_____

_____

_____

_____

_____

_____

3. *Programs.* In the space provided, write a clear step-by-step program for each of your goals. Some of Simon's steps were:

—Get the fine arts brochure.

—Get some suggestions from Arlette. See if she would like to see some plays together.

—See Jim and find out what he likes from the fine arts offerings.

—Each week, plan the use of 10 hours of TV time. Use the TV guide to check on interesting programs; substitute quality for quantity.

—Plan at least 10 more hours of leisure time. Each week on Sunday, plan two events that involve getting out with someone to a play, concert, or other cultural event.

—After 8 weeks, reassess my feelings about my use of leisure time; set further goals.

Program Steps

_____

_____

_____

_____

_____

_____

_____

_____

_____

_____

4. *Evaluation.* Determine the criteria you are going to use to evaluate the success, partial success, or failure of your programs. Simon wrote:

I want to feel better about the way in which I use my leisure time. I feel that I'm too passive and even lazy in my leisure life. I will feel successful if I become more consistently active in planning and doing leisure things. A second criterion relates to being honest with myself. I want to see if putting more cultural events into my life is really what I want and enjoy. I don't want to be sitting at a ballet pretending that I like it when I really don't. I want to like these things, not just think that I *should* like them.

Criteria

_____

_____

_____

_____

_____

_____

_____

_____

_____

_____

Summary

Researchers know quite a bit about what people do during their leisure time. They know relatively little about people's feelings concerning their leisure activities. The material in this chapter is intended to help you consider your leisure activities and your feelings about the ways in which you use your free time.

In the next chapter, we will use the concept of "life-style" to integrate all the developmental tasks that we have considered.

13

Life-Style: Integrating Developmental Tasks

The Task of Integration

At this point, you might be asking yourself "How can I pull the developmental tasks together into a unified whole?" It doesn't help, you say, to know that this is a complicated task. On the other hand, perhaps you've already come up with some tentative answers to this question. One answer is "Well, life is going to happen whether I pull these tasks together or not. Some people who don't know anything about developmental processes and tasks seem to get on all right." Or, on a more positive note, feeling that you now have a more practical understanding of the possibilities of community, you might answer "I'm not sure, but somehow I hope to accomplish these tasks through participation in a community—the community of my friends, the 'community' I form with the person I marry, my church community, or perhaps a community of people at work. These communities will help me to integrate developmental tasks. After all, I don't have to face all this alone." In this chapter, we examine *life-style* as a process of integration.

Leaving the Transitional Years

Up to this point, we have emphasized that a transitional period is a boundary zone in which individuals modify or terminate relationships with people and institutions, question values and ways of doing things, experiment, and either confirm old ways or initiate new ways of doing things. In this chapter, we reemphasize the initiation of new structures and turn our attention to the fact that transitional periods *are* transitional—that they come to an end. As we have seen, one sign of this transition is that the work of terminating, questioning, and experimenting seems to become less and less important. Your new commitment to life becomes more important. The choices you make during the transitional years add up to a new life structure, even if these choices include a renewed commitment to old values and traditional ways. Renewed commitment to traditional practices after a period of questioning and experimenting can be as valid a sign of growth and development as the initiation of something new.

Life-Style

We use such expressions as "I envy her life-style," "He has a bizarre life-style," "Their life-style is quiet and serene," and "I'm dissatisfied with my life-style." Since we are going to use this term as a means of integrating much of what we have seen so far, it is important to get a concrete idea of the way in which it is being used. Let's start with your understanding of the term *life-style*. In the space provided, write whatever comes to your mind when you think of this term.

_____

_____

_____

_____

_____

_____

_____

_____

Conduct a class discussion in which you share your understanding of the term *life-style* and come to a basic agreement on its meaning.

Self-Reflection Exercise: My Current Life-Style

1. Using your understanding of what *life-style* means, present a picture of your current life-style. Do so by making a statement regarding your style in each of the developmental-task areas we have considered. For instance, consider what one student, Ken, wrote about his current style in the area of competence:

> Right now I'm trying to be especially competent in the biological sciences. I spend a lot of extra time in the lab. It's my top priority. I want good grades in pre-med, because, more than anything else, I want a crack at med school. I was fairly good in basketball in high school, but now I barely get enough exercise.

Ken's life-style revolves around career preparation. Gladys had this to say about love, marriage, and family:

> I don't have one very close male friend. I'm overweight and fairly depressed. I'm told that I'd be much more attractive if I'd lose a few pounds, but I don't do it. I don't see myself as loving or lovable. What can I say about my style in this area except that it doesn't exist? I'm dissatisfied but doing little about my dissatisfaction.

Make a statement concerning your style in each of the developmental-task areas. It might help to review what you wrote about yourself in the self-assessment exercises in previous chapters.

a. *Competence*—what I currently do well or am trying to do well.

_____

_____

_____

_____

_____

_____

_____

b. *Autonomy*—my current style in terms of dependence, independence, counterdependence, and interdependence.

_____

_____

_____

_____

_____

_____

c. *Values*—the values that are currently most important to me to the point that they affect my decisions and behavior.

_____

_____

_____

_____

_____

_____

d. *Identity*—my current sense of who I am and how this is confirmed by those about me.

_____

_____

_____

_____

_____

_____

e. *Sexuality*—my current style in terms of a sexual relationship with another person.

_____

_____

_____

_____

_____

_____

f. *Friendship/intimacy*—my current style with acquaintances, friends, intimates; my interpersonal or social style.

_____

_____

_____

_____

_____

_____

g. *Love/marriage/family*—my current style in terms of a love relationship with another person and a deep commitment to another person.

_____

_____

_____

_____

_____

h. *Job/occupation/career*—my current style or approach in orienting myself to my present work or a future occupation.

_____

_____

_____

_____

_____

_____

i. *Relationship to society*—my current style in relating to the world, neighborhood, community, organizations, government, politics, and so forth.

_____

_____

_____

_____

_____

j. *Leisure*—my current approach to the use of free time.

_____

_____

_____

_____

_____

2. Describe the "center" of your life right now (if you feel that you have one). Another way of putting this is: "Where does the main flow of your energy go?" Jenny wrote:

> School is my center right now. It takes up practically all my energy. My friends tell me that I put too much of myself in it, but that's what I want to do right now.

Terry's picture was quite different:

> I don't seem to have just one "center." My job is a center, because I like it and it provides me with the money I need to do other things. My relationship to Janelle is a center. A lot of energy goes there. My family is still a kind of center. I go home fairly often. And I don't see it as something I have to do.

Describe your center and any "satellite centers" you might have.

_____

_____

_____

_____

_____

_____

_____

_____

3. Describe the principal values that you see as means of integrating developmental tasks. Values can be like threads, tying these tasks together into a unit. Describe your real values, not your notional values—that is, the values you actually follow, not the ones you would like to pursue. Ken, a student who is preparing himself for a medical career, made the following statement:

> To be honest, I think that ambition is my strongest value right now. It ties everything together for me. I don't mind putting long hours in studying and in the lab, and it doesn't bother me that my social life is suffering right now. I want a career in medicine and all the good things it brings—prestige, money, and an exciting life-style. It seems that I can get all of that and still be a very useful member of society.

As you try to describe your integrating values, don't be afraid to admit that they are still tentative—not yet fully formed.

_____

_____

_____

_____

_____

_____

_____

4. Write a paragraph describing how you feel about your present life-style.

_____

_____

_____

The Meaning and Scope of the Term *Life-Style*

In one sense of the term, everyone has a life-style. However, in the case of many people, much of their life-style is not a question of choice; rather, it is dictated by social, economic, and cultural conditions. Middle-class North Americans have, at least relatively speaking, a great deal of freedom of choice; they can choose their style of living. According to Dennis Brissett and Lionel Lewis (1979), there is a

> growing emphasis on what Joseph Bensman and Arthur Vidich call the "consciousness of choice" among the middle classes of American society. Many Americans have come to assume that they have the possibility and, in fact, the right to choose their own style of living. Curiously, they feel a new self-reliance while experiencing the options within the rather limited confines of the organizations and norms that constitute their social worlds. Part of this consciousness stems from the recognition that, although their choices of activity are often severely limited by other than self-imposed considerations, they usually can choose the style in which they wish to act. The choice is not life, but life-style [p. 63].*

In other words, within certain limits, you can choose the ways in which you respond to the developmental challenges discussed in the previous chapters. The way in which you pattern these choices or allow them to be patterned for you is determined by your personal life-style. Limitations arise from the "confines of the organizations and norms that constitute" your social world—that is, from the four levels of systems described in Chapter 1. As Brissett and Lewis point out, "the choice is not life." The developmental challenges that have been reviewed in this book constitute "life," or at least a large part of it; you can't ignore or avoid them. Nor can you avoid the ways in which these challenges are shaped by the social

---

*From "The Big Toe, Armpits, and Natural Perfume: Notes on the Production of Sexual Ecstasy," by D. Brissett and L. S. Lewis. This and all other quotations from this source are published by permission of Transaction, Inc., from *Society*, Vol. 16, No. 2, pp. 63–73. Copyright © 1979 by Transaction, Inc.

systems and culture in which you live. That, too, is "life"; but you do have an opportunity to make choices that your ancestors did not have and that perhaps most people in the world do not have today. This opportunity stems from the fact that you live in an affluent society and have the kind of leisure found in such a society.

> The old ethic that people should work still prevails. What a person can choose, however, is, to a certain degree, the style of work, and to a much greater degree, the life-style surrounding the work. . . . Work itself, in fact, has become concealed by the work style and life-style alternatives it makes possible. Unlike the era when persons had to justify their play as work, we now seem to be entering an age where work itself has to be justified as play. The disguise of play both creates and reaffirms the "consciousness of choice" [Brissett & Lewis, p. 63].

In using the phrase "the disguise of play," these researchers are cautioning us against pretending that we have more freedom to create our own life-styles than we actually do.

As social critics, Brissett and Lewis point out that our limited freedom can lead to a preoccupation with the self. They quote Tom Wolfe's description of our society's version of the alchemical dream: "The old alchemical dream was changing base metals into gold. The new alchemical dream is: changing one's personality—remaking, remodeling, elevating and redoing one's very self . . . and observing studying and doting on it. (ME!)" Wolfe suggests that our life-styles can become more important than the communities and societies that sustain us and give us our freedom.

Life-Style as a Purposeful, Integrating Concept

The term *life-style* needn't have negative connotations; it can be very useful as a purposeful, integrating concept. In this sense, a life-style doesn't refer to a plan for the pursuit of pleasure, an exaggerated preoccupation with the self, or a description of the pattern of behaviors and accomplishments that happens to evolve from the choices made by any given individual. Rather, it is *a process of life planning* that is based on the planning and problem-solving process discussed in Chapter 3. In this respect, a life-style includes the following elements: (1) an awareness of choice, (2) an ongoing review of personal values, (3) concrete goals and clear-cut programs, and (4) ongoing evaluation.

Awareness of choice. The first element is an awareness of the areas of life in which you actually have some choice. The self-assessment and analysis-of-systems exercises you've done are means of increasing this kind of awareness. They've helped you to become more aware of your own inner resources, your personal limitations, the resources that are available outside yourself, and the limitations imposed by your environment. For instance, if you do very poorly in math, a number of careers that depend on mathematical ability are closed to you. Many people are locked into a dissatisfying life-style (for instance, in terms of occupation) simply because they aren't aware of their alternatives. Brainstorming—that is, listing all possibilities and generating as many alternatives as possible—is an important step in the planning/problem-solving process.

An ongoing review of personal values. We don't mean to intimate that you should constantly change your values. On the other hand, some of your values can and do change; they mature. Once you realize that life-style options are open to you, it is a question of setting priorities—of determining which options you want to pursue. Your choice will be determined by your values. If your values are unclear, it will be difficult for you to choose.

> Patti had leisure and she had money, but she was still bored. She simply did not know what to do with her leisure time. She knew a lot about the options that were open to her, but she did not know how to choose among them, because she did not know what values she wanted to actualize in her leisure pursuits. She had vague ideas of "altruism" and of "self-improvement" but these values were unclear; they were not strong enough to move her to any kind of action.

A coherent set of values helps you to introduce order among your life-style choices. For instance, you can formulate a set of strong family-related values to limit the demands of your job or career.

Concrete goals and clear-cut programs. Once you realize the variety of your life-style choices and determine what you want to get out of life, you need to establish concrete goals and develop programs that will turn these goals into accomplishments.

> Bess was in her mid-20s, she was single, and she had a fairly good job. She came to realize that she was letting her job take up most of her energy. This wasn't necessary, because she didn't advance her career by putting more time into her job. It seems that she was doing so because she still thought of work as her primary value. Her social life had become somewhat aimless. She came to realize, however, that there was no reason for her interpersonal life to suffer from the "blahs." She was intelligent and personable, and she had little trouble making friends. Since she was relatively new to a large city, she had to decide how she was going to develop a social life. Her first goal was to involve herself in activities in which she would meet people. She did this and found a number of people with whom she wanted to involve herself. In order to give herself more time for her social life, she avoided overtime on her job. She was on her way to a more fulfilling life-style.

Since your life-style is, to a certain extent, a process, you need to learn to reformulate your goals and programs to keep up with your own development and your changing environment. For instance, you might choose to live and work in a small town, where the pace of life is slower than it is in a big city. You choose a town that is relatively close to a large urban center (with cultural amenities and other advantages that only size can offer); however, you remain open to reformulating this goal as you and your environment change.

Ongoing evaluation. This refers to periodic evaluation of the life-style you have developed and its relationship to the values you want to pursue. For instance, after involving yourself in working for the committees of your local church for a year or two, you find that this activity is interfering with the time you want to spend with your children. You try to realign your priorities. Or, you find that your leisure pursuits are infringing on what you see as a reasonable commitment to your aging parents, and you do what you need to do in order to restore balance.

Although many people today talk about career planning, it seems that few people talk about *life planning*. In fact, we believe that, in many cases, the former takes the place of or swallows up the latter. Donna, a middle-aged mother of four children (the oldest in his mid-teens), mused on her family and her life:

> My husband has a good job with a large department store and mail-order firm. But the price we have had to pay for the job has been quite high. We have moved 8 times in the past 14 years. New cities, new schools, new friends, new churches—this is our way of life. Corporations are talking about not doing that as much today, but that's a bit late for us. In a sense, everything has centered around Tom's career. He and I have talked and argued about this from time to time, but we have never really done anything about it. We haven't even considered other choices seriously.

A career can become the focal point of an individual's life or a family's life: a job or a career is chosen and, somehow, the rest of life has to fit around it.

Householder as an Integrating Approach to Life-Style

Robert Havighurst (1953) uses the term *householder*, which we believe can be quite useful as an approach to integrating various dimensions of a life-style. Often, when two people marry, they become householders for the first time. (This does not necessarily mean that they buy a house, but often enough it does.) The household becomes central in their lives. They ask themselves questions such as: "What kind of living arrangements do we want? What kind of house or apartment do we want? Where will it be? How settled or mobile do we want to be? In what kind of community do we want to live?" In both real and symbolic ways, the household can become the center of life.

As most people grow into adulthood, their lives become more stable. As Roberts (1970) puts it:

> They normally assume family responsibilities. They also often seek social roots in the communities where they are living, forming personal friendships and becoming involved in clubs and associations. In order to maintain the responsibilities and the styles of life that they have developed during their free time, people will seek security and stability in employment. . . . [T]he manner in which careers become increasingly stable as people grow older is only fully explicable in terms of the way in which the patterns of life that they develop outside the workplace lead to new demands being made on employment [p. 37].

Often, the central social setting outside work that has the greatest impact on work is the household, where work, friendships, participation in the community, and participation in other associations come together.

Four Types of Life-Styles

In Chapter 6, we discussed four types of personal-identity formation—foreclosed, defended, diffused, and flexible. In this chapter, we revisit these approaches from the broader perspective of the development of a life-style, for we believe that they apply to the manner in which you integrate the major developmental challenges of life and establish patterns of living.

Foreclosed Life-Style

People who maintain a foreclosed life-style do little life planning. They do not investigate the alternatives to the "standard" life-styles they see in their communities and among their families and friends. This does not mean that their life-styles are exactly like those of their parents; their styles differ, because they are influenced by a changed environment and a changed society. Changes in their life-styles are determined by the changes that take place around them.

> After services one Sunday morning, Father Kelly talked about Kevin, the lay person who had read the Bible passages at the morning liturgy. Kevin was in his early 40s. "You remember Kevin from grammar school, don't you? He was one of the wild ones. I don't mean bad, but he kicked up quite a few storms while he was in school here. Who would have thought that, after college [Kevin had gone to college in the city], he would have settled down in the old neighborhood and become one of our best parishioners just like his folks. His kids are in the parish school now, but not kicking up as much trouble as he did.

Father Kelly could be describing an instance of a foreclosed life-style. In spite of his supposed "wildness" earlier in life, Kevin chose, or perhaps fell into, a life-style that is quite similar to that of his parents. This does not mean that his choice has been a poor one or that he regrets it and is unhappy. In his case, quite the opposite seems to be true. Nor does it mean that Kevin should have chosen a different life-style or that he would have chosen differently if he had investigated other options.

The development of a foreclosed life-style *can* lead to painful consequences.

A woman we know (we'll call her Nadine) was less fortunate than Kevin. She was an only child who grew up very close to her mother. Her father died when she was 14, and, from that time on, she accepted her mother's values and dictates almost without question. Her mother's style of life was not restricted or repressive. She enjoyed good company, literature, the arts, and travel, and she had the means necessary to do so. Nadine developed similar tastes. Nadine was 29 and still unmarried when her mother died suddenly. Although she was upset, Nadine did not collapse psychologically. One year after her mother's death, she came for counseling. She felt aimless. She had changed jobs twice in the past year and had moved to a different part of the city. She came to realize that her life structure and her life-style were, in a sense, not hers. For the first time, she had to pattern her life herself, and she felt somewhat helpless.

Unlike Nadine, you are on the near side, rather than the far side, of life-style formation. The more you inform yourself of the different patterns that are open to you (and the more choices you make based on your investigation), the less likely are you to find yourself locked into a dissatisfying life-style. The choices you make now can be the beginning of a life-planning process that will help you to avoid the pitfalls of premature foreclosure. Now is the time to experiment, to push back the walls, and to think of alternative ways of approaching life. This doesn't mean that you must choose radical alternatives; mere consideration of alternatives can make a difference in the way in which you choose a life-style.

Defended Life-Style

In an interesting experiment conducted some years ago, people were asked to enter a room in which they were to sit and fill out some forms. As they entered the room, they were given either a red or a green arm band and asked to wear it as they filled out the forms. In the room, they wrote in silence. Later, during a "debriefing" session, they were asked how they felt about the task and how they felt about the other people in the experiment. Even though the "reds" had not interacted with the "greens," they had some negative feelings about them; the "greens" felt the same way about the "reds." The simple, seemingly meaningless difference in the color of an arm band aroused suspicion and other negative feelings.

There seems to be an important lesson here—one that human beings haven't been able to learn in the course of history. There is a tendency in human beings to fear people who are "different." People who have a defended life-style not only lock themselves into traditional patterns of living in which they are secure but they also spend considerable amounts of energy defending themselves from what they see as the encroachment of people who have life-styles that differ from their own. Those who have milder forms of this malady merely feel uncomfortable around people whose life-styles differ from theirs; they voice their discomfort to members of their own group. In more extreme cases, they might attack those who are "different." They see pluralism as a threat, and they do what they can to avoid it by forming groups in which they are not bothered by others or by moving to communities in which pluralism is not an important issue.

People who have foreclosed life-styles reflect very little on the styles of other people, whereas individuals who have defended life-styles are often extremely aware of others' styles, and their awareness leads to discomfort and fear.

Pamela came to a large state university from a small town in the Midwest. She came with a parental injunction to pursue a course of studies related to farming and farm-support services. Her parents managed a small feed cooperative. They belonged to a fundamentalist sect that emphasized the dangers of worldly contamination. Pamela, a strong person in her own right, came to the university prepared to battle for the important religious and cultural values in her life. She joined a local fundamentalist sect, even though she had to travel 30 miles to attend meetings and services once or twice a week. She was bright and assertive in class, but she socialized relatively little on campus. When she did socialize, she had an "edge" about her. She did not hesitate to condemn the immorality and superficiality she found around her or to praise the people she saw as strong and upright. Although she could be very pleasant, it was not easy to be with her, since she was always "on the alert." She joined two clubs that were related to her agricultural interests, but she felt awkward whenever work gave way to socialization at meetings.

The point of this example is not to question the values espoused by Pamela, her parents, and her community; however, Pamela's defensive posture, which alienated people who had no intention of trying to talk her out of her religious or cultural convictions, can be questioned. Pamela felt that she couldn't be herself around people who had established life-styles that differed from hers. Sensing this, people resented her rigidity and defensiveness and eventually were more than glad to leave her alone.

By citing the case of Pamela, we do not mean to suggest that only people who experience a conservative upbringing develop defended life-styles: the life-styles of libertarians can be just as defended.

Tom, who drank freely, experimented with drugs, got by with as little work as possible in school, and experimented with sex as freely as anyone on campus, expected to be criticized by others. In anticipation of this criticism, he defended himself by calling others with more conservative approaches to life "square" and implying that they didn't have the guts to live as fully as he did. He associated with people who admired his boldness, even though most of them didn't have the nerve to imitate him.

Diffused Life-Style

People who have diffused life-styles have not made clear-cut choices regarding their values and the ways in which those values relate to the pattern of their lives. Rather than make choices, they let life happen. For instance, they don't choose marriage partners in an interdependent way; rather, they drift into marriage. Perhaps "drifting" describes much of their style of living. There is no clearly identifiable center in their lives.

Randolph made few critical choices during his transitional years. He knew that he was no longer a kid, and he tended to terminate adolescent approaches to life; but he didn't replace those approaches with well-defined adult choices. He married, because the woman he was going with insisted on it. He found a job as a clerk in an insurance firm, because it fulfilled the minimum standards of employment he had established for himself. The job had a temporary feel about it—it gave him something to do until the "right" job came along. Most of the things he did had a temporary feel about them. His diffused identity led to a diffused life-style. To this day, he hides his talents, alternates between dependence and isolation in his relationships with others, sees his marriage as temporary, knows he is underemployed, has little sense of community, ignores the wider social and political scene, and generally wastes a good deal of time. His wife works, and, since they have no children, they are comfortable financially. Since Randolph doesn't know what he wants, his wife tends to fashion her own separate life-style. In their own way, they are practicing separation in preparation for divorce.

There needn't be a one-to-one relationship between diffused identity and diffused life-style, as in Randolph's case. Even people who have a relatively well-defined and flexible sense of identity can allow themselves to be trapped in a foreclosed or diffused life-style, simply by failing to investigate possibilities or deferring choices in important developmental areas of life.

Flexible Life-Style

People who have flexible life-styles are stable; they have a center. They've developed a coherent set of values that act as integrating forces in their lives. For instance, their jobs or careers do not swallow their family life. They do not have to divide their lives into compartments—work in one, family in another, and religion in still another. They are aware of people who have life-styles that differ from their own, but they don't waste a lot of energy envying them or feeling threatened by them. Unlike people who have diffused life-styles, they do not easily become the victims of fads. On the other hand, they are open to change. Their life-styles develop as they develop. People who have diffused life-styles might drift from job to job, whereas people who have flexible life-styles are open to new occupations and careers.

> Tim and Margot were married in their early 20s. Tim became a successful accountant in a large firm. They had three children during a 7-year period. During the summers, they rented a house for a couple of weeks near a beach area. Ten years after their marriage, Tim quit his job. He and Margot bought a small inn near the area in which they vacationed. They decided to become innkeepers, even though their income would suffer. Their move involved a fair amount of risk, but it wasn't impulsive—their decision had matured during a 4-year period. They enjoyed living simply in a small community. The inn included a small house in which they lived; the house, together with the inn, constituted their household. They became *householders* in a number of senses of that term.
>
> Today, Tim and Margot are living with their choices, although they have discovered that the inn consumes more of their time than they had anticipated. Tim feels that he can do consulting work for firms in the area without being swallowed by the business world again. That would provide income that could be used to hire some help in running the inn. Family life is still a major value for them, but now it involves working together. They would like to reach the point at which they could invest themselves more deeply in community activities. In one sense, they are "struggling," but they are financially secure and reasonably happy. Their life-style fits their values.

People who have flexible life-styles are open to reevaluation of their goals and the ways in which they pursue them. They might well have a deep sense of tradition, but they are not tied to the past.

We do not suggest that all people who have flexible life-styles make changes as dramatic as Tim and Margot's, nor do we mean to imply that such changes never involve misgivings, pain, and disappointments. Furthermore, we do not suggest that the options open to the family we have described are available to most of the members of our society. As Rubin (1976) points out so graphically in *Worlds of Pain*, such options are rarely open to members of the working class. She describes the ways in which many people become trapped in depressing life-styles, even in an affluent society. The fact that you are a college student indicates that you might have more life-style options than the average member of society.

Self-Reflection Exercise: My Dream as I Currently See It

In the exercise that was presented at the beginning of this chapter, you were asked to review your current life-style. In this exercise, you are asked to look to the future. After reviewing what is said about the Dream in Chapter 2, write a statement about your Dream with regard to each of the developmental-task areas.

Remember that your Dream is not pure fantasy; rather, it is a way of saying "I want something out of life." Try to visualize models who are living out your Dream in each of the task areas; this might help you to make your Dream more concrete. (You can choose public figures or people you know and respect.) Even though you are talking about your Dream, be as specific as you can in the statements you write. Follow these three steps in writing each statement:

1. Review the statements you made in the exercise at the beginning of this chapter regarding your current life-style.
2. Next, write a statement concerning your Dream. What would you like your life to be like in the future? Begin each statement with the following formula: "Within _____ years, my life in this area will, ideally, ..."
3. Finally, explain why you think your Dream is possible.

1. *Competence:* _____

_____

_____

_____

_____

_____

2. *Autonomy:* _____

_____

_____

_____

_____

_____

3. *Values:* _____

_____

_____

_____

_____

4. *Identity:* _____

_____

_____

_____

_____

5. *Sexuality:* _____

_____

_____

_____

_____

6. *Friendship/intimacy:* _____

_____

_____

_____

_____

7. *Love/marriage/family:* _____

_____

_____

_____

_____

8. *Job/occupation/career:* _____

_____

_____

_____

_____

9. *Relationship to society:* _____

_____

_____

_____

_____

_____

10. *Leisure:* _____

_____

_____

_____

_____

In the space provided, summarize the important elements of your Dream as you see it now. Include a description of your center and your satellite centers. In this summary, indicate the relative importance of the various parts of your Dream.

_____

_____

_____

_____

_____

_____

_____

_____

_____

_____

_____

_____

_____

Group Exercise: Current Life-Styles and Dreams

1. Describe what you like best about your current life-style. Then share one or two misgivings.

2. Share one or two important elements of your Dream. Describe any revisions you have made in your Dream since this course began.

3. Present a brief summary of the life-style you would like to create for yourself during the next 5 years. Include some of your hopes and fears.

Action Plan

1. Goals are valued accomplishments that satisfy needs or wants and contribute to the solution of problems. As you compare your present life-style with your Dream, you begin to see what you must do, or what series of steps you must take, in order to implement your Dream. In the space provided, list three goals or valued accomplishments that will bring you closer to your Dream. Be as concrete and as specific as possible.

After reviewing what she had learned about herself, one student wrote:

> *Goal 1:* A job that puts me into managerial training or has some chance of leading to a managerial position.
> *Goal 2:* A stable, intimate relationship with a male friend—a relationship that could lead to marriage.
> *Goal 3:* A network of friends in the city—a group of people who like to get together with one another.

Goal 1: _____

_____

_____

_____

Goal 2: _____

_____

_____

_____

Goal 3: _____

_____

2. Use the planning process outlined in Chapter 3 to determine how you could reach your goals.

Summary

In psychology textbooks, we often find statements concerning the way in which life should be lived—or at least the way in which some people *think* it should be lived. On the other hand, in novels and plays, writers often try to give us a feeling for life as it is *actually* lived. We could call the material we find in textbooks the *logic of life* and the material we find in novels and plays the *literature of life*. We suggest that both are important. Our emphasis here on such things as developmental tasks, life planning, working knowledge, and skills is not meant to present life as a technological enterprise. Even though you pursue life with a sense of mastery, life will outdistance you in terms of its own mystery. Planning does not take the surprise, the unexpected, the mystery out of life.

In *The Eighth Day*, by Thornton Wilder, the hero, John Ashley, is falsely accused of a crime. With the help of some unidentified men, he escapes from the train that is taking him to jail. His escape takes him on a strange pilgrimage to the Mississippi delta and on to South America, where he meets life in ways that are totally foreign to his life in Coaltown, Illinois. He finds himself sleeping among thieves and prostitutes, grappling for his own safety, getting involved in people's troubles, and talking about the mysteries of life with a woman who is half mad and half mystic—until it finally becomes clear to him that he now understands life as he has never understood it. He has glimpsed its mysteries in most unexpected ways. He takes this as a sign that he should return to his country, his home, and his family, whatever the consequences. He takes a freighter that is moving north along the western coast of South America. When the freighter goes down in a storm, John Ashley is drowned. It seems that, once he had glimpsed the mystery of life in his own way, his work was finished, and he could move on.

There aren't many hints in this text concerning the ultimate meaning of life, nor is a program presented that will help you to understand its mysteries; that's too much to expect of a book as rational as this one is. We hope that your search for an understanding of life will be, like Ashley's, a lifelong search.

References

Andrews, E. *The emotionally disturbed family and some gratifying alternatives.* New York: Aronson, 1974.

Balliett, W. Profiles: Super chops. *New Yorker*, January 29, 1979, pp. 37–44.

Bandura, A. *Principles of behavior modification.* New York: Holt, Rinehart & Winston, 1969.

Bandura, A. *Social learning theory.* Englewood Cliffs, N. J.: Prentice-Hall, 1977.

Bane, M. J. *Here to stay: American families in the twentieth century.* New York: Basic Books, 1976.

Beck, A. T., & Young, J. E. College blues. *Psychology Today*, 1978, *12*(4), pp. 80; 85–6; 89; 91–92.

Berger, P., & Neuhaus, R. *To empower people.* Washington, D.C.: American Enterprise Institute, 1977.

Brissett, D., & Lewis, L. S. The big toe, armpits, and natural perfume: Notes on the production of sexual ecstasy. *Society*, 1979, *16*(2), 63–73.

Carkhuff, R. R. *The art of problem solving.* Amherst, Mass.: Human Resource Development Press, 1973.

Carkhuff, R. R. *How to help yourself: The art of program development.* Amherst, Mass.: Human Resource Development Press, 1974.

Chickering, A. W. *Education and identity.* San Francisco: Jossey-Bass, 1969.

Chickering, A. W., & McCormick, J. Personality development and the college experience. *Research in Higher Education*, 1973, *1*, 43–70.

Cooley, C. H. *Human nature and the social order.* New York: Schocken Books, 1964.

Dulles, A. *Models of the church.* New York: Doubleday, 1974.

Dychtwald, K. Sexuality and the whole person. *Journal of Humanistic Psychology*, 1979, *19*(2), 47–61.

Eddy, H. P. (Ed.). *Sex and the college student.* New York: Atheneum, 1965.

Egan, G. *Interpersonal living: A skills/contract approach to human-relations training in groups.* Monterey, Calif.: Brooks/Cole, 1976.

Egan, G. *You and me: The skills of communicating and relating to others.* Monterey, Calif.: Brooks/Cole, 1977.

Egan, G., & Cowan, M. A. *People in systems: A model for development in the human-service professions and education.* Monterey, Calif.: Brooks/Cole, 1979.

Ellis, M. J. *Why people play.* Englewood Cliffs, N. J.: Prentice-Hall, 1973.

Erikson, E. *Young man Luther.* New York: W. W. Norton, 1958.

Erikson, E. Identity and the life-cycle. *Psychological Issues* (Vol. 1). New York: International Universities Press, 1959.

Erikson, E. *Childhood and society* (2nd ed.). New York: Norton, 1963.

Erikson, E. *Identity: Youth and crisis.* New York: Norton, 1968.

Gartner, A., & Riessman, F. *Self-help in the human services.* San Francisco: Jossey-Bass, 1977.

Gilbert, T. F. *Human competence: Engineering worthy performance.* New York: McGraw-Hill,

Giroux, H., & Penna, A. Social relations in the classroom: The dialectic of the hidden curriculum. *Edcentric,* 1977 (Spring-Summer), 39–46.

Grant, G. (Ed.). *On competence: A critical analysis of competence-based reforms in education.* San Francisco: Jossey-Bass, 1979.

Hall, E. *Beyond culture.* Garden City, N. J.: Anchor Press, 1977.

Havighurst, R. J. *Human development and education.* New York: Longmans, Green, 1953.

Heath, D. Academic predictors of adult maturity and competence. *Journal of Higher Education,* 1977, *48,* 613–632.

Hettlinger, R. *Sex isn't that simple.* New York: Seabury Press, 1974.

Huizinga, J. *Homo ludens: A study of the play element in culture.* New York: Routledge & Kegan Paul, 1949.

Hunt, D. E. *Matching models in education.* Toronto: The Ontario Institute for Studies in Education, 1971.

Keen, S. Some ludicrous theses about sexuality. *Journal of Humanistic Psychology,* 1979, *19*(2), 15–22.

Keniston, K. *All our children: The American family under pressure.* New York: Harcourt Brace Jovanovich, 1977.

Kohlberg, L. Stage and sequence: The cognitive developmental approach to socialization. In D. Goslin (Ed.), *Handbook of socialization theory and research.* Chicago: Rand McNally, 1969.

Kris, E. *Psychoanalytic explorations in art.* New York: International Universities Press, 1952.

Lasch, C. *The culture of narcissism: American life in an age of diminishing expectations.* New York: Norton, 1978.

Lessor, L. *Love and marriage and trading stamps.* Chicago: Argus Communications, 1971.

Levinson, D. J., Darrow, C. M., Klein, E. B., Levinson, M. H., & McKee, B. *The seasons of a man's life.* New York: Knopf, 1978.

Lynch, J. *The broken heart: The medical consequences of loneliness.* New York: Basic Books, 1979.

Marcia, J. E. Development and validation of ego-identity status. *Journal of Personality and Social Psychology,* 1966, *3,* 551–559.

Maslow, A. *Toward a psychology of being* (2nd ed.). New York: Van Nostrand Reinhold, 1968.

Masters, W., & Johnson, V. *The pleasure bond: A new look at sexuality and commitment.* Boston: Little, Brown, 1970.

McLuhan, M. *Understanding media: The extensions of man.* New York: McGraw-Hill, 1964.

Mead, G. H. *Mind, self, and society.* Chicago: University of Chicago Press, 1934.

Nevins, S. The challenge of embodiment: A philosophical approach. *Journal of Humanistic Psychology,* 1979, *19*(2), 23–33.

Newman, B., & Newman, P. *Development through life.* Homewood, Ill.: Dorsey Press, 1975.

Newman, B. M., & Newman, P. R. *Development through life: A psychosocial approach* (Rev. ed.). Homewood, Ill.: Dorsey Press, 1979.

Perry, W. *Forms of intellectual and ethical development in the college years.* New York: Holt, Rinehart & Winston, 1970.

Riesman, D. Society's demand for competence. In G. Grant (Ed.), *On competence: A critical analysis of competence-base reforms in education.* San Francisco: Jossey-Bass, 1979.

Riesman, D., Denney, R., & Glazer, N. *The lonely crowd: A study of the changing American character* (Rev. ed.). New Haven: Yale University Press, 1969.

Roberts, K. *Leisure.* London: Longman, 1970.

Rocky Mountain Planned Parenthood. *So you don't want to be a sex object.* Denver. 1973.

Rocky Mountain Planned Parenthood. *You've changed the combination.* Denver. 1974.

Rokeach, M. *The nature of human values.* New York: Free Press, 1973.

Rubin, L. B. *Worlds of pain: Life in the working class family.* New York: Basic Books, 1976.

Rubinstein, L., Shaver, P., & Peplau, L. Loneliness. *Human Nature*, 1979, *2*(2), 58–65.

Shepherd, J. F. *College study skills*. Boston: Houghton Mifflin, 1979.

Silverberg, W. V. *Childhood experience and personal identity*. New York: Springer, 1952.

Simon, S. B. *Meeting yourself halfway: Thirty-one value clarification strategies for daily living.* Niles, Ill.: Argus, 1974.

Simon, S. B., Howe, L. W., & Kirschenbaum, H. *Values clarification: A handbook of practical strategies for teachers and students*. New York: Hart, 1972.

Skinner, B. F. *Science and human behavior*. New York: Macmillan, 1953.

Smith, M. *A practical guide to value clarification*. La Jolla, Calif.: University Associates, 1977.

Toffler, A. *Future shock*. New York: Bantam, 1970.

Votichenko, M., & Winter, S. A radical therapy view of sex. *Journal of Humanistic Psychology*, 1979, *19*(2), 63–64.

Walker, R. E., & Foley, J. M. Social intelligence: Its history and measurement. *Psychological Reports*, 1973, *33*, 839–864.

Watson, D. L., & Tharp, R. G. *Self-directed behavior* (2nd ed.). Monterey, Calif.: Brooks/Cole, 1977.

Weick, K. *The social psychology of organizing*. Reading, Mass.: Addison-Wesley, 1969.

White, R. W. *Lives in progress*. New York: Dryden Press, 1958.

White, R. W. *The enterprise of living* (2nd ed.). New York: Holt, Rinehart & Winston, 1976.

Whitehead, E. (Ed.). *The parish in community and ministry*. New York: Paulist Press, 1978.

Whitehead, E., & Whitehead, J. *Christian life patterns*. Garden City, N.Y.: Doubleday, 1979.

Williams, R. L., & Long, J. D. *Toward a self-managed life style* (2nd ed.). Boston: Houghton Mifflin, 1979.

Name Index

323

Subject Index